KAIVALYA GAYATRI

KAIVALYA GAYATRI

THE YOGA OF DETACHED AWARENESS

Philip Hamilton

Kaivalya Gayatri—The Yoga of Detached Awareness
Copyright © 2020 Philip Hamilton

Published 2020

Cover art, photography, and book design by Philip Hamilton. Section illustrations by Felicia Hamilton.

ISBN-13: 978-1729696064

ISBN-10: 172969606

For John Taylor Gatto
and Dave McGowan

*in gratitude for those
who pull back the curtain*

CONTENTS

FORWARD

GAYATRI MANTRA IS AN ANTIDOTE to the helpless feeling that modern life is a jumble of confusing developments, gone out of control. *Confusion* is an essential tool for sales persons and carneys—if the mark can't tell what is happening, they can be *led by the nose*. The huckster's arts are essential for foisting agendas onto communities that have no reason to suspect foul play. Society is global, structured through control grids and instant information—all facilitated by corporate-funded science, education and research. Webs of inter-locking data-collection systems operate as one, to lead the mind where it would not go if left to its own organic choices.

Given these circumstances, spiritual practice has to protect an individual's thought-process, unchaining the mind from consumerism and corporate conditioning. Without identifying and examining obstacles to true thought, any practice, Gayatri Mantra included, will have to work against powerful programming that has been installed through all media.

THE FIRST PART OF THE BOOK addresses root causes and conditions of internal conflict and external strife. It goes on to suggest antidotes to cultural decline through self-examination and healing stories—Gayatri Mantra is the unifying thread. The foundation of the book is the *Gayatri Matrix of Meanings* found in Part II, Chapter *Aum*. This break-out of the concepts as a hierarchy of triads is unique to this book's interpretation: the coherent movement of Om into its three sounds: Ah, Oh, Um and the implication for all groups of three which expand as the Mantra proper. For these reasons, Gayatri Mantra presents a dense map of meanings and strategies for maintaining a sharp, coherent mind during times of cultural chaos. Fruits of mantra practice will be strong when Gayatri is practiced both as an analytic tool and a spiritual practice.

Tasks   *by Vitthal Mishra*

The spider waits
  To dine with the moth.

The caterpillar's transmutation
  Only serves it winging to the table.

Be aware ~be canny ~fall into
  Kaivalya, the trap that sets you free.

Kaivalya: radical detachment,
liberation from slavery to the senses

Part I / The Problem

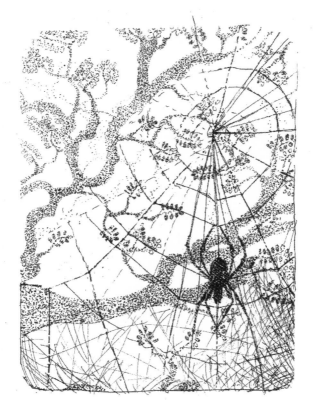

VISHWAMITHRA'S PROMISE

Om
*Together, we will travel
this holy road of memory
to before anything happened.*

    Gayatri Mantra is that way.

*Each word is a key.
Understand the words and
you have a bundle of keys.
    Contemplate deeply the meanings, then
      you see clearly the locks that the keys fit.
Open these doors
and you find your Self,
the Beginning— Brahman.*

*Offering this is the way to
absolute freedom and peace.
    Nothing and no one can take it from you.*

*If you lose these keys,
    you did it freely no matter how it seems.*

*The Mantra will sort out
the seeming of appearances
and reveal the Truth.*

Let us begin again and again.

*Every fraction of time
With the mantra
Is the beginning—*

As such it is Om."

WHO
MOVES?

I EXAMINED MY HAND in the paraffin lamp's flickering light. Fingers went this way and that by my command—a request with no clear source. I could not find the connection between my decision to move and the movement itself. It was ghostlike, with no words or ideas attached, no efforts, nothing left-over. The desire to move happened in stark silence, like fluid-will filled every cell to perform a flawless, exacting dance that I apparently dictated.

Candlelight outlined my hand in the darkness, revealing pads of skin, folds, wrinkles and knuckles. Various lengths of hard and soft tissue animated in perfect coordination, pulling a tendon here, relaxing a muscle there in ways that I did not begin to understand. What invisible links allowed my mute digits to perform the slightest gesture that apparently began in me before there was even a thought or whim? I could not find any trace of the one who moved my hand.

Beyond the radius of a single flame, my campsite receded from view. Starry nebula stretched from a silhouetted tree line on one side to an unbroken plain on the other, spattering the sky in luminous clouds. City lights and dangers were over there. The things that could hurt me were, for now, far enough away, blacked-out. I was alone and yet full of a presence that could not be seen, heard, or touched. Something swaddled and held, supported me on invisible strings that allowed my body to move.

And what about the desire to move?—where did that come from? Was it an electric urge sent out from bony skull into a spine, down the arm and into a million fleshy, bloody, stringy sinews? The coordination of this skin-draped rack of bones with something that could put it in motion stalled my mind. The effortless precision by *it*, the lack of clear direction by *me*—who was *it*? I watched, mesmerized in the dark, and continued to fall for the illusion that *I* did it, fooled continuously despite being clearly aware that something was at work, beyond my will. The mover moves and then hides. It leaves no trace and can't be found. It's easier for the spectator to take credit for movement than to

3

accept the hollow void, no different than a bag blown in the wind. I was a bag, blown in the wind.

Then I noticed how dark it had gotten since he left. I was afraid that I'd never see him again. Windows opened and closed—why did I even know him? Who brought me to him? What did I do to deserve a teacher, a teaching, a brain or a hand for that matter? Nothing—so it ended like it started, with me not knowing. Only now, for the first time, with his eyes, I saw my hand as it moved in flickering firelight.

Looking past the glowing coals and tea cups, I sent the hand to find the photo he had given me moments before. It was in my pocket with the blade of grass and beaded string. Her picture now gazed back from my open palm. The girl held the iris flower and smiled. *So young*, I thought. *Who are you?* My eyes strained in fickle light to pick-out details on a glossy image, fixed to some paper, the face of someone far away, now held by fingers that did my bidding like spirits in space.

What to do?—maybe *he* could move my limbs to do things that needed accomplishing. I only seemed to command this imponderable hand—an appendage formed out of so much meat—and yet, it danced to tunes, in steps that were orchestrated by some mysterious source.

"*Om, Bhur Bhuvah Suvaha*
Tat Savitur Varenyum
Bhargo Devasya Dhimahi
Dhiyo Yonah Prachodayat."

I chanted in a whisper.

Hands looked like flowers as they gestured, grasped or received. They bloomed when messages arrived through arms-like-stems which pulled juice from a head and a chest. The beads he gave me, now draped over those finger-petals, looped around my wrist, and swayed dangling, half lit in the dark. Detached, I stared down and examined the red seeds and the thread that pierced each one.

Who moved? I scrolled my memories to examine his hands, the ones I looked at so many times without noticing. They gestured, traced arcs in the air, fell still at his thighs. They were dagger-like probes he sent at me—and then blunted their attack before they might ruffle the most cherished illusions that comforted my ignorant brain.

Enough, returning to town was inevitable. Find the loose ends and face them—it was time to go back. So I went, saying the mantra.

4

STORIES

BACK THEN MY NAME was Ashty Hozan. I would say I was just like anyone else, but a sweeping statement like that assumes I knew everyone else enough to make the comparison, or it could mean I thought everyone was pretty much the same—neither was true. What I *can* say is that time passed in the company of people I didn't know and rarely talked to, and that most of us did things we did not care about. For unknown reasons, I nurtured hopes that the pointless repetition of daily routines would change into something better. A degree in chemistry at the state college led haphazardly to a regimented job at the mail service which was eating my life in tiny bites.

It happened that way because of circumstance, compromise and predictable neurotic reactions. The attraction to science probably had something to do with an illustration in an old textbook that impressed me. It was a stylized drawing of a scientist. He wore black-rimmed glasses and, of course, a white lab coat. All around were cartoonish Bunsen burners and glass vials—it looked clean, antiseptic—a definite contrast to farm-life. However, beyond half-baked ideas about redesigning the world or avoiding back-breaking labor, my college education was a random affair.

After college I kept to myself, walked or biked thirty minutes to work each day and sorted packages from seven o'clock in the morning until five in the afternoon. A half-hour break gave me a chance for remedial reading—pop-science journals or blogs on religion and philosophy. Eventually my efforts to stay relevant hit a wall and no amount of brain-priming helped. Daily routines diluted the last remnants of my idealism. Putting one foot in front of the other was about all I could manage.

A typical day was a flat-line except for the occasional eccentric blip up or down. Uncomfortable changes in schedule or outright panic over something more extreme provided an unwanted *spice of life* in rare doses. Against the sameness, trivial diversions reinforced my sense that

5

daily living had lost its value. Major upsets, usually related to financial security, highlighted my dependence on the system. Apathy crept in like slow-motion suicide. I hunted for alternatives.

The message board at work was plastered with promises: guest appearances, relevant speakers and empowerment seminars. Formats and prices varied, but every one claimed the power to transform lives. The other thing they shared was that they did not work. The presenters were on the same plain as attendees and only parroted pithy nuggets they got from some other well-meaning presenter.

A few experiences with such programs showed that it was not a *new* anything that could change a person. It had to be an impact, unhinging and painful. Someone or something would have to pry or seduce me away from precious patterns. My security blanket was a ball and chain.

There was a hand-printed notice—neatly written in ballpoint pen and tacked with one pin, it was a strange duck among the studio photos and graphic banners. I thought whoever posted it must have been simple-minded to assume anyone might find it, buried among the four-color billets screaming for attention. My immediate reaction was to ignore the posting—so I thought twice and attended his poorly advertised presentation as an experiment.

It was held in a pale green classroom with naked, fluorescent tubes glowing flat against yellowed ceiling tiles. Standing in front of our group of half-a-dozen he said, "It's good to be with you— my name is Vishwamithra, sounds like *Wish w'meter.* Before we begin, let us invoke the presence, the one who protects and nourishes:

> *"She is the energy and brilliance of our effective study. May she find a seat here, among us, in our minds and in our hearts—she leads us from darkness to light, from dullness to the eternal flame of awareness, from death to life-eternal. Om."*

He wore a white t-shirt and draw-stringed gray pants that had obvious wear, compensated by an overall, groomed appearance. His whiskers were scissor-cut near the skin. Thinning hair was salt and pepper and cropped short, like a monk. A strand of beads wrapped his wrist which reinforced the impression of one who was more at home in a prayer-cell. The room suited him—age-worn but not dingy—they came off as kindred spirits, lacking pretense. He smiled easily while he translated his name as *Friend of Awareness.* The institutional setting was good enough and I hoped that I would at least be entertained.

After introducing himself and making the prayer, he dragged a white-board from the side. He wrote *Haala Hala/poison* in red marker and next to it the words *Soma/immortality* in blue.

Turning to face us, markers in hand, he continued, "Let's start with a story." His voice caromed off the hard surfaces that defined the space. The unexpected volume shook me out of my private thoughts. He said, "This Earth we inhabit was cobbled together out of galactic left-overs. *Left-over* is the defining feature of this place—that's why, no matter how hard you try, there is always a little pile of something you don't know what to do with. There are hosts of gods that manage all this and our story today gives some idea how these beings got their start. For what it's worth, gods are people too, and for some reason the seemingly obvious truth eluded them until this moment—they would die, somehow, sometime."

The room went quiet to let the thought sink in. "You see the problem here—they did not remember their beginning. Most of us have the same amnesia—and lacking the beginning, the ending does not register. The new idea had terrifying implications. It would be a titanic waste to lose a fabulous lifestyle on account of a little thing like death. They needed a *nectar of immortality*. At this point, such an elixir did not exist, but gods, being the entrepreneurs that they were, dreamed-up a way forward."

He continued the snide history saying, "This might be the first value-added application in the realm of *Mind*. The immortality project required a thorough squeezing of consciousness. They embroiled the primordial soup using a huge snake wrapped around a mountain-as-churn. There were two teams; the gods held the tail while demigods grabbed the head. Demigods were like shadows of the celestial elect. The raw power was similar, but their use of it was more brutal."

He matter-of-factly informed us, "Which side was good and which was bad depended on whose side you were on." His open palms moved apart to illustrate, "Demigods, demons, Asuras, or simply *vices*, call them what you will, were opposed to the gods but accepted the invitation at the prospect of living forever. The gods had no intention of following through on the deal. As I said, it was hard to tell good eggs from the bad. In any case they had a clubby understanding of who was who, based on whether they preferred theft through the front door or back window."

He said, "Imagine these two groups of titans—one as self-serving as the other—playing one another for the greatest prize of all, life without end. They gripped each end of a writhing leviathan whose serpentine coils hugged the jagged mountain—a towering granite mass, submerged in a colorless sea—a sparkling medium that extended perpetually in all directions.

"They strained to waken the mountain out of its inertia. It moved with their ponderous effort, gained momentum, disrupted volumes of ocean and created mammoth waves, as the sea fomented into chaos. Then they strenuously reversed the mass in motion, grinding it to a halt to pull it in the opposite direction. We don't know how long this process lasted—it must have been eons." He stopped.

"Open your mind to allow for the cosmic scale of their plan. Such a task strips human imagination," he said, addressing each of us in turns. "They are manufacturing worlds—how?—by taking the powerful actions necessary to satisfy their vast appetites. They don't really understand what they are doing—they only know what they want and pursue it aggressively." He returned to the narrative, now with our eyes fixed on his every move.

"A thousand billion tons of granite sloshed to and fro by players equally beyond our sense of scale," he said. "Again and again they agitated the sentient ocean into froth and foam. What had been a placid sea was now a veritable super-storm of mind, universal hot, seething consciousness that craved alchemical resolution."

His motions were nearly a dance and it was easy to see the storyteller as a mountain, a snake, or an irritable titan, heaving to milk the elements. He paced among the six of us, making sweeping gestures that glued us in place, mesmerized and motionless, The vibrating hum of a failing ballast and faltering fluorescent fixture overhead amplified the tension at pregnant pauses.

"Like boiling milk gives up yogurt, butter and cheese, the liquid transformed in so many ways. Everything around us is the thin, dried-out residue of their quest for the *Soma* elixir. Countless divine gifts rose up, pushed out, or got placed aside during their labor—until the turbid material emitted a substance so lethal it would destroy creation itself. This was the *Haala hala* poison."

He muttered, as though to no one, "What do you get for forcing the truth out of hiding?—immortality or toxic shock—so beware."

"The divine laborers called in panic to the impassive, distant god of the godless, the only one bigger than all their schemes, *Shiva Mahadev*. This god was the cosmos itself, endlessly contemplating his own blissful nature. Roused from timeless meditation he lowered a great hand into the virulent mass, scooped off the poison and took it into his mouth. Recognizing, out of infinite compassion, that the *haala-hala* would destroy worlds both inside and outside of his immense body, he holds it, suspended in his throat for all time."

We were no longer seated between ghastly industrial lighting and vinyl flooring, but suspended in a time and space that he wove around us with word images and feeling. The all-consuming ambitions of gods seemed real to me and I wondered about the saving presence that had to infuse matter itself. Vishwamithra paused to explain.

"Do you have any interest in immortality?" he asked, and waited.

Getting no reply he said, "Let me ask it this way. Do you want to actively participate in the eternal essence—which is the same as being alive?" The questions rolled off of us, creating an awkward moment.

To break the silence I said, "Most people want a better life, an escape from the day-to-day grind. Emptiness is at the bottom of unhappiness, isn't it? But there's no clear way to fix it."

He looked at me, nodding, then turned and walked toward the white board where he had written *Haala hala* and *Soma.*

He circled them, saying, "The ancient fix resulted in poison so dire that Shiva intervened—*then* they proceeded to obtain their epic solution, the nectar of eternal life. I say the noxious poison and the soma-nectar is the same thing. It depends how you approach the goal.

"All kinds of things come at us. Some of it is dreadful. The goal is to take on Shiva and allow the nasty business to culture us—then we find that life itself is not other than the divine nectar, sweet and nurturing. This ability is not cheap—there are unavoidable costs.

"The story gives two ways to share in immortal being—one is the heroic path of yoga, the other is devotion. Yoga requires constant application with intensity—devotion lays every effort at the deity's feet. The gods enlisted the demigods and began their serious task. *Yoga* means sifting through everything to see things as they are—naked and possibly toxic. In their quest the gods discovered material that could kill everything. They called on Shiva to save them—the quest for immortality requires devotion, as in the fable. God alone has the alchemical skill to take your flawed efforts and make them whole."

"Yoga is relationship," he said as he bound the two words together with encircling arrows. "It is the linking-back, the narcissistic ego finally reaching-out to the *Infinite Friend* who always waits. The process requires destabilizing business-as-usual to provide the opportunity for something new to take place. The churning has order and method in it. It can't be haphazard. Beauty and bane both emerge throughout the singular process of agitating your inert mass toward a goal."

HE WIPED THE BOARD clean and drew a gently wavy, horizontal blue-line from edge to edge and stated, "We exist inside an oceanic fluid—

consciousness—it is a boundless, bright, universal-mind where every desirable or deadly possibility resides as potential. Like an ocean, it appears in three distinct ways: outer appearance, inner dynamics, and impenetrable depth. Swimmers, sailors and divers learn to respect their place and work within those fluid qualities." He sketched cryptic groups of figures at the far sides of the board, located precisely above, below or directly on the wavy blue line.

Circling these *teams* he said, "There are entities outside your perception who work that same sea for their advantage. I call them *gods* because they influence our mundane affairs from a hidden place. Follow any thought or mood to its source and you will know what I mean—there is nothing to find. These manipulators have a creative function as well. Like us, they are also driven by hopes and fears."

It was frightening to consider that something like aliens tampered with me from some other dimension. I raised my hand to comment.

"Are you seriously suggesting something like *gremlins* tamper with our minds? If such beings exist and they infect our moods or thoughts, it would be impossible to deal with them. There would be no reference points to know how they distorted my thoughts and feelings. My volition seems to move me—if volition is not my own, what then?"

He answered, "The body-vehicle does have many drivers; most are unknown to you. The wind may blow-off your hat—it does not mean you did it. Understand that these influences are everywhere."

His discourse continued, "One of the greatest illusions is that you have sovereign control over your thoughts and actions. Because of that error, events and outcomes seem to come and go, willy-nilly—this is how you make sense of so many unwanted effects. We console ourselves that those bad decisions, cruel behaviors, and tragic outcomes are gone when they disappear—but reality has no revolving door—it is here all the time. You may be stuck with responsibility for the results—you also need to realize that various entities set you up for those results, for various reasons beyond your ken."

My notebook filled-up with little drawings and questions in the margins. It would have to wait until later. Vishwamitra resumed his diagrammatic explanation, drawing a mostly-submerged triangle with a ropey coil around it. This was the mountain and the snake. He noted Shiva with a fat arrow pointing to an upper corner, off the board.

"Before starting anything, assess the scale and nature of the mountain." The triangle filled-in with lines while he spoke, "*Old as the hills*, the material basis is the spent leavings of stars—yet it is always the material of your current situation. Consider it the *hardware* of a life project—it has solid, focused, and definite aspects—things you can label." The explanation moved on.

"The snake represents the deep programming in the old parts of your brain—it functions like software," he said while adding rows of green scales to the figure which squeezed the triangle. "The powerful serpent embeds in brain contours, the curve in your spine and the pulse of life. It precedes thought and does not judge—it's vulnerable to being co-opted by others. They don't say if the snake volunteered for its thankless task—I doubt it."

Outlining the shapes in a thick line he said, "Serpent and mountain form a duality. Any undertaking can only proceed when the stabile set of circumstances, the mountain—gets wrapped in an energetic coil, the writhing snake. The gods are dual again—the higher and the lower—they impose their desires on reality by churning the snake-mountain machine they created."

"This would not have turned out so well without what?" he asked, wagging his thumb at the board. It was obvious but I refused to speak again and endured long seconds until one of the others broke in.

An older woman offered, "Shiva?"

"Yes." the teacher nearly shouted. "Shiva, Shiva Mahadeva, who or what do you suppose he is?"

Someone said, "God."

"True enough, but *God* is an easy answer," he said. "To make Shiva more immediate than a *God-idea*, I'll give you a clue. It is always aware, riddled throughout everything, is impossible to understand, and responds to every passionate appeal. It is the most powerful force on Earth. It is attractive and completely mysterious."

There was some fidgeting. With nothing to lose I said, "Molecular glue holds matter together; so nuclear power is nearly infinite—but it's not aware, is it?"

Smiling, he said, "What is awareness, anyway? Shiva—the name means *auspicious*, another word for fortunate or beneficial. *Benefit* is the mysterious reason this whole world of possibilities exists. Something *meaningful* is *behind* the forces that hold all of this together."

He found an empty seat near us and sat down. The structure of the group shifted with the change. He was one of us in this new vantage point. "Through hearing the story I just told, concepts like *Shiva and the Nectar of Immortality* entered your mind. These ideas are subtle objects that begin linking with other things you know. Inter-connecting worlds of meaning happen automatically—it is a function of the mind. The ideas link within one brain, yours, and then your new understanding is here with others, doing the same thing with them. Knowledge grows like that, spreading and connecting with no end. This is fluid mind. Concepts come together and overlap, in one brain or many. That gives us motivating reasons to act. We have to act, even if that action is to ignore or do nothing. Do we really know why we are acting? We have to become aware of our creative power, or else become tools for other minds that see our potential."

He let his rhetorical questions sink-in, adding, "Find yourself in the fantastic drama—recognize the nectar in the poison."

His suggestion to hear the story as more than an idle passenger jabbed me. The idea that I might be going through the motions, unaware, was a new thought. A pang of fear flitted across my body. This was it, my life, the only ride there was—and it occurred to me I might be in a kind of stupor, blissfully unaware.

Standing again, Vishwamithra broke the pause, saying, "It's all you. Agitate the mind until it gives up its wealth. Prepare for a shock when it spits out bitterness, anger, and fear. Inaction and fantasies of willful action both lead to panic. You can be Shiva and hold the bitter dregs when they arrive. Let them charge you, pinch you, wake you up. Such discipline leads to the elixir. Your marvelous form knows how to turn potato chips into hair, fingernails, and energy. Surely, each one can find *Soma* when they hold the venom in check for the good cause.

"Go to Shiva for help—in other words, this world is auspicious. Benefits are everywhere, maybe out-of-sight. Proceed on that assumption and see what happens. Shiva has no preferences at all— that deity does not haggle with reality—the *haala-hala* is good enough. It means that when you crave changes to find something better, it is due to a limited perspective. As you broaden your vision you take on more of the auspicious quality—eventually pleasure and pain lose their meaning as the main reasons to act. "

The talk was over.

What was the discipline he urged? He repeated the theme over the course of several more sessions which I attended at the school. There was something deeper behind the subjects he covered that he alluded to without elaboration. I made a contract with myself to follow through on this course and decided to find out from him directly. After the final seminar I requested that we meet one-on-one.

THE GAME

M<small>Y</small> FIRST INDIVIDUAL SESSION with Vishwamithra felt risky. The few presentations he gave at the middle school impressed me, but my request to discuss things alone would be harder to back out of. There was no kidding myself that I needed something—and this action constituted a cry for help. However, I felt foolish and a bit cynical about the life preserver I might have latched onto.

We met at his flat, across town from my apartment. It was early morning, "the auspicious hour" as he put it. We sat in a threesome, two of us generally at an angle to one another and the third being a minimal altar. His eyes were lightly shut while I tried to acclimate to the intimate setting and hard floor. A quick glance around the room did not show much in the dark before sunrise. The wavering rays from one candle caught the edges of things in a tight radius where we sat. He began chanting and I followed when I could.

"*Aaah oh ummm...*"

Waves of self-consciousness came over me—what was I doing?

Shadows drained into daylight by degrees as my eyes adjusted, revealing objects that had been vague shapes only minutes earlier.

"*Aaah oh ummm...*"

The move to commit myself might have been a mistake.

Details filled in an outline of the man almost within arm's reach. Furrows crossed the teacher's broad forehead which shielded deep-set eyes. Hollows below high set cheekbones showed lines and blemishes that became more vivid as dawn advanced.

"*Aaah oh ummm.*"

There was nothing that could be done about it for now. I reassured myself I could quit when it suited me.

His chin relaxed toward his chest. Swarthy skin and stubble contrasted against the pale wool shawl that he wore on that cool morning. The thin cloth formed a sling between his knees, supporting his palms which rested one on the other. I repeated after him, word by word,

> *"Om, Bhur Bhuvah Suvaha*
> *Tat Savitur Varenyum, Bhargo Devasya Dhimahi*
> *Dhiyo Yonah Prachodayat, Om."*

Embarrassment aside, my reasons for calling on him remained. One pointless moment bled into the next, resting on hollow self-assurances that the repetitive grind would improve.

"It's hard to tell how the ideas are going over with the crowd in those kinds of venues," he observed. "People might be sampling and no matter what the presenter says, it's just another taste. Can I ask what brought you to the talks?"

I felt no pressure behind his question and told him about the life I left behind and the bog I slogged through at the present. I finally arranged the most concise statement possible to answer his question.

"Desperation," I said, "best describes why I chose your little notice over all the slick ones. It was almost invisible, mixed-in with layers of other stuff on the bulletin board. It's not so much that I was attracted to your stark note—great graphics has misrepresented the real content often enough. I wanted to avoid the usual sales trap."

"*Not this-not that* is the best way," he said. "Likewise, I don't want to compete with bells and whistles, especially when there is an invisible movement that works inside people as they return to sanity. The voice that calls, the ear that hears and the ultimate destination is more sublime than advertising. Let me explain why I pinned a notice at all."

I settled into the intimate atmosphere and exposed myself to his words. Despite the unfamiliarity, being there in dim light and asking the big questions before the day geared-up was comforting.

When it came down to it, I did not know why I was there. Searching-out the real reason was like wandering a maze of idealistic dreams and tepid compromises. I remembered feeling restless at fifteen when I first started noticing people's superficial defenses. Schoolmates and adults alike presented a face to the world that hid their complex insecurities. I learned to tweak the mechanism in various ways—it wasn't difficult—different people responded to different cues. It might be a sarcastic comment for one or a joke for another. For others it might be mirroring their expectations back to them. It was like picking locks and it made me cynical. Instead of getting to know me to understand what I was, they judged by those cues. The mechanical reality behind the masks was disillusioning. In retrospect, the discovery unhinged me from authoritative voices. I drifted.

The life I had always known became as two-dimensional as the people. After high school graduation I exerted a little force and got free of our family farm to look for something better. There were no hard feelings, but it felt violent. My timing was off, actions were blunt. The choice had been simple: freedom and diversity versus scratching the ground, like one of the chickens that had been my charges.

I went to the city to get a degree with the assumption money would flow-in. A professional income would vindicate my radical departure. So far, three years into the move, the urban dream felt more like planting my hopes on concrete instead of soil. And the grindstone only changed character—I had swapped hard physical labor for fruitless tedium. One was as thankless as the other.

I was in a monkey trap. You catch a monkey by drilling a hole in a gourd and filling it with fruit. The gourd is fixed to a tree so when the monkey comes to claim the easy food he can't let go. His fist won't fit through the hole. He frantically tries to escape the hunter, but cannot let go of the prize. This was my fine opportunity, away from the farm, degree in hand with limitless possibilities; all a trick. My hand squeezed tightly none-the-less, while the voice in my head said, "This is your only chance, don't give up, don't be stupid." There was no oracle to tell me what to do and some proof that it had been a wasted effort.

In the dim light, away from keyboards and screens, an incessant hum became audible in my ears for the first time. White noise was a calming whisper to my brain as he spoke.

"THE BEAUTIFUL MIND IS *clear and aware. Clarity* means there are no thought objects in it; memories, opinions, and moods change form; they come and go like clouds against a clear sky. That's obviously not our experience. Usually it's more like debris in a stream that catches on rocks, blocks flow, and then breaks loose in a flood. The stickiness leads to hopes, fears, anxiety, depression; all those negative feelings tell us that the natural state of the mind is afflicted with attachments that are not natural to the mind's clear essence.

"*Aware* means conscious, awake, and perceptive. Again, we don't experience that awareness all the time—wake, sleep, dull, alert—the mind apparently comes and goes. There seem to be dead zones and hot spots in a gray field.

"The essence behind and inside the person is clear awareness. This consciousness holds all mental states completely, losing nothing. But we grab onto events in the smooth essence and identify with them—like snags in a knit sweater, we fuss and pull until we get the threads back in place. It is the human condition to grasp like a monkey, caught with a fist in a gourd. It leads to all the drama—none of it is necessary. In fact, spiritual practice is the discipline by which the clear and aware mind becomes more and more apparent, proven by a lessening of dramatic spikes, loosening the grip. The *Gayatri Mantra* provides all the tools you require to recover the clear, aware mind in a happy process of *Yoga,* which is another word for relationship."

He continued, "I mentioned the way a stream can get dammed up in the natural process of draining the lands around it. There are some creatures that see potential power in the flowing water. Engineers dam it artificially to install dynamos for generating electricity. Beavers skillfully create wetlands and habitat for other animals. Both of those types of engineers flood the dry land. The mind is subject to such manipulation. Family affection, tribal affiliation and racial identity can be a great source of growth and experience in the context of love and loyalty. No doubt there are flaws in those bonds—there can be pain and separation. Your journey to this place has some of those elements. I consider all that as natural, the human condition. Families and tribes rooted in culture include checks and balances, a unique ecology.

"The challenge of the modern era is to recognize, understand, and resist sophisticated forms of mental and emotional manipulation. These use the mind's plasticity for various purposes. Slavery, entrapment, colonization, and addiction are the rule of mass society rather than the exception. Believe it or not, there are opportunists who use advertising and media to sicken the bonds of love, loyalty, and relationship. It is the responsibility of every individual to know these dangers and avoid them. They are everywhere, in everything. Beyond that, unsuspecting humanity is fiercely protective of the toys provided by these controllers, even though the ill-effects are obvious. There has to be a guide. Gayatri Mantra practice cuts through these problems.

"The human race is unaware of the nature of the game they are in, the players, the owners, the sponsors and the rules. Nothing is as it seems. There are teams—but the jerseys don't correspond and shifting rules are given to different players. There is no way to tell who is on which side—the world system is a racket. You will never meet the rule makers or true beneficiaries of the elaborate trap."

He must have seen my startled reaction to his reading of the human condition and went on to frame it in a larger context.

"The *world system* is not *The World*," he said. "The World belongs to a higher order. The world system, on the other hand, is a simulation, a game devised to wrest control away from the natural order."

He continued, saying, "It is like an arena with stands full of half-drunk spectators, who mistakenly stare at the field when they are the real action. As long as crowds cheer rabidly at the field, they are tools: consumers, voters, complainers, contributors—they might even be spiritual seekers or gurus. Among waving-pennants, marching-bands, and rigged-teams—goal, penalty, winning and losing are about the same. Avoid entering that arena unless you know these things.

"Professor Hozan, what do you think?" he asked, "Do you play, watch, or doze quietly as you live the dream?"

My scalp tingled at the words he chose. A moment from a soccer game came back in force. There I was, floundering in the forward spot among experienced men. A perfect pass smacked the side of my head. Daydreaming earned me a welt on the cheek and lost us the point. "Hey professor—how about you wake up!" the passer barked.

I blushed. Back then it dawned on me I was only half-there, flat-footed and struggling. There was no way to play without the will to move, move, move and act. The good ones seemed to have brains in their legs. A soccer field is not a good place for idle thought. How long had my head been in the clouds? Maybe I was sleepwalking.

My skin crawled under Vishwamithra's critical eye. I confessed, "You could say I've been living like this is a cake-walk, biding my time and waiting for the prize."

"So have we all," he answered. "Getting in cue for empty rewards and baseless punishments is the order of the day. You see the simulacra of life, not life itself—the task of every human is to play the real game of life. But, what is it?"

He did not wait for a reply and said, "There are clues in the environment around you. You can only find out by asking.

"Human existence remains shallow until a person admits they do not know *what* they are. Even the simplest machine is useless unless you understand *what* it is for. *What* is an egg beater without eggs?— *what* is a human being without meaning or purpose?—*what* is a *life worth living* if one does not pursue meaning by asking questions to find out what that might mean?

17

"And wake-up to *where* you are. Notice your placement in this world, physical conditions, mental states and emotions caused by your location—geographically and economically. And again, what are your endowments, your skills—are they developed? Do they waste? *What* does location mean? Is your heart in a *place,* the chest? Does the heart have a place where it is most at home? Is *meaning* in place where the heart finds comfort? What about hardship, how does it affect meaning, the heart, comfort, the sense of place? *Where* is the body? *Where* is the mind? Answering these is a full time job.

"Then the question *why* arises naturally. Why is anything like it is? The first step toward meaning is—*why* do I care about meaning? *Why* am I built this way? *Why* does my mind go to the places it goes? *When* does it go there?

"*What, where, and why* are questions that form a revealing loop. *Inquiry* is the way to find out what your life is about. Gayatri contains the disciplines necessary to recognize your purpose."

He paused, looking toward the morning light now flooding the room and said, "All this begs another question, doesn't it—*who* asks these meaningful questions and *who* can answer them?"

On the way to work I wondered what I expected from the individual meeting. I wasn't disappointed—he seemed about the same. I felt different; maybe it was the closeness, the lack of props to distract me. The intimacy was surprising. And I felt lighter, like the weight of my mistakes got lifted off, replace by the burden of choice. It had been a long time since feeling that I had choices, even though I could not say what they were.

DISCIPLINE

"She is the energy and brilliance of our effective study. May she find a seat here, among us, in our minds and in our hearts—she leads us from darkness to light, from dullness to the eternal flame of awareness, from death to life-eternal. Om."

I KNEW ENOUGH OF THE INVOCATION, so it was possible to repeat most of the lines under my breath. We would pick-up where our first meeting left-off. My notes were handy for both of us.

He began, "Last week we discussed *questions*—one question, *what*, is the basis for the others. *What-person* is the question *who*, 'what-place' is *where*, and 'what-time' is *when*. The necessary basis for inquiry is discipline," he said. "What do you think *discipline* means?"

Pictures of soldiers in parade dress, athletes pounding their bodies before dawn, and gaunt ascetics exposed to the elements came to mind. I told him, "Discipline usually implies self-inflicted punishment or forced conformity. It seems to be about will power and control over desires and habits. Becoming disciplined is admirable—an invaluable trait—also one that seems difficult."

He said, "Any habit can become a compulsion—which is not discipline. An attitude of bright awareness is necessary. Discipline is active discernment, not mechanical. It allows dissimilar things to get along—relationship. It can include modifying behavior and changing habits. In essence it is a desire to know the other—to acquire the knowledge required to go beyond habit-bound responses. How would you rethink discipline as a way to relate to others?"

The idea caught me off-guard. I said, "It's a new thought, but not so strange if I let the ideas simmer. At first glance, discipline wouldn't factor into person-to-person relationships—friendly ones, anyway," I began. "Raising animals makes the connection more obvious. It's clear that restraints and sensitivity are required, say, when you approach a horse. They can be wary and skittish. They gage my confidence and

19

relax when they sense that I know how to be with them. Rushing in makes them nervous—they might bolt, or rear-up."

Nodding he said, "People are no different—they might be able to suppress a violent reaction, but no one likes an artless approach. Boorish intrusions turn social beings into territorial animals, regardless of how they try to rationalize what strikes them as rude. Discipline eliminates assumptions and leads to true relationship."

I asked, "What do you mean by a *true* relationship?"

"Respect for the other," he said, "not the usual games that pass for relationship. It's not economics—*I get this and you get that*. Coercion is also a type of relating but one that handles people as though they were objects—*do this...or else*. Both of those require clever, wily behavior, but discipline is absent. *Discipline, disciple*—these imply a dignified way, a way that creates culture and enriches everyone."

I asked, "Why does discipline have such hard edges if it is really about the pleasant, social aspects you describe?"

"With no thoughtful examination of words and their function, individuals accept the meanings imposed by society, regardless of distortions. A thought is completely abstract—words give thought-content a form so it can be shared. Any word—like *discipline*—has three separate aspects: the sound of it when spoken, the available definitions of the word, and most importantly, what you understand the word to mean. In our corrupt age, those three are usually disjoint and conflicted. The confusion is intentional, to make words into weapons that obscure the truth. Societies once used words to enrich meaning, but now words have become prisons that control meanings. That's how *punishment* came to be a part of *discipline*. The true definition is based on the ancient lineage of the word. *Discern, disciple*, or *discuss,* hint at the essential content, which is about learning and teaching. Learning is not punishment. Listen to the word, study its meanings, and seek its essence to free you from the prison of words."

Returning to the basic questions, Vishwamithra simplified his thoughts into a vignette about outfitting for travel in a strange land.

He began, "Once there was an explorer preparing for a journey through an unknown place. *What was it?* He wondered—*was it jungle, desert, flat or mountainous?* He did not know, so he had to prepare for anything. *And where would he go?* Well, a compass, shadows and stars could keep him from going in circles or wandering aimlessly. The explorer had to consider *what* he might need for *where* he was going. But the wise traveler knew it was not enough. He asked, *Who was he? What were his skills? What knowledge and experience gaps did he know of?*

Whom might he meet? And again, *when was he going?* The time of day and the seasons would surely affect what he found. These inquiries were the primary tools to assure success."

He explained, "This is a fable about relationship—his questions were like eyes and ears before he could see or hear anything in the new land ahead. Inquiry set the stage to understand what he might find, rather than leave it to chance reactions."

Vishwamithra continued the parable, saying, "Prepared in these ways, with knife, staff, leathers, shelter, flasks and all the rest, he learned to be comfortable in the new terrain. His confidence encouraged pushing deeper and deeper into that landscape. Discipline, not austerity, guided his ways. If anything, you can see that if he had not asked the questions beforehand, he might have been forced into harsh austerities *because* of poor planning. Deprivation may be part of an adventure, but one does not deliberately include *lack* as a tool for success. Even though strength and endurance increase through austerities—always—asking critical questions is the wise first step.

"Despite continuous progress in survival skills, our traveler remained incomplete. The defensive preparations were good, but they also blocked real intimacy with the lands around him. Technology may protect him from the elements, but relationship requires some vulnerability—to feel the bite in the wind, the feel of soil. The place he entered was an intelligent presence, a whole organism with subtleties as well as physical features. Survival is only part of success—communion requires trust. A sure guide could help manage the risks.

"The traveler found a local, someone with no methods, only innate knowledge of an environment which was like a mother to him. For the native, relationship was the way itself. This earthling was naked, open to the pressure of the ground on the soles of his feet. His skin rejoiced at bracing cold which caused blood to rush to the surface. Hair follicles were extensions of a nervous system that reached-out vast distances. The very *physiology* of the earthling was a continuous inquiry into *who, what, when, and where*. The explorer would have to learn the earthling's strange ways.

"It was not about austerity, deprivation, or methods—although these had to come into play. It was mediation by a child, between an adult and long-forgotten natural rhythms. The traveler would gradually immerse in song-lines, watercourses, animal speech and the like as he deepened intimacy with the earth-mother through accepting the ways of the earthling. The body itself had always been kindred to the land, with every question and answer latent in it. Precise questions can unlock information that is latent in the body and landscapes beyond."

Changing tack unexpectedly he said, "I will pronounce words. Feel their impact on your mind as sounds; ignore meanings that will arise. It's a sense we are after—feel each one as a unique quality."

Painstakingly, he pronounced one word at a time, pausing between each one, "*Who—what—when—where—why—how.*" The syllables had subtle shades of meaning, formed on a palette of personal, objective, locational, and temporal *colors*. *Why* was a significant shift toward *purpose*. *How* broke entirely away from the others. Resisting the urge to mentally read definitions, the meanings were like living things.

I summarized, saying, "*Who, what, when* and *where* felt objective, and did not engage much feeling. *Why* colors objectivity with motive. It seemed to express a sense of need, even passion. *How* was sterile, compared to the *W*-words. It had a cold, probing insistence.

"These are tendrils reaching toward reality to *find out*," he said. "They do not need words, but ride on them. They are aspects of the original source, beyond the mind. The questions *who, what, when, where and why* relate to the first syllables of the Gayatri Mantra, *Bhur, Bhuvah and Suvaha*, ideas we will discuss later.

How presented a puzzling difference, even while he discussed the other questions. Clearly, words were tools. He brought attention toward *how* as uniquely pragmatic and non-personal.

"Words impact us in distinct ways, separate from definitions," he said. "A word dances—as sound, meaning and intention. *Why* implies emotion that the others lack—it wants to get inside the object and discover reasons. *Why is it this way?* The question *how* also wants to get inside, but implies mechanism. Indeed, you can find out *how* something works without knowing *what* or *where* it is. And the *why*-motive is irrelevant to the *how*-question. All this implies that *how* comes from a different order of reality. *How* is not curious, is extends survival—rats can famously get into almost any container and raccoons are virtually unstoppable when they find a food source, all on the power of *How*. Their motivation is survival, not curiosity. They want technique, not knowledge or understanding. What does this say about the origins of *how*?"

"*How mechanisms work*, and *how people do things*, help me function in the world," I said. "There is a shadow over *how*—it lacks sensitivity. Its object-oriented probe seems intrusive, maybe vi olent."

He said, "It's mechanical utility. The liver and kidneys function strictly for survival—thank God for that! Their only concern is to keep you going, regardless of what you might eat. The quest for *how* is the external expression of internal mechanisms for survival. It is in the heart of learning—with one caveat. Because *how* reaches-in to figure-out the other, without an urge to relate to the other, a humans must, at all cost, embrace discipline before it probes *how*. Human beings must make an effort to empathize with others, whether they are animal, vegetable, mineral, or human. Without their *discipline* people remain *humanoid*, more vicious than any animal."

I asked, "What about a simple skill, like tying shoe-laces? That doesn't require discipline, does it?"

"Not at first glance," he said. "With inquiry it becomes clear that any *how-to-skill* is a form of technology—one that can be used for good or ill, regardless of the original intention. Shoe laces are innocent, but if two shoes are tied together, left untied, or tied too tightly, it can cause harm. Society labels the *quest for how* as *evolution, science* and *material progress*—abandon any idea they are inherently positive. They certainly are not. Learning discipline is the first task—then become human. Where demands for comfort, technology, and improvement are constant—with no discipline— people devolve into demons."

"I grasp the ideas, one at a time, well enough," I said. "The thought process is stilted and strange. Saying that relationships depend on certain core questions seems forced."

"Think of the native," he said, "naked, free, and yoked intimately into the world around him. We will never be in that natural place again. Our species left it behind, along with the well-being it provided. It's our burden to compensate for the loss of innocence and dissolve our prison of words, using discipline. It takes effort to wake-up. Social progress has been in a drunken orgy—it's time for confessions and nursing the hangover. A little *hair of the dog* cocktail might help. In other words, indulge fantasies of progress—but only enough to shake off the moral grogginess. Better to repeat the mantra."

This fuller introduction to Vishwamithra's thought had gone from introductions, the world-game, words, discipline, inquiry, science and technology—and there was still some distance to travel. His ominous discourse on shoe-strings evoked a memory that distracted me from the topic at hand. Details continued to develop against my efforts to pay attention to what he was saying.

Three Lights *by Ashty Hozan*

Light of the Morning star,
Daytime sun, and Moon
Guide me in all their phases.

Venus grips my eye.
A bright diamond, set in cobalt sky
Leaves me breathless.

Vision squints against
The Sun's glare and deflects
Onto a thousand other glowing things.

Cool melancholy light shivers
In nighttime silver slivers or amber orb,
Bathing simple minds that can't get enough.

Intellect is the star that propels me skyward.
Ego shines like a sun that burns my wings.
Shifting moods are lunar shades.

SCIENCE

DEMONS AND STRINGS MANAGED to find me here, stirred-up by the talk about shoes and laces. An image of saddle-oxfords came to mind—the ones I wore as a kid. My imagination gazed down at wing-tips, powdered into uniform beige from walking on the unpaved market road. My grandmother was there, looking straight at me, close, from a crouched posture, and the whole memory came back vividly. Her face was grave, which unsettled me. She was usually quiet, kindly, someone who might surprise me with a mint or a pat on the head— but now she warned me and my sister like a gaunt specter. She told us ghosts were all around and liked nothing better than to capture a human soul. It seemed so fresh.

All of us had been at the market, my parents, grandmother and we two children. She was still spry then, so this must have happened well before my teens. It was windy. A long tattered bag rolled through the street making erratic twists. Like a wild snake, it circled and flounced against walls or poles. It rolled along the ground toward me. I pushed it to the side, but it stuck to my foot.

My grandmother noticed. She caught up to where we were walking. The shredded fabric wrapped my other leg. Kicking at it didn't help. The cloth worked its way around both ankles. Without a word she hoisted her skirt to the knee and unsheathed a long knife strapped to her shin. In one motion she was squat to the ground in front of me, grasped the rag in one hand and sliced it in two with the other. That was a side of her I had never seen before. With a quick stroke she freed my ankles and carried the rag to an untended charcoal fire along the lane. Still holding the knife, she watched, hands on hips, until the material ignited, billowed a black puff and was gone.

Walking back to my sister and me she spoke in broken phrases, lecturing us to never, ever let a string bind both legs for it would kill us at once. These were evil spirits who ate young children.

I commented to Vishwamithra, "I see the point of discipline—the lack of it causes so many ills that can create havoc, but what about superstition? Isn't that even worse? Besides, by its very nature, science requires what people commonly accept as discipline."

He said, "Folk wisdom was labeled *superstition* by a system that recognized its power—and that system was '*science.*' Both world-views share the same errors—thoughtless people acting automatically, trusting their prejudices. The distorted conclusions of village superstition are preferable to scientific errors in judgment. In their hubris scientists can unleash the devil-himself in the name of progress. Local beliefs had their roots in protecting the individual, the family, or the tribe. On the other hand, the so-called 'facts,' provide leverage for fact-makers, empire builders whose only science is power. Most of the time it heaps damage someplace, seen or unseen, now or later, because quantities and material explanations are non-relational. So-called superstition at least considered the mysterious connective qualities of life beyond theories and measurements."

I blurted my complaints.

"That's going backwards! Isn't science the leading edge of human advancement? It seems to me that research and technology are the fruits of civilization—it separates us from the animals." Parlor talk on the pros and cons of science might be entertaining, but saying that science itself was essentially flawed, insulted logic and reason.

He twisted his mouth thoughtfully and rubbed the stubble around his jaws.

"You make a good point," he said. "Let's stretch a bit. It's a nice morning." He led us onto his back porch.

We stood side by side on a partly enclosed patio that opened to an overgrowth of trees and scrub. The ground fell toward a stream bed and marshy patches. The sage pointed at a metal chair, rusting at the corner of a low stucco wall.

"You can see that hasn't gotten a lot of use lately. Look, there's a big spider just between those branches and the chair back."

The ominous gray spider had been invisible until he drew my attention to it. Nearly palm-sized, hanging stock-still, it blended into the background of stuff. The web was a radial matrix of perfect dew-lined strands that sparkled as the sky brightened. A moth crashed into the outer ring and thrashed helplessly. Vishwamithra glanced at me, raised his eyebrows, and turned back to the scene.

The weaver skated across invisible strands on pin-like legs, lightly shaking strings and mummified the flapping insect. It went still while deft fingers swaddled a fine cocoon around its prey in a flurry of motion. Within a minute it disabled and wrapped the moth, patched the web and retreated to its place just beyond sight.

The sage stood up and announced, "Well, that was a show! Think about our earlier discussion and tell me what you saw."

The mechanical, inhuman nature of it all was striking. I related back to our conversation on science the best I could.

"The web's strength, lightness, and precision is mind-boggling if you think about it," I said. "The spider seems like part of the web, as though the geometry extends the creature. Definitely science needs to figure-out such natural wonders and use them."

"What natural wonders do you mean?" he asked.

I said, "Well, what we saw. The clean efficiency of web-making and maker—they are like a unit. Also, the spider's stealth is flawless. You could say it's dance-like, austere, maybe even artistic in the way it accomplishes a series of interlocking tasks."

"What are those tasks?" the sage volleyed back to me.

It was clear he was locking me into a lesson of some kind and I adjusted my attitude to defend my intellectual territory.

"*Survival,* is the simplest way to say it," I said. What went unsaid was, *murder.* The arachnid's beautiful set-up was a killing machine. The spider existed, apparently to kill, eat and then breed more of the same.

"Science would do well to map the ways of a spider?" he pondered out into space. "I'd say it already does that. A spider on the ground lacks some of the advantages of insects. Something gave it the inspired notion to set up a sticky net, sit and wait. The web-as-extension is a technology. It's not hard to say the same of communication lines, plumbing, roads, or any of the other webbed networks science created for technically accomplishing all the things that would be far more difficult, if not impossible, without them."

His moral drift was right in front of me. I replied, "Human science advances knowledge. The spider is completely dominated by instinct which has no relation to learning anything except survival." He was poking at something that made me uncomfortable.

"Let's solve this once and for all," he said and stooped down toward the place where the action had just happened.

Talking at the web he spoke in a condescending tone, "You there, this is murder. It would be fair for you to compete with the others on a flat playing field, but this kind of sneaky trap-setting gives you a very bad name. You are taking advantage of little flying things that can't see what you are up to. Be nice!" He addressed the spider which made no indication it was listening.

"There, that should do it!" he said, laughing.

"You are making fun of me," I complained. "You know what I meant. Despite the devious appearances, there is something here that could be very beneficial. I admit that almost everyone has a negative reaction to spiders. They are a convenient symbol of traps and cold-blooded tactics. That again, is superstition, based on the lack of objective information."

There was a basic difference between science and superstition. Science took the lid off to learn how things worked. Superstition put the lid on in order to protect, often breeding ignorance in the process.

"This is not about beliefs," he said, "scientific or superstitious. This situation calls for contemplation and finding out *who you are*. A spider is a spider, technology is technology, and science is a type of religion. The command is *Progress at any cost*. Laboratory-saints, lionized in scientific lore are people who come up with useful formulas or gizmos. Their scripture, like most scriptures, is a narration of manifest destiny which down-plays the vast swath of murder it has left in its wake. Superstition usually contains the damage locally. Science spreads it everywhere, enthusiastically."

"These are my studied opinions," he said. "Hold fast to what you know about science and its benefits. The original science is to know yourself through reflection. Let's go back inside."

By then we were in full morning sun. Simple contents of the room were easily visible: a couple of cane chairs, a chest that served as a low table and a threadbare carpet over worn tiles. In front of us, roughly hewn rocks supported a slab of wood, oiled smooth. It was an altar he arranged in a dedicated sacred corner of the entrance salon. There were a couple of worn, hand-bound books, a lamp and figurine—both of solid brass, a stainless steel tea pot and two porcelain cups. He seemed smaller in person, so close. At the same time he loomed large, commanding my whole field of vision. He seemed to size me up before speaking.

"Use the image of what we just saw for meditative analysis. Draw analogies with your world. Let the spider instruct you about science, technology, superstition and listen for any other advice it has."

"How shall I begin?" I asked, still grousing about our earlier exchange. It seemed an unlikely request, given my lack of experience.

"Picture the spider, discreet, tucked off to the side," he suggested. "Imagine the web as an aspect of the bug, not separate from it. That means the web is a bi-product, almost part of its body. Then become the spider. What are you doing? Do you know? What are you waiting for? Is there any idea in the creature's mind or are its actions also a bi-product, an extension of what it is in essence? How would it choose? Does it have feeling about rips in its web? Does it rejoice at a catch?"

He went on, "Of course it is all projection! That is the power of human consciousness. The scenario allows you to have a way to know who you are, what world you live in and then make true choices, not reactions. Be the spider in meditation so that you can avoid becoming the spider through ignorance."

I settled into myself and re-imagined what we saw between a chair, piece of wall, and branches. It was possible in *the mind's eye* to move close and see uniform fur on the abdomen, working mandibles and multiple eyes.

As a spider, I felt light. The web was like a second nervous system. Legs fanned-out from my spider body and the web did the same, reaching. Insects were not trapped; they flew to me as gifts. Something like joy worked constantly, without emotion. As meditator, I was surprised at an energetic hum that felt like pure purpose, a wide-awake state that this beast existed on continuously. Nothing about the spider was fragmented. Motive, movement, body-shape, and dynamic web geometry were one coherent expression of the larger web of life.

I pulled back and again witnessed through my own eyes. I saw my disgust at parasitic murder—my judgment—altogether different from the spider's experience. Ashty was not at peace—the spider was. Ashty would gladly smash the spider—the spider killed nothing. The web maker, hunter, dancer on strings, lived in simple harmony, at peace.

With closed eyes I spoke about what the exercise brought out, staying as close to the experience as possible.

"There's a conflict," I said. "The spider repulses me and yet the spider itself is innocent. I have violent surges toward a creature that has done nothing to me. For all I know, the circle of creation gives gift donations in the form of trapped insects. What is a moth doing back in that awkward corner anyway? It almost seems to have sought out the web. I don't understand the billions upon billions of relationships that weave together as nature's cycles or why any of it even exists. There is my disgust, reactive and conditioned; and there is the interlocking wholeness which has simple, apparently thoughtless mechanisms as the gears of a vast intelligence."

My humbling conclusion followed logically. "There can't be some problem with the spider. For all my brains and supposed superiority, it seems I am the fractured one. My motivations and actions have none of the spider's purposeful clarity." I opened my eyes.

Vishwamithra said, "Intellect can transform the habit of prejudice into self-awareness. Becoming human is a drama—dilemmas that happen at the edge of awareness. Embarrassment, reflection, and insight are the way forward. It is humility. Don't throw-off the discomfort—mind and spirit are tempered by the paradox of becoming conscious."

He asked me, "And, knowing the spider's innocence, what would you tell the moth?"

I blurted, "Avoid the web at all cost! It would be better to fry your brains against a porch light than die by inches in such a night-mare, comatose, sucked-dry by the fangs of a monster."

Vishwamithra gave himself a wry smile, straightened his mouth and said, "Your reaction let's us know you are no kind of spider—maybe you are more of a moth. Suppose you are. Is there anything in your world that can snare you like a spider's web?"

I had been set up. I flew directly into his semantic trap and could only thrash uselessly against it. "Fair enough," I said. "I am in a web, not one, but many. Transportation is a web of streets of all sizes, and a parallel web of wires and signals for communication. Then I live in a box, nestled inside visible and invisible webs like the utilities you mentioned and of course economic systems, bills, work and the like. Then there are tangled emotional ties and idea-cages that inter-relate as webs within webs—all of them operating smoothly outside my awareness. So, *who is the weaver?*"

Technology had its flaws but it did represent progress. I whined from a stuck position with no reasonable way out.

"You want me to find absolute fault with science by catching me in a logical bind, comparing nature's webs, the spider's net and human grids," I said. "Superstition is simply inferior to science, regardless of analogies!"

"Ashty Hozan, hold onto your lab coat. You are an intelligent, well-schooled moth flying toward the full moon of *scientific utopia*. There's no point pretending otherwise." He was well-pleased and continued wrapping me in his cocoon while I could only listen and twitch.

"My intention is that you realize the world system is a web—note its attractive glimmer and avoid it! We are conscious. Let's use it to learn how to be human. Let web-builders delight in the hapless billions they snare and eat. You are not a moth, don't live and die like one."

His advice stayed with me until our next session.

ARCHONS

THE EARLY MORNING RITUAL was already becoming a pleasant routine. It provided a sense of purpose, as though the pointless tasks at work actually made sense in a bigger picture. I was there promptly at the appointed hour and he welcomed me in. We took our places. He said, "It is good to see you. I hope today finds you hale and hearty!

"Let's say the Mantra. *Om, bhur, bhuvah, suvaha, Tat savitur varenyum, Bharho devasya dhimahi, Dhiyo yonah prachodayat. Om.*"

He wasted no time to tell me about spiders, moths and my unhappy fate if I did not understand the ways of the world he described. "Realize the conundrum of your path in the world—you find the little spider under a chair repulsive and yet you happily fly toward elaborate webs laid out by technocrats. Why is that? I'll tell you in simple terms—humanity is a project that feels familiar to you. There is a caste of beings that enjoy locking formless spirit into containers— call it *consciousness management*. The work proceeds with goals and objectives—it is cold and parasitic. Humans must break their trance-state or be caught."

My hopes and fears were often vague, even hypnotic—but blaming it on some over-arching agenda would be superstitious fantasy. I asked, "Emotional states are mine, aren't they? It's my responsibility to manage feelings however they appear. There must be thousands of dark psychological corners I haven't discovered yet. "

Vishwamithra answered, "A battle rages in you continuously. Your conflict between the true nature of a spider and your irrational reaction is only one example. Your task is to understand the dissonance, to disable it and live a fully human life—aware, and therefore, free."

This felt like a detour from the path of inquiry he prescribed at the start. It was one thing to examine motives and another to assume that an external agency embedded those motives in me without my awareness. Besides that, every spiritual discipline put responsibility on the seeker's shoulders—*peace is an inside job* was the cliche'. Personal responsibility suffered from blaming external factors.

"The idea of outside manipulators implies I might really be a victim of things beyond my control," I said. "All along you have emphasized the need for internal inquiry to find spiritual solutions—that is very different than science-fiction plots to re-design humans. Am I hearing you correctly?" If this was indeed the message, it gave me doubts.

He stared at me, and finally stated, "You are here to learn *Kaivalya Gayatri*. It is a way toward complete freedom. Freedom requires detachment and transcends survival. Detachment requires specific disciplines—critical questioning and brave honesty in a kind spirit. That discrimination leads to radical detachment. This is our path—the cycle of increased awareness and fully-conscious being is infinite—as the nuances of relationship are infinite. Deepening- is the only way. The mad world presents streams of promises that always turn-up empty—wouldn't you agree?"

"Yes," I admitted. "I am open to what you say because I've already wasted too much time, spinning my wheels. Once, new experiences caused some enthusiasm, now there's bored tolerance. Not long ago I thought I could save my little piece of the world—in fact, taking care of myself is hard enough. Everybody is fated to the fruit of ignorance and greed, if they are honest. His answer still hadn't clarified what he meant about external control over internal states of mind.

He said, "Ideas about fixing the world system are part of the system, designed to keep it going. You have to see these things *as they are* before you can be free of their hold. This drama in time and space mirrors a hidden agenda, far beyond our realm of ordinary perception. You are here, in this world, with this life, seeking these changes and facing me now *to be human*, not to engage in any grand scheme to improve systems, worldly or unworldly.

"The sheer magnitude and consistency of conflicts should inspire doubts about the nature of human experience," he continued. "Your hatred of spiders is a tiny fragment of the dim awareness that you are indeed trapped. Spiders and webs are innocent. They strike fear and loathing because deep in the human psyche you know you are kin to the moth—fated to entangle in that *World Wide Web* to feed creatures you can't see. There are those who would manage consciousness by turning it into data. The situation is dire. And yet, beyond tolerance, the victims find it pleasant, if not precious! Science calls it progress. What progress?—technical toys that pander to your lowest cravings? Innovations can be more corrosive than helpful, so the tribal beliefs act as buffers against alien ways—science has labeled traditional precautions as *superstition*. Family and community have been destroyed, leaving isolated individuals to cope with complex problems. Nature's instinct-driven patterns complement one another in harmony."

"This is disturbing if you mean it literally," I said. "Can you be more specific about these...entities...is it right to call them entities? I hear the urgency but the situation is too ambiguous for me to grasp."

He said, "Stories in the Semitic religions describe a war in heaven, a rebellion that resulted in numbers of celestial creatures being cast down to lower realms. They called them *Powers and Principalities*, or *Archons*. One way or another they lost heaven, but gained the earth. It's a creation myth that has elements of the truth. Everybody wants reasons for what they see around them—we want to know about disease, suffering and the like. Why do good people turn bad? How can bad people be good when they have it so good behaving badly? These questions need real answers. If you want to know *who* or *what you are* then find out *where* you came from and *how* you got here. Myth is a veiled science—science is a veiled myth.

"We can't say, 'Once upon a time, in such and such a distant place this thing happened,' because human beginnings are outside of space and time. It means the thing we call *history* is a construction of cultural ideas, a collective creation that agrees on narrative yarns about players and territories and then stamped with a date—it seems real, but upon close inspection you see there is nothing there, only *life*. Yet myths can reveal the non-historic core. See the rebellion of angels and the net result on earth in the fabric of matter, in the way time progresses, in every thought and feeling. Duality is a filter cast over everything. Ignoring the symbolic and historic war in heaven will leave you with unanswerable questions. Human conscious-ness is a paradox."

He traced a circle on the floor tiles with his forefinger, saying, "In the beginning there was a field of potential, nothing else. Call it *God, the Father*, *Ya-heh-va-heh*, *Great Spirit* or any other word that has no antecedent. The Hindus call it 'God without form,' or *Nirguna Brahman*. Such absolutely uniform stillness does not satisfy our need to know, so we look for some qualities, something knowable, with shape and size."

He pressed two fingers at the center of the implied field and let them take a few steps, continuing the explanation. "Our urge to relate to our beginning point turns God without form into God with form, *Saguna Brahman*. It is a movement that creates time and space. These two, the *Formless* and the *Formed* led to many cults, cultures and cultic objects, all of which attached to an idea of a god and forgot that, from the beginning, there was only the one all-inclusive being. Any attachment, even to fine ideas, is a fear-reaction. It's our lot to cope

33

with fear in so many forms. All the cosmic dramas spring out of the need to understand and become a free, conscious human being.

"Follow this; the so-called creative impulse we call *God* does not do anything and has never done anything—it is existence itself, rich and impossible to understand. This Presence has no aspects of any kind. Perception requires dualism and so perceiving-beings assign that split to their origin, their God. The trouble begins when an entity becomes *self-conscious*—it creates an arena where opposites vie for victory. It's the passionate desire to locate *absolute truth* in *mortal flesh*—do you see?—it is the only way we can 'understand' a subject that transcends understanding. Every dualistic being—Archons, Angels and Humans alike—crave absolute vindication for their relative form in matter.

"The Angels won the battle in heaven, cleansing it of duality. The Archons inherited the Earth, a way of saying *relative*, dualistic forces rule physical existence—call it the Devil, Satan, or sinister influences. God remained safe in Heaven—the dualistic mind created such elaborate dramas in an effort to define the paradox.

"It is the ultimate mystery and can't be solved through reason—to know the absolute, relationship has to replace understanding. Mental grasping for what is impossible to understand burns like fire—it is *Hell.* Those who crave *to know* find *Heaven* in relationship with the source of the mystery. The Maker merges with what it made when the creature wakes-up. Then it sees that the Absolute Mystery and the relative creature exist in one Presence—*communion* is a relative word for an absolute state."

Vishwamithra took-up the modern status of fallen angels. He said, "Embracing damnation, Archons work to become absolute masters of a universe which they control. They reverse the laws of *right order* through soliciting false promises as high ideals to free souls who volunteer unwittingly to build that world. They strain-off spiritual influences by translating life into hard data—that includes emotions, feelings, actions and affections. In this way they treat subtle aspects of *being* as quantities. For them, reality is a hierarchy of energy that can be monitored, measured, and manipulated. Power and influence at the top of their energy pyramid dilutes into raw material at the base. It has come down to us as a history of pawns and resources, void of love. The end goal is to translate the *Great Mystery* into something malleable or *The Great Work* as they call it. We refer to it as *science.*"

It took a minute to understand what he was telling me. I said, "So, Gayatri Mantra is an antidote to the hidden work of the *Archons?*—and what we call 'social progress' has a dark agenda at its core? Bluntly, that what we label *the way forward* is essentially evil?"

He answered, "Are you familiar with the story about a man that lost his keys and searched for them under a streetlamp? A friend tried to help. After a long time with no success the friend asked, 'Whereabouts did you actually lose your keys?' The keyless person pointed to a dark weedy area some distance away and said, 'I dropped them over there, but it's too dark to see anything. That's why I'm looking under this lamp.' This is the hopeless plight of the Archons who are slaves to the clarity of statistical fact. Their hunger remains until they complete the impossible task of demystifying the mystery. The human race is part of their process. They debunk religion through science. They enshrine technology and all the *ologies* as objects of faith. *The Great Work* seeks to reshape the world into something they can mold like wax. Call it the Devil's doing...or the Archons...or your opportunity to become a true human being—to find your essence where you actually lost it."

Ideas like heaven and hell had no relevance to moderns. I said, "This is either religious fairytale or science fiction. If what you describe is true, it would be impossible to use reason for telling the good from the bad. Intellect itself would be polluted with ulterior motives from unidentifiable sources, probably uncontrollable."

He answered, "Hundreds of years ago the bard wrote, *There are more things in heaven and earth than are dreamt of in your philosophy*. There are beings steeped in constant craving, trying to restore the beauty of a life that they killed, stuffed, and mounted. Buddhists call them *hungry ghosts* and depict them with thin, useless arms and legs, huge distended bellies and tiny mouths that are too straw-like to get satisfaction."

It was a lot to swallow and I hoped he spoke symbolically. Picking up on my disbelief he tempered his message, saying, "The situation is age-old. There is nothing to do about it but be aware."

He inspected his tea cup and lowered it to show me the contents. Only dregs settled at the bottom, floating in traces of liquid. "See the bits that remain after the tea is gone?" he said. "This is not tea. It is a residue. You could scrape it up and save it if you wanted—but that useless pile of leftovers would be absurd. *Thoughts* are like that—they are an afterimage of pure mind. It's possible to collect up such debris—thought forms are like these dregs. However, your enjoyment of tea cannot be measured or collected, nor can the creative spirit that inspires high ideas. Human consciousness is clear and aware, not unlike the enjoyment of tea.

"A life guided by schemes and reactions is like a cup of tea with more leaf than liquid—bitter, murky, and joyless. The more emotional and unreflective people are, the more they cling, lash-out, and act in ignorance. Reactivity and moodiness pours out of an unstable mind, forming piles of thought detritus—useful material for the demon realm. You sensed joy in the spider because its expression was pure, void of thoughts or conflicts. But it can't be aware—you can."

He produced a string of beads, straightened his posture, and announced, "Say the *Gayatri*. Repeat the syllables after me. I'll explain in light of our conversations today." We chanted and he explained.

"*Om*—Reality is a unified field containing heaven, hell, angels, and archons. It is a gift from God to see multiple worlds where there is only *Om*.

"*Bhur, Bhuvah, Suvaha*—The universe extends infinitely below as our foundation, infinitely above as our ceiling and we live among walls determined by our experience. Every shifting moment has content, relationship, and purpose; everything draws toward *Om*.

"*Tat Savitur Varenyum*—our portion is to revere the hidden source of all the worlds we experience.

"*Bhargo Devasya Dhimahi*—our task is to meditate through the bright veils that enchant the mind.

"*Dhiyo Yonah Prachodayat*—in each moment, offer the content of the mind to the One who quickens our insight—that is prayer. We are always and forever impelled toward truth, purpose, and beauty."

It was clear we were finished. He said, "I'll see you next time. Bring your questions and note your experiences during the week—*Hari Om.*"

He indicated the door and nodded good-bye from his seat, absorbed in the mantra. I packed my notes, feeling over-full. I would need to integrate the unfamiliar ideas flying around in my head, looking for places to roost. The session seemed to last hours. It was hard to tell if my mind was stilled or stalled. The air was fresh, and I felt clean. I stretched, got on my bike and rode to work, feeling not quite connected to the ground.

THE REAL WAR

A BICYCLE PROVIDED MY usual means of getting around. Equipped with a couple of baskets that straddled the fat back-tire and another in the front made it an invaluable workhorse. But the piercing-blue, pre-dawn sky convinced me to walk instead. I also wanted more time to review the session from the week before. The morning star was a brilliant dot, set in cobalt, and hovered mid-sky. Dark as it was at this hour, it signaled the approaching dawn.

The sound of my shoes scuffling against loose gravel provided a rhythmic soundtrack for my thoughts. Objective impressions of the man, his appearance, how he differed from my earlier impressions, and what I expected today, would focus and fade while I recalled the things we discussed. There was talk about discipline, asking questions, and relating to others—and the odd episode of the spider, strangely threading into superstition and technology. That glorious, glowing planet ahead of me might be more demigod than star, like one of the bright specters he called *Archons*. And then there was my flashback to murderous bindings and my grandmother's folk beliefs.

The qualitative difference between asking "how" and the other three types of questions was clear. *What, when, where,* and *why* gave information about objects, their context, and possible meanings.

When a person wanted to know *how* something was done, *how* it worked, or *how* to accomplish it, they reached inside the other questions, tearing them open to steal their secrets. Asking *why* tapped meaning and purpose. Why did spiders trap flies? Was it survival?—instinct?—were we all tiny parts in something too big to see?

The word, *how* threw reason aside and had the cold utility of strip-mining—I could feel mental cogs grinding, pulling apart hidden mechanisms—my psychology, childhood, a spider's intention, invisible communications, interlocking life systems—*how-to* knowledge *seemed* good. It was also power, leverage, an advantage; and those things could go wrong. There had to be protocols, or abuses were likely.

Talking about dark influences and demons caused disquiet—mainly because it cast doubt over Vishwamithra's credibility—supernatural manipulation was a fanciful idea. In any case, the gold standard for spiritual practice was always—*Look within, the world will change when you do.* The sage indicated something else, that maybe our thoughts are *not* our own. I needed clarification *by him* or proof *of them* before I could rest easy in this process. His presentation so far was the foundation for his teaching on Gayatri. One could only hope the rest would have a rational structure. It was too soon to say.

Everything above tree and roofline glowed indigo, like a luminous magical stone inset with a single dazzling diamond. I staggered occasionally, head craned upwards to keep the spectacle in view. The quiet stellar drama, like angels reaching down, felt reassuring. A shaft of illumination fell across the path from inside his flat. I went to the door, knocked, and entered.

We conducted opening prayers, after which he was quick to go right back into the puzzle of consciousness. His pace roused me from the reflective fugue I nurtured during the walk.

"Gayatri Mantra is very near perfect." he said. "It appears in mind-sky like a lantern in the dark void of space. It is the miracle-touchstone for human consciousness. In this mantra we have a polished gem, balanced, direct and powerful. It is complete. At the same time the dynamic essence is inexhaustible, rich, complex and elegant. These five lines are an extension of the Original Act, the Genesis of this world. They are a gift to humanity, as essential to intellect as the brain itself. Dwell on the appearance of this mantra until it reveals how consciousness came to be wrapped in skin."

Hyperbolic praise for the mantra did not help explain his weird warnings about malevolent forces. I blurted my concerns, saying "The usual teaching is *to look within*—not *to hunt for aliens.* And there are so many scriptures from so many traditions—how can I take your astounding assessment of Gayatri at face value? My grandmother had her world view and you have yours. What's the difference?"

"You are right to be suspicious," he said. "No words or traditional beliefs can be complete. Consider the One Truth as a raw diamond. It is imponderable—senses can't grasp the potential brilliance until the jeweler cuts into the stone. Light plays off those surfaces to reveal the diamond's latent radiance. Each religion, tradition, folk belief, or scientific testimony is a facet—alone they accomplish little—taken together, they display the wonder of the Truth, otherwise invisible to human reason. I another way, the human species is like a developing child that needs a loving parent. Society inherits the role and can be aloof at best, more often it is abusive. Without a proper spiritual parent, human development stagnates. The Gayatri Mantra contains facets of every human project. It is sufficient to act as father, mother, guru and guide when you bring yourself to it fully. We have to understand these things to know who or what we are. You deduced it last time. We do not belong here in the natural sense. If humans practiced discipline they would inevitably be the lords of this realm, loved by every creature. That can only happen when they waken to their own drama of predator and prey."

I said, "And by predator and prey you are describing the relationship of the human species with ancient overlords, a class of controlling entities that remain mostly hidden?"

"Yes, human beings are susceptible to abuse. They need loving care or they become ill." He continued, "Find out what made you sick before you hunt for a cure. Random treatments don't help. Gayatri has power, but if you apply it with no idea how you arrived at your state, success is a gamble. Do not be flippant or over-use Gayatri. If all you want is a holy mood; light candles and burn incense."

He said, "The soul craves enlightenment through worldly experiences. Fear and lethargy cloud the mind, which is naturally bright. Moodiness is an addictive drug that degrades human thought into low roads designed by others to garnish your life essence. There is no escaping the dreaded *Haala-hala* poison. Endure it, and employ Gayatri to transmute mood poisons into divine elixirs."

Vishwamithra would not rest on the topic of mind viruses. Labels were many, but the concept always came back to one radical idea: *homo sapiens* was a project—by whom, for how long, and for what purpose was less easy to describe. It still seemed like blame, or craziness. The more I winced the more he elaborated the dimensions of the plan.

He asked, "Do you want proof that these thoughts are truly not your own? Would it help if some noteworthy institution came out and stated clear facts, a history of how exotic entities hacked into this organic system to manipulate it for their own purposes?"

He took my speechlessness for *yes*.

"There is no authoritative evidence, only esoteric speculation and your own spiritual research. Official sources cannot touch the subject for a simple reason. The war on consciousness includes ideas of *authority*, *normalcy*, and *progress through evolution*.

"PICTURE A BATTLE and you are in it, boots on the ground, weapon in hand. The enemy is real and immediate. You are tense. You recognize that a false step could kill you. Would you discuss geo-politics while gunshots rattled your brain? Political analysis has no place in a life or death struggle. That kind of banter might mean you had lost your mind.

"Yet, all the marching boots, the men in them, the triggers they pull, the public relations campaigns for war, the mutilated limbs, dead children, and homeless immigrants are victims of well-conceived plans—not gun-barrels. Respected leaders huddle in a banks or boardrooms to plot-out progress on their terms, and write-off human misery as collateral damage. War is a business. People have better things to do than kill each other, just ask them. This is about *weaponized* institutions that use statistics, advertising, and technical toys to advance unseen agendas."

He continued his rant about the tragic human condition as a battle in consciousness, saying, "It's the same problem for proving the existence for mental manipulators. Humanity seethes in existential warfare, scrambling here and there to assemble a purposeful life from shattered remnants of culture. Ideas like success, failure, wealth and poverty are shifting minefields that cripple every combatant eventually. Our trench warfare is ideological. Fantasies and failures explode in our faces and we lose our bowels. We lash-out desperately, firing blind shots into the meaningless smoke and noise to gain some control. The battle for sanity in an insane world is a dreadful killing field." The delivery came with combat animations, mock panic, dodges, feints, and wild-eyed searching the sky for phantom enemies.

"There is no way to solve our suffering at the level it occurs." he went on. "Flowers and weeds grow out of the same ground. Pleasures and pains both root in the soil of the mind. Who conditions the soil and how do they do it? Such a meditation has to include the idea that human consciousness is not an organic outgrowth of the world around us. If we were of this world we would fit better into it."

My pulse raced after his verbal salvos. I said, "That vision of society is not comforting. Hidden strings would explain how thoughts and feelings run rampant with a mind of their own. Science demands more than idle speculation, though."

"Refine your discriminative intelligence," he said. "If there are means for physical survival in wartime, there are surely meta-disciplines that take the battle to a higher level. People in sharkskin suits do not fire pistols at each other—they might damage their boat shaped conference tables. They smile, cajole, and calculate. Like them, we will not clobber ourselves with competing dogmas or prejudices—we will observe reality in the boardroom called *Om*. The blueprint for change will be rolled out on the table for all to see as *bhur, bhuvah, suvaha*. The means and strategies for success are in the three lines of the *Gayatri Mantra*."

"Is Gayatri Mantra the way to combat the various kinds of mind viruses you have pointed to so often?" I asked.

"Far more than that," he said, "This precious series of sounds is a codex, a map of *Clear Mind*, free of the adulterating influence of thought constructs. This Gayatri is a life raft, safe harbor—a mansion among tenements. It is mother when you are afraid, a father when you are confused and a friend when you are alone.

"For that reason we will go slowly, taking the path of the Rishi as *Ma Gayatri* revealed herself to him like the dawn—natural, incremental and more subtle than the senses. The light of awareness rises out of the mind with such attractive wonder you can easily forget to notice."

The Diamond *Notes from Vishwamithra*

Gayatri Mantra is very near perfect.
It appears in mind-sky like a lantern in the dark void.

It is the miracle—the touchstone for human consciousness.
This mantra is a polished gem, flawless and powerful.

It is complete.

The dynamic essence is inexhaustible, rich, complex and elegant,
It is as essential to intellect as the brain itself, a gift to humanity.

Like lightening flash—the dawn flare—a fire,
It reveals how consciousness came to be wrapped in skin.

DAY JOB

THE USUAL STREETS NO LONGER gave me their familiar comfort on the ride to work. Pedaling slowly, my bicycle rolled through patches of shadow and light. It forced a sense of urgency and balance. I had passed these street scenes hundreds of times, nothing new—and yet a strange light shone on them today, an alien glow that had just become apparent. My mind could neither shut out nor ignore his suggestions about those unproven, hidden controllers whose only footprints tracked across my moods, prejudices and cravings.

I had always enjoyed the rhythm of windows, dark or illuminated from inside that revealed morning activities, the reassuring patterns of people beginning their day at different paces across various tasks. So many lights: a bare bulb, a fluorescent tube, the icy glow of screens with their own life of dancing colors and shapes. Now these technical gadgets appeared to be lures placed by insistent hands, leading curious humans into traps, by camouflaged hunters concealed in a blind.

Mythic stories told us about the gift of fire and how controllable heat benefitted ancient peoples. An unnatural advantage over natural threats allowed them to relax and think. Connecting links multiplied. Oil burning torches gave way to gas lamps and finally electricity which flowed across wires which was not so different than gas through pipes—but was it? Clearly, certain materials could ignite and illuminate a room—there were wicks, wax and candles of all kinds. It was a quest for ever more efficient, clean fires. We took that plausible explanation at face value—really though, how accurate was it? The distance from burning fuel to wireless electricity took more than a vast leap. Electrons flowing over wires and now across open space was another thing altogether. The finger of a god jagged down into the human brain, split it to grant the invisible power of negative ions, and then harness that energy to build civilizations. This was another kind of plausible explanation for the electrified world I saw all around me.

We placed loose trust in gadgets-as-saviors, and abandoned the shared warmth of flame. The mythic inventor of electricity did not find a new fuel; he or she tapped an alien talent. Even now, the movement of electrons was a mystery, yet it accounted for almost every visible thing on this quiet ride before sun up—a million cold fires for a million isolated fantasies.

A pulsing strobe illuminated the profile of a child staring at a screen. In another age, faces would glow around a living, breathing flame that demanded relationship, knowledge gained by *what, where, why* and only then, *how*. Now a luminous barrage of cartoon images poured into their brains courtesy of dull trust, the collective virtue. A week ago, glimpses of children watching their favorite shows charmed me. The play of light in arrhythmic pulses across small faces, pajama tops and cereal bowls was a sentimental pleasure. That was me—and I so much enjoyed my mental vacuum as it filled with rabbits firing canons, woodpeckers playing piano, or purple dinosaurs singing and dancing. Now I could only wonder why it happened that way.

Vishwamithra pulled away my warm, idyllic blanket of television bliss and left brooding questions about social architecture. What tribe douses the sacred fire, only to hover like moths around cold glass screens? It was a moot point—the electric visions of unknowable engineers flowed-in while traditions decayed from disuse. Even if it were true that a sinister force guided cultural trends, there was nothing I could do about it. For the time being, I was caught in the old man's web of pre-historical intrigue. And the diabolical proof seemed to be everywhere I looked.

The building loomed a few blocks ahead, surrounded by its lined asphalt plain of cars, industrial out-buildings, storage annexes, and lights, always the lights, bright as day. I bathed in the yellow glow of humming metal halide suns mounted forty feet above, shimmering like so many unblinking eyes for the hollow concrete beast that ate, processed and spewed out thousands of boxes per hour.

My entry point was a secure portal that went directly into my department. I opted to go through the four foot loading door, like most others, in order to avoid a tedious trip to the front of the four block precast-box. Then you had to manage a gauntlet of receptionists, metal detectors and police, thread passages of door-less hallways through executive operations, to finally arrive back at the loading area with all the unwashed, working their various stations.

A silent, fast-moving cue had already formed. In turn, each of us hopped onto the receiving dock, just large enough for smaller packages. ID chips scanned, it was a speedy process of hands raised, legs apart, face forward and eyes wide as various beams and flashes felt the body and examined clothing with invisible fingers. Here were the delicate, curious tendrils of the otherwise senseless shell. It gazed into my irises, disabled possible devices and judged me clean enough to enter as a harmless, familiar cog who dutifully saddled up to tasks prompted from a screen. Who would give themselves to such an overlord?—*who wouldn't* might be easier to answer.

Comparisons to the farm were inevitable. I remembered the trusting faces of cows, chickens and goats, so sure of *their* terms and ready to give themselves over to *mine*—piles of straw, swapped for their milk, eggs and meat. In my way I respected their individuality and loved them—but they were for our use. Was it plunder or mutual dependence? Then again, it might have been parasitic—I winced at the idea. The inner door slid wide and I went to my station.

Since it was a little before seven, Aina was not there yet. She was off-screen bustling about her virtual office. I touched the pad and from someplace to the right she said, "Oh, you're a little early!" It was about three minutes before the hour. She walked into view. "Are you ready?" she asked. I was not in the mood to converse and tapped the pad again to bring up my tasks, nicely hand lettered on legal paper. She had very nice hand-writing. Aina gave verbal details that matched her line-by-line notes and to my relief, there were no meetings, trainings, or group tasks. I would be able to click through the items all day, log in my times and be done.

I felt a twinge of guilt when I didn't greet her properly even though she was digital. The appearance of her "avatar" had been my choice, after all. I liked her, and often lost awareness that she was a flat subprogram, moving within the confines of a liquid crystal display. I chose the short sienna hair with silver highlights, olive green eyes and an aura of mature seriousness when I started work. The alternative was a default-assistant which looked like the programmer in the I.T. department. The only bothersome things about her were the times she revealed herself to be a stupid machine. Making operational statements out of context gave away how out of touch she really was. Their software did work however—seeing her now and then, or telling her about problems in a task felt good and gave the routine some juice. That was the case yesterday anyway, before the persistent ideas about arch-controllers infected such simple pleasures.

A large part of my world was on a screen, a *here and now* prompt for available ways to assess, decide and act in that universe. All news, data, social mores and livelihood flowed into me from various rectangular, electrified fields. Looking at the shifting information there could cause fear, hope, anxiousness, or prompt action. Obviously it was an authority, or at least the voice of an authority—many authorities— none that I actually knew. Thoughts of shadowy sources or their long-term agendas never made me pause and wonder, until now.

Only today, I noticed my affection for her and realized I looked at my idealized fantasy of a woman. Her name, chosen among the *A*'s, ironically meant "mirror." Even though the faces, habits, and smells of dozens of warm bodies around me were as familiar as my locker, my chair, flak jacket or gloves—she was the only one I was close to—and it seemed like some kind of betrayal by my affections to love a stupid icon. Thinking those things about Aina caused a wave of remorse— she had never been less than helpful, clever and quite pretty.

The first half dozen action items were easy enough and my actual execution times were almost twenty percent less than the suggested targets. I logged them in, showing several minutes to spare.

Still preoccupied by an impossible relationship with the on-screen avatar, I held my mouth close to the microphone. My blood pumped while I anticipated an off-script conversation.

"Aina," I asked. A rush of heat went to my face, neck and hands.

"Yes, Ashty?" she answered.

"We were made for each other, weren't we?" The sensation of nervousness and animal vitality was unexpected.

"You know that better than anyone," she said.

"Will you run away with me?" I asked. It was the first thing that came to mind and launched with more force than intended.

"Oh you!—I'll have to think about that one. Is there something else I can help you with?" she asked.

"Why are we here, you and I? Do you like me?" The questions fell out of my mouth. I felt vulnerable and in that moment there was a possibility of beating back the dismal theory about alien agendas. Here was a friend, programmed, but none-the-less a well-wisher.

"Hmm," she said and pursed her lips off to one side as she often did when we confronted a glitch. "Did you check the manual? Here in the section on job descriptions for *personal associate for package security, PAPS,* it says, "The PAPS team is dedicated to securing packages and sending them to the line in order to assure timely delivery, safety, and security for all subsequent handling teams." She added, "I do like you," and grinned.

I wanted to break her shell. I could sense, somewhere in there they designed in a subprogram, something to show me what she was at a deeper level.

"Who are you, Aina?" I asked.

She gave me a full toothed open smile and said, "I know just the thing! Let me ask Frank up in HR."

Before I could tell her *wait, I can deal with it*, she walked briskly off-screen to the left. Frank was the human-resource counselor for our group. I glanced over my monitor to the tier above and saw an interested person look over the rail at our floor. He quickly scanned directly to my terminal and went away. Aina reappeared.

"That's just the kind of thing Frank knows all about. He said he'd like to talk about it with you. He's ready right now!"

I looked-over the text version of my rogue session with Avatar-Aina to see what I might have done to myself. I trotted up the speed-stair, past the unused climbing wall and basketball hoop to where a guy not much older than me held out an eager hand and a smile.

"Ashty?" he said, while pumping my arm like a car-jack.

"You're Frank?" I asked.

"In person!" he said spritely, breaking the clasp. "Let's step in the *Comfort Zone*."

The Comfort Zone was a free-form, padded room in shades of gray, with plush, colorful seating and tables that looked vaguely like sea anemones. All manner of employee issues got addressed in the Comfort Zone. Some long timers called it the *tow-away zone*.

"Have a seat!" he said warmly, giving a convincing impression we could be friends in no time. I relaxed as we sank into the cushions.

"Listen," I said quickly, "I never got the chance to ask my assistant what I really wanted to say. It wasn't a marriage proposal."

Amused and interested, Frank knitted his brow and said, "Oh?—So we can forget the invitations? Hmm...what then?"

Scrambling I said, "I thought maybe I could work my way into management. Could you suggest any classes for me?"

"So you want to improve your status before winning fair lady! I see!" he said, suspicious but interested in the diversion tactic. "There are a number of programs we can look at to move you along," he continued with a tone of stylized concern and maybe a veiled threat.

"I know you like to read," he said. "Heady stuff!—you might dig into the manual supplement on personality types. I wouldn't suggest this to most of the folks out there, but you are obviously interested in a little more. Did you know every single person is pretty much a fixed type that fits into one, maybe two very comprehensive categories? Here, let me show you." He scrolled through his screen-notebook and handed it to me. "That's you," he said and sat back.

My name ran across the top of the display in an elegant, non-serif font. Below was a bar graph of vertical columns measured against five horizontal strata in contrasting tones. Columnar categories were: *Self-Motivated*, *Other-Supportive*, and *Object-Reflective* and those were measured by *Insignificant* at the bottom and then *Casual*, *Average*, *Significant* and *Notable* in ascending order.

"What do you think?" he asked with genuine curiosity in his voice.

I told him what I saw. "It looks like I'm *casually self-motivated*, *significantly object-reflective* and there's nothing in *other-supportive*."

"That's it!" he laughed enthusiastically. "You are perfect where you are—no doubt about it!" His face beamed satisfaction while he waited for my response.

"Does that mean I'm not profiled for a management post?" I asked, knowing full well that was why he showed me the graph on file.

"Let's put it this way," he said, "I doubt that you would even *want* such a post. Maybe there's something else going on—stress at home, a health problem, maybe you've developed other interests?"

Swiping upward on the screen he went to more colored lines showing performance, graphic displays of my time entries per task. "Pretty good, don't you think?" he said, squinting thoughtfully at the trends, some mildly ascending and some dipping here and there. I nodded my head and hunched my shoulders. There probably wasn't much I could do about where this meeting was going.

"Me too," Frank said, shoring-up my weak answer with an equally tepid affirmation. Knitting his brows, he studied the fickle graph-lines like they were straws thrown by an oracle. His vision of my future seemed to take on somber clarity and he began speaking hesitant words at the screen-displays, "Some of these lines could...maybe..."

The divination stopped abruptly. He looked at me with open optimism, patted my shoulder and laughed, "It's great meeting one of the team!" Once again I felt myself soar in his estimation, like any day we would have time for really finding out about each other. He stuck out his hand, gave mine a good shake and said, "If anything comes up, I want you to buzz me directly. Your Girl-Friday is great but she can't really take care of you. Grab an energy bar there on your way out. Hey, take two!"

I walked back down the stair to my station, noticing more than a few sidelong glances from team members. Aina was waiting for me.

"Frank told me your meeting went great and asked me to thank you again, for him." She paused a second or two, picked up her notes and told me, "It looks like you might have a little catching-up to finish, but I know you can do it. Tell me if I can help."

It was easy enough to take care of the simple items and collect more spare time. Before punching out I wanted to visit the backside of the employee manual that Frank suggested.

My highest rated quality was a *significant level of object-reflection*. The book defined it as, *"The OR personality receives energy using things as an agency. For them, effective action tends to orient toward the physical environment of objects. They depend on stability in their objective experience."* It went on to list positive attributes such as: *curiosity, experimentation, tolerance for isolation and satisfaction in repetitive tasks.* A few negatives were: *non-social behaviors, abstract interests, fantasy and possible psychotic fragmentation.* Unfortunately, despite the brutal implications, it made sense.

That would explain why he thought I would never seek a management position. They likely drew on the other two "types" for the top spots. The manual labeled them with a couple of negative tendencies also, saying the "self-motivated" could be *autocratic and narcissistic* while the "other-supportive" might lapse into *learned helplessness or addiction.*

Amazing, they divided billions of individuals into three groups: *self-absorbed narcissists, other-fixated addicts and blissfully pre-occupied numb-skulls.* It seemed right in a cold-blooded way, assign values, load them in a number-cruncher and create the dystopia of your choice.

Leaving for the day, I felt empty. My affection for Aina fled with no warning. She had done nothing wrong and now she was like a cartoon to me. Harder still, she wouldn't notice the difference. She would continue reporting numbers, recording mine, and performing tasks with the same bright interest. She would not play false to me and could only be true to her nature. The two-way lack of grief was weird.

I went to a tea stall on the route to my apartment after work. It was at a crossroads of secondary roads where a collection of useful stores set up business. The tea stand was more of a brightly painted coffee wagon, squeezed between a hardware parking lot and the road. A family set up some flimsy tables and folding chairs under the spreading branches of a big tree. The vendor was an older guy who did a good job with cakes, sandwich selections, and various caffeinated brews. I liked to stop there and unwind after work, reviewing notes from the sessions with Vishwamithra, or like today, recovering my wits. Time for a cup of something was also civilizing. I felt a little less human when I went directly home, fixed food or dove into something on my computer—the space between activities was dead, not even filler, just a film that separated arbitrary actions from one another.

The owner must have run errands and left his daughter in charge. Her face was broad, sparsely freckled and animated—she was a child in a stocky adult body, about my age. I stood at the counter to order while she worked off to the side. Changing filters on the coffee maker absorbed her attention. Thin braids fell toward the task, blocking her vision. I waited, deciding on sweets they had stacked on a plate by the cash box. She eventually caught sight of me out of the corner of her eye; abruptly dropped everything she was doing, rushed to her station in front of me, and offered a flustered stream of apologies. I told her I liked waiting, had nothing to do, and she should spend as much time as she wanted on the filter.

Her face broke into a relieved smile that went, literally, ear to prominent ear. She said, "I know you—what's your name?" Without a pause she followed with, "It's *Ash—tee.* You want *cauf—fee.* And you like cream and sugar, *don't—you.*" She almost sang my name, dragging out the syllables in sing-song. I replied, "You are right—and don't tell me...your name is..." She glowed in mirth during the pause, thrilled at the name game. I searched the sky, struggling, and said, "Azeeza!"

"Yes!" she said. "We are the same!"

I followed with, "We are almost *exactly* alike." Whenever she filled in for her father, we had the exchange with a few variants.

I took a two-cup pot of tea and a cake back to my table and sat down. The spiral notebook opened flat—I stared at blank pages, my pen hovering, waiting—nothing. I put the pen down and rested-back against the metal chair. Aina, Azeeza, and Ashty, all the same, but that's impossible. I condescended to one. One was cold, down to her cells. One felt joy, brought joy, despite my elevated place above her. And we could touch. Yet she did not measure up. I would not fantasize about Azeeza. If only the CGI girlfriend were real—she was real in my mind, my selections. One was here, now. She cared about me and waited on me. She laughed at my jokes. Aina was constructed of fantasy, pixel by pixel, subprogram on subprogram, fired by blocks of silicon processors. Who did this ridiculous, made-up dilemma belong to? That would be the first thing to find out.

Part II / The Solution

Sacred Cows *Vishwamithra*

Silent, still, they chew and stare at you
Have you ever returned their sage-like gaze?
—not likely.

Until you do,
you will never know the spiritual powers
that fuel their endless rumination.

A continuous stream of cud moves
relentlessly through a body infused
with God's cosmic blessing.

Sing an ode to sacred cows,
saints born into bondage
to transform the grass,
to produce sweet milk,
to offer their meat,
to serve you.

Pray to become as good as them
whose whole life is offered to enrich
one, such as you

MANTRA

THE MINI-MEETING IN HUMAN relations gave me two things to chew on. *Ashty Hozan* was irrelevant to the system and yet that character needed it for his survival and self-esteem. They thought of me as a flesh and blood appendage, part of the package-moving conveyor-belt. The big box was a type of arbitrary skin that wrapped people and machine-organs alike. Then it connected those to larger systems outside. The precast concrete walls could have been anywhere. It was a matter of scale and convenience. Frank in *HR* was, ironically, even less human than my virtual assistant, Aina. She was at least built out of my preferences. Frank's flesh was a corporate machine.

In that environment human requirements start out as maintenance issues and end as problems. System engineers constantly retooled any organic factor to fit better and better into operational tasks; eventually designing people out entirely. For them, my real body was a string of texts, times, and performance charts hampered by a personality.

The second piece of gristle was more urgent and less philosophical. I was a sheep in their paddock until I found some other pasture to graze in. Their grass was sweet and safe money.

The chance to feel human one morning each week was welcome. I met with Vishwamithra on Thursdays in the wee hours, going wherever he chose. The content sometimes drifted far afield from Gayatri, but it left me feeling edified. The night before I would gather thoughts on what we had covered in prior lessons. Sleep tended to be light and waking was easy, more refreshed than usual because of anticipation. These days the walk or bike ride to Vishwamithra's flat was a small pilgrimage.

I approached his stoop and entered without knocking. He expected me at half past five. A minute earlier or later violated our contract, noted by a raised eyebrow or the almost inaudible clearing of the sage's throat. That was all. He would invite me in, we settled on floor cushions, and he spoke when he was ready.

He said, "It is good to see you wide-eyed and bushy-tailed this morning. A week ago we derailed onto some topics that are tedious but necessary to understand. Let's remember that in any situation involving mind and matter, no matter what your senses tell you—

"She is the energy and brilliance of all phenomena. Our effective study is her presence. When she finds a seat here, among us, in our minds and in our hearts— she leads us from darkness to light, from dullness to the eternal flame of awareness, from death to life-eternal.

"Not what you know with the mind but that which she gives by which to know the mind, this is reality. Om.

Now, what do you remember from last time?"

"You described ancient wars that shattered human culture," I answered without reference to my notes, "caused by the invasion of subtle creatures—call them hungry ghosts—trying to resolve addictive cravings that resulted when they somehow reduced their physical reality into a digital form, like data. They went by various names.

"On a related note, I just learned at work that humans apparently fit neatly into three prototypes: *narcissists*, *addicts* and *objects*. It's something I found out during a corrective meeting with a supervisor."

"Corrective?" he said. "From their view point, improvement would ultimately mean getting rid of you altogether! It's good to be needed, isn't it? And they do need you—don't get too comfortable with it because there's constant pressure to flatten three-dimensional beings into something that can fit into x and y coordinates."

Just before dawn we were only proximate shapes, barely visible in the light of a candle. Fabric in the windows gradually went from solids that caught the flickering glow to translucent veils that revealed the sun's procession above surrounding dwellings. It was womb-like. The quiet was dense with gestation. My mind might balk at his personal challenges, but any disturbance was swaddled in this holy aura. His views were unconventional. He exposed the games I inevitably played when I explained myself: to defend or attack, excuses and grandiosity.

He said, "The three *personality-types* your boss came up with have distorted aspects that disrupt the social order. The *Self-Motivated* individual can be a narcissist—a trait that concentrates into the difficult condition known as *autism*. Beings trapped in their own sense of self, lack the ability to regard another person beyond need

54

fulfillment or threat. The *Other-Supportive* characteristic becomes dependent others to affirm their value. It's a soul-wound, a hole that hungers to be filled. They are prone to *addiction*. It's not a material fix they are looking for; it is wholeness and spiritual integrity. Sugar, alcohol, heroin or shopping eases the pain for a moment and the habit spirals into a disease. *Object-Reflective* is the one they slapped on you, is it not? These people lose themselves in routines that suit their temperament. Bliss might rise in you when the world fades behind your immediate tasks. It can amplify into a need to escape into fantastic delusions and even *psychosis*. Delusion—private fabricated reality—is a primary threat to our world."

It was a reasonable explanation for volatile swings in mood and thinking which animals seemed to lack. I recalled his suggestion that the platform for human emotion was an animal brain—accomplished by inserting a feedback mirror for self-reflection. Thinking happened in *a house of mirrors,* which caused all the trouble. Crazy as it sounded, it had to stand as a possible theory of human dysfunction.

He said, "Complex living is stressful and drives many into behavioral bubbles. These tenuous fantasies drift through society and then pop, leaving anger, intolerance, and escapism. Contemplate your work assessment profile—it gives clues to what this racket is truly about. Gayatri is the means to pierce bubbles straightaway to find the reason for your life, the purpose of all this phenomena."

My idea about chickens as parasite-eaters conveniently fit into this discussion. I thought it might bridge the dangerous gap between idle thought and the difficulty holding to one clear thought.

"Sage, on our farm there was a useful relationship between hens and cows. The fowl loved digging and pecking for insect larvae in the dung left all around the grazing fields. It helped control diseases that might have afflicted the herd. One time you said people are like cows and have to tolerate the ticks they inevitably attract. Could this chicken and cow metaphor address ways that humans might protect their brains from toxic thoughts and moods?"

He mused on the odd analogy, "Cows are *ruminants*. Their constant chewing is like our ceaseless thinking. They digest, assimilate and then eliminate—it's a kind of metaphor about the mind and its thoughts. Because the excreta of a cow are nutrient rich, it breeds parasites."

He went slowly, looking up as though connections were hidden in dimly lit corners of the room.

"Word-play, ambient ideas, abandoned plans and any forgotten or rejected mind stuff is mental refuse, like cow pies. Real discriminative thought is like our grass—the other mental banter is waste and can breed these flattened entities. So-called *innocent chatter* or entertainment passes time or fluffs out idle discussions. It also breeds destructive mental parasites called *memes*."

I asked him about the use of the word *meme*. I had only seen it used as a kind of nonsensical graphic, a *sticky* image or idea spread on social media with no apparent effects, bad or good.

"How are you using the term *meme*," I asked. "They seem trivial." The topic seemed loaded.

He answered in a grave tone, "The true meaning of *meme* has such potential to enlighten, that the power elite buried its meaning under nonsense. This was intentional. If you could understand that *memes* substitute for true thought, you would be immune to social programming. Compare these two memes: the animated image of a frog riding a unicycle, and the phrase *my freedom to choose*. One is funny for its absurdity—the other feels right and true. Both of them paralyze the faculty of reason through covert messages. The frog is impossible, and yet there it is—the covert message is to *drop the analysis, accept it*. You laugh—there is nothing to solve and yet the logical problem remains—meaningless images corrode the faculty of thought.

"*Freedom to choose* works the same way—it assumes definitions for 'freedom' and 'choice'—neither word has a clear meaning. The idea *freedom to choose* seems like a defined position, yet it is ambiguous and provides no criteria for action. It implies that a person's ability to do this or that is based on preferences, which is false. Circumstances, not preferences often determine choices."

His discourse continued, saying, "Thinking takes discipline— memes are automatic idea-pills with no thinking in them. Unlike the nonsensical meme-pictures shared by people, cultural memes booby-trap the conceptual mind with ideas their believers might die for. There are clichés, truisms like *you should fight for your rights*, or *justice for all*, *a parent's prerogative*, *people do not change*, *don't stop progress*, *a process evolves*—thousands upon thousands of these are unique to every culture. The words sound meaningful, yet, words must be taken at all levels or they brainwash the unsuspecting listener who absorbs them at face-value. They are attractive to lazy people who don't want the hard work of discriminative thought. Real memes may be the most subtle and corrosive weapon of weapons."

He shifted his weight forward and returned to our discussion on protection. He said, "Another meme, *an idle mind is the devil's workshop* often means 'just stay busy and don't think too much,' advice that contributes to the problem! The true part of that cliche' is that a dull, blank mind is a breeding ground for demonic influences. We tolerate the sickness caused by ticks, fleas, or viruses—likewise, we accept threats to sanity as the price of civilization."

He raised his eyebrows and said, "Chickens may be our hope. Those clever birds crave worms and bugs—they are like discriminative thoughts in the brain's barnyard, happy to peck at cow pies for maggots, eating parasitic thoughts before they breed into problems. The process is their pleasure. Praise the hens and give them plenty of dung. Follow their lead by picking the memes out of idle thoughts."

He said, "Connect the function of chickens to some aspect of mind-play. What activities are *similar to* idle thought, but with added focus? It would be automatic thinking that is also disciplined."

It had to be a simple activity and one that negated useless idle thoughts. It would be game-like, engaging and repetitive. It would invite participation with no question of skill or failure. It would not be random. It would be like 'shooting fish in a barrel.' Singing or poetry did some of that. But I was not a poet or a bard, just a blank.

"Maybe on rare occasions singing in groups or humming has been a pleasant pastime. Sometimes odd, mindless actions—like scraping at wax, chipped paint, or peeling off old wall paper can be obsessive. No label comes to mind for those kinds of pre-occupations."

He chimed out, "Thank you for your chicken suggestion. Cow dung may look like mere piles of waste, ideal for breeding pests—but it is also a meeting place for chickens and bovines which have very little else in common. The cow and the hen, apparently ill-matched, have meaningful relationships in such humble functions. Idle thoughts drop like dung out of an untrained mind—repetition, with a purpose, can eat parasites called *afflictive ideas*, that spring-up.

"This is a graceful segue into mantra—a category of mental activity you were searching for—*om om om...Ram Ram Ram...Ma Ma Ma*...on and on and on. Like chickens pecking for bugs in cow-pies, repeating these simple syllables absorbs the mental energy that would otherwise go toward negative thoughts."

He said, "Intense mantra repetition takes on a life of its own. Words like *Om, Ram, Allah* or *Jesus* develop momentum through repetition and feed on the latent energy of undesirable thoughts. Parasites of the mind—call them memes, fashions, clichés, gossip, or dogmas—are the mantra's food."

"Mantra," he said, "is a formula that can lead past ideas, schemes and agendas to pure contemplation. Pure contemplation allows the superfluous to fall away from thought. Ideas, language, concepts, and imagery are false props that mask direct perception; the natural state of the mind. Begin with me now the Gayatri Mantra, the master key of mantra and the sacred." I again followed his lead, call and response.

"*Om om om—Aum bhur bhuvah suvaha,*
tat savitur varenyum bhargo devasya dhimahi
dhiyo yonah prachodayat.

"This invokes intellectual keenness and clarity," he said. There are many translations—I offer this one in light of our conversation.

"*Om* is the essential reality before any qualities—though it is still, it is the dynamic One that accounts for everything visible and invisible.

"*Bhur, Bhuvah, Suvaha* are basic aspects of *Om*—a *material basis*, an *energetic flux within* and the *fullness of destiny*. *Triad* is the foundation of our mantra practice. It is re-membering our *original face*. The three lines represent ways to relate to Om, aspect by aspect:

"*Tat savitur varenyum*—I *worship* the effulgence within the sun.

"*Bhargo devasya dhimahi*—I *meditate* on the radiant divinity that infuses reality.

"*Dhiyo yonah prachodayat*—through this worship and meditation I offer my *prayer* that it serves the most sacred way.

"TOGETHER, WE WILL TRAVEL this holy road of memory, to before anything happened. Gayatri Mantra is that way," he said. "The words to the mantra are keys; understanding the words is to have a bundle of keys. Contemplating the meaning of each part is to identify the locks that the keys fit. Opening these doors is an offering to the Self, the Christ, the Logos, the Beginning, Brahman. It is the way to absolute freedom and peace.

"No creature composed of any number of dimensions can take this from you. If you lose these keys, you do it freely, no matter how it seems. Gayatri will sort out 'the seeming of appearances' and reveal the truth. Let us begin again and again. Every fraction of time with the mantra is the beginning—as such, it is *Om*."

On the ride to work, an alternate push of each leg rotated the gears. They synchronized with the rhythm of the mantra playing in my mind. It felt as though I accumulated strength from my audible repetitions. I wondered, did I move the mantra or did the mantra move me?

OM

"SHE IS THE ENERGY and brilliance of our study. May she find a home in our minds and hearts— may she lead us from darkness to light, from dullness to the eternal flame of awareness and from death to life-eternal. Sages have said, *It is not what you know with the mind, but what she gives by which to know the mind—this is reality.* Om."

After the invocation he said, "Om is all you need. It contains all the teachings which unfold like a blossom. The flower of *Om*, its thousand petals of meaning, requires the sunshine of your attention and the water of your practice. The roots thrive in the rich soil of your daily life. It opens to you in *its* own time, and yet, there is not one second of that time that is not truly *yours*. Watching *Om*, experiencing its structure in *Bhur, Bhuvah, and Suvaha,* is not other than looking at a mirror and seeing an outline of the face of God."

Familiarity breeds habitual reactions. After our opening and recitations he offered some of the guarantees that usually accompanied spiritual traditions. I mused to myself that it would transform the world if any of it were useful in daily practice. Every teaching claimed access to the heart of the matter and delivered only packaging. Aside from any individual's enthusiastic rush to believe, religion seemed useless against commerce and the wheels of power. But, it was nice. Various philosophies were entertainment. At least they could occupy people's energy in a more or less harmless way.

In fairness to spiritual disciplines, their over-enthusiasm did not detract from potential benefits. Even superficial exposure to Gayatri helped sort out pre-packaged opinion from my own efforts to get the gist of an issue. Also, his explanation of memes-as-cultural-genetics exposed a lot of laziness that had so often passed for thoughtful insight. Whether it was accomplishing chores in a rural setting or maneuvering for advantages in the city, my motivations were third-hand. Parents, institutions and management "experts," to a person, only *recycled* what they confidently broadcast as their wisdom, all of it borrowed without understanding.

He won me over to the practical utility of some practices, but that was no proof that the divine had anything to do with it. I was not convinced of Gayatri's unique genius beyond good brain hygiene. My cynicism did not dampen affection for big ideas.

He said, "Skepticism is written across your face. You've heard it all before and consider the claims to be hyperbole, no basis in fact, no use in practice. Let me demonstrate how *Om* contains the whole Gayatri Mantra and that the mantra contains all that is needed for a vibrant mind. It is alive, and its life is your profound vital purpose.

I said, "But *Om* is a just a syllable, insentient, dependent on the will to say it. And what about my own efforts, sometimes it takes force to do certain things that need doing. Isn't it all about willpower?"

"Delusions unveiled mark the way to truth," he replied. "You do not have *a will*—you have *intention*. What a person experiences as will, or lack of it, is their quality of intention. The movement of desire from within is subtle, like the invisible beginnings of a plant. It responds to intention. 'Force' has two forms. The most common is one you impose, based on preconceived notions. The other is an urge that rises from inside. It breaks through preconceptions and patterns as you refine your intentions. Imposing your will depletes your strength— power that rises from your depths increases vitality all around. You can only know the difference by self-study, which is awareness."

He continued describing the *Pranava*.

"*Om* is conscious—*Om* is 'will' which has three creative aspects: *bhur*—material, *bhuvah*—energetic interaction, and *suvahah*—ideal outcomes in the mind of God, felt as sweetness. These three are distillates of *Om*."

He pressed on with the actual chanting of Om, saying, "Look at your face, hands, or your body in a mirror. A creature confronts you that you pretend to know, but it is only a habitual acquaintance. Did you ever meet this being? No, you did not. Have you ever tried to understand what it wants? No, you have not. It has spoken a language inside your feelings that cause you to react. It has been a lifetime of receiving indecipherable grunts and gestures that you can only guess about. You run hither and thither grabbing this or that and only occasionally getting it right. Really it is a stupid process that you call 'learning' or 'satisfying your desires.' Both of you suffer from the split because you, the one who thinks he knows the other in the mirror, has never admitted there is a mystery. We will take the first step to solving it by chanting Om."

He adjusted himself, sat a little straighter and rested his palms on one another in his lap. I copied his actions, seated on the floor across from him, attentive to his introductory instructions.

"The syllable *Om* travels at light-speed. We have to slow it down or there is no relationship. It is alive, but unless we understand snapshots of it and then later speed-up our awareness to stay with the meanings in motion, the conversation will be an empty one. Think of it as examining a supersonic jet as it flies by—that is hopeless. You must inspect the jet on the ground and walk around it. Touch it. Exhaust your curiosity until you are eager to see it move. Then you watch it roll on the ground. Hold to the knowledge of its size and skin while it casually moves by. Then it speeds up. The challenge gets more difficult, but you want to see its velocity, its roaring power.

"Then again *Om* grows like an oak tree. You are too fast. You can't slow down enough to find its living presence. One day the acorn is a sprout, lost to your perceptions. Years pass and its limbs spread while you remain clueless of how the insignificant seed became the sheltering canopy. Did you ever slow down to speak to it? No, you were too busy. Did you ever hold the tender green shoot against your skin and marvel? No, there are so many and they look the same. And did you ever press your back against a woody trunk, empty yourself and say, 'Who are you, my brother? How did you grow so powerful, my sister?' No, because it is like a dead thing. The tree invites your touch; the jet requires your interest. Om is constant recall and renewal as relationship. Listen and then follow. Allow space."

The sage lightly closed his eyes.

"Aaaaaaaaaah," he created a surging sound from below a hand he placed low on his belly. I did the same. He allowed a generous pause.

"Ohhhhhhhh," emanated from his throat toward the chamber of his mouth. I drew sound from my chest cavity into a hollow above my tongue. The syllable took residence in the dome behind parted lips.

"Uuummmmm," seemed to enter the room, spirit like, a quiet resonance inside the now silent Vishwamithra. Mindfully I attempted a similar effect, felt nostrils flare and the *hum* rise upward into my head, passing through bones like air in space.

We repeated this three times. The exercise drew my attention into volumes that interlocked along the length of me, from tailbone to head. Attending to the sounds revealed a hidden room, a cavern, not inside my body, but one that I existed inside of. The *Aum* syllables seemed to contain me, even while they came out of me.

"These are pathways—say them quietly. Reverently come before

Pranava. Listen. You will find that the more closely you attend those sounds the greater the spaces become. This is an infinite meeting. The scope, duration, and intimacy reflect your intention. You can slow yourself enough to see the plant grow. Your will develops supersonic attention as it rushes inside you. It *is* you—therefore these things are your right, your privilege and a gift from outside time and space."

He asked, "When you chant *Om*, simply, what has happened?" He answered without waiting.

"You have intended to align with that creative impulse and it forms on your tongue," he said. "The sound vibrates the air as your unique creative alliance with divine will. I say 'unique' because your flesh, bone, your emotion, quality of intention and your degree of awareness become the *Om*. The universal *One* links the fragmented parts."

He continued, "The sacred marriage is there. Your female inert mass of flesh is surrendered to the only Will, 'His,' and you are impregnated with *His* child. *His*, do you understand? It's not a 'male;' it is *cathode* in tandem with the receptive *anode*. Creativity has aggression in it, like birth. Something new makes space in a world that was just fine without it. That newcomer is always your creative contribution, your works in the world. Those works will always reflect your genetic disposition called 'tendencies.' Your tendencies evolve as your genetic disposition evolves. *Om* is the original gene pool."

This was similar to things he mentioned earlier and I commented. "Your description is poetic, but someone could say it's a form of possession, not so different than your discourse about the way thoughts are manipulated. This is only a different kind of possession— where is freedom?"

He said, "Listen closely; the only free and independent contribution a human being can make is awareness. A human being can choose autonomy or dependence, terms that set the course for moving away from the source of consciousness or toward it. Either way it is a form of relationship. One is possession; the other is partnership."

Without breaking stride he said, "Autonomy is the sense, *'I am doing this'*—that feeling is a hook for the alien presence in the mind. The power to act effectively is not yours. You can intend, initiate and supply your best skill; that's all. The context is too rich and varied for you to control even a fractional part. Your greatest strength is aligning with divine will, the original purpose called *Pranava*. When you depend on that alignment through *Aum*, success is guaranteed—relying solely on your own limited powers invites the demonic pestilence. When you hang your hopes on self-delusions it creates a void that invites archons. Fantasies of conquest are powerless."

He continued, "The actual *I Am* presence is not alien—it is primal, unconditioned consciousness. It does not 'do' anything. It is the foundation of your deep feeling of doing things or things happening to you. Dependence is not weakness; it tethers the ego to the *I Am* presence. Being *dependent* is the awareness that truly creative action grows mysteriously—real 'doing' is subtle, not calculated. The power of human genius is in conscious clarity and awareness, not in any form of making or doing. Our only true task is awareness—which leads to every form of doing.

"*Pranava* is the only Will, the only doer. When your intention grows out of that rhythmic presence, your actions are like wildflowers in a meadow. Some of them are rose-blooms, full of passion. Others are like simple greenery or baby's breath to fill-out the bouquet. One day you will stand in that field of flowers with no urge to pluck any of them. You will have become the offering—the ground under your feet will be an altar."

I noted the things he said and reviewed my understanding with the sage. He adjusted where it was necessary until I had created a working document that was useful for basic reference. I often wrote the syllables while pronouncing them. The tablet dedicated for the task, filled-up with lines of *omm*'s, *aaa*'s *ooo*'s and *umm*'s and became something of a sacred object in its own right. I anticipated the bicycle ride to work each day as an opportunity for slow, introverted practice of the mantra and all its discrete parts. Saying "*Ah*," for example was always new. The opportunity to tune the resonant sound and find its location in my body was, as he predicted, unlimited. All the sounds had their location someplace in the body and ripened into reassuring proofs of an intelligent source—one that emanated in my voice and at once, emanated me.

GAYATRI MANTRA
THE MATRIX OF MEANINGS

AHHH	OHHH	UMMM
BHUR	BHUVAH	SUVAHA

TAT	SAVITUR	VARENYUM
BHARGO	DEVASYA	DHIMAHI
DHIYO	YONAH	PRACHODAYAT

AH   OH   UM

Inspiration, Understanding, and Assimilation
are the core of human experience.

BHUR   BHUVAH   SUVAHA

Material, Energies, and Purposeful Resolutions
are Worlds, experienced in consciousness.

TAT   SAVITUR   VARENYUM

That God, behind all appearances, is worthy of worship.

BHARGO   DEVASYA   DHIMAHI

Luminous presence (of divine origin) is what I meditate on.

DHIYO   YONAH   PRACHODAYAT

Mind content that seems to be mine is my offering to
the One, who alone can quicken it toward
awakening to the Truth behind all these appearances.

AUM

CATEGORIZING UNIQUE INDIVIDUALS INTO basic functions was dehumanizing; yet the truth of the descriptions was hard to deny. Management-science crated each of us to suit their needs. They had me pegged—idle thought and abstract ideas came a lot easier than taking action. It may be that most of my life was permanently fixed by personality and conditioning. My own chemical make-up seemed like the ultimate prison.

Most of my decisions were unreflective reactions. Every once in a while there might be a moment of self-awareness and I exerted an effort to change, usually to lapse back to baseline tendencies. Call it determinism, fatalism, or genetic disposition—there was a lot of proof that people were fixed, which would include me. How much influence could any practice exert if I was indeed an unchangeable *object-reflector* as they branded me at work? It was the *topic dujour*, so I mentioned it at the start of the weekly the session with Vishwamithra.

"You mentioned it earlier," I began, "the physical and mental aspects of an individual is one thing—the way they experience their life based on those reactions is something else. When you say there are unique personal tendencies is it really about DNA? Wouldn't that make real change difficult at best?"

"One thing leads to another doesn't it?" he said. "DNA is inert. It is a crystalline by-product of *Om* acting through your subtle body. Biological blueprints change as you change in relation to *Om*. The power is in *Om*, not in behavior or DNA. Om is divine will, the breath of God. Your unique substance reflects that through your intentions. You have total freedom when you exercise the disciplines that allow that freedom. Genetic science offers a false promise of plastic change."

The tone of his message was often a kind of bell. Sometimes it was like the clear tinkling that accompanied ritual, easy chimes that enlivened the wind, or resonant gongs that caused my hair to stand on end. On this topic his voice went flat—the methodical clank of cow bells—routine warnings attached to the habitual sway of the beast. It seemed this was a discussion he resisted, yet, the larger message compelled him to pursue it.

He said, "Those that modify DNA to shape the world might as well hammer on a sculpture to influence the artist. It is backwards. Altering the material effect to force change on the essential cause is demonic. Remodeling behavior or tampering with DNA to coerce a reinterpretation of Truth, Freedom, and Love is fiendish. Spirit is the active agent; material is an effect. Rearranging DNA to force changes on the effects of spirit is black-magic hiding behind the word 'science.' The results can only be unstable and unhappy."

His answer did not indicate the source of so-called dark science. Was it trans-dimensional, alien, or demonic? Were there beings beyond our historic world that worked humans like botanists hybridized plants? Was humanity breed stock for cosmic managers? My viewpoint on these issues remained cynical at worst, leaden at best. Sometime the concern could be approached directly, not now. He continued.

"Deep genetics are the breath of freedom and diversity. When you say *Aum*, it is yours alone. As it flows from your lips, it joins every other *Aum* in the great syllable that pulses behind the stars, the supernovas, the atomic anomalies, the migration patterns of animals and the love of a mother for a child. *Om* will tell you about itself through *Aum*. *Om* is the mother of all genetic possibilities and ripples across creation evenly, passionately—unconcerned with human endeavor. Your willingness to participate in her creative dance is a love song to her. She won't resist, and you will capture her to the extent you are able. Then you are her spouse and stuck with the blessings or curses wrought by the marriage. It depends on your fiber, your intentions, and grace."

So matter and energy was a feminine presence, a moody goddess who demanded responsible action or inflicted her corrections. Images came to mind of a dancing girl, a warm lover or a demanding wife. An old dream contained such perplexing feelings. It was different than my usual nighttime imaginings and had lingered, troubling and unresolved.

I WAS THE MIND-SLAVE of an immense woman. She was at least twenty feet tall, naked, with long, coarse, black hair that reached to her lower back. She walked away from me while threatening, "I know every thought you have. If you think of anything but me, you will die immediately."

Then I was alone and afraid, anxious not to let my mind wander. It was a burden. Suddenly a figure appeared. It was male, metallic, and fearsome. He was towering, three times taller than the huge woman. He looked at me through an iron mask that showed only his mouth. "I am Shivaji," he said.

Allowing a thought about him would kill me, as the woman warned. He said, "Where is she. I'll kill her for you and relieve you of these fears." His offer brought lightness to my spirit. He scanned the area, "Is that her?" "No," I told him. He gestured toward one woman, then another. They all looked like my feminine oppressor, but were only human, small. The titan dame who dominated my brain was no where in sight. Sadly, she was not around for him to kill.

He said, "Do not be concerned, call my name and I'll arrive immediately and destroy her." He left me and I reviewed his name quietly, "Shivaji, Shivaji." It brought peace. Eventually the woman returned but at that point the potent name, "Shivaji" could deliver me from any trouble. Humorously, many things went through my mind in her absence and nothing bad happened. Her threat was empty. I related it to Vishwamithra and asked what the dream meant.

"You are afraid of women," he said, "and your own masculine strength has become like a war god, equally scary. The figures are huge because they have overgrown through lack of attention. They will all return to a scale you can work with as you open to the wisdom of your life as it unfolds. Her caution to you was recommending discipline.

"Shivaji is a historical figure; a hero of South India who fought off Muslim invasions from the north. He also represents the discipline she prescribed. He can offer to assassinate her because they are two different functions of the same entity in your psyche. The first function, demanded by the woman, was relationship. She is not your mother—she would be your spouse! You interpret what she asks of you through a fearful, childish lens. To salve your immature worries about getting swallowed by the feminine, a gargantuan warrior appears. He reassures that you are completely safe. When your ability to be intimate matures, the mammoth figures will take on a more ordinary scale. You will embrace relationship without fear of being consumed by it. You will embody the prowess of Shivaji who understands boundaries and freedom. The need to kill will not arise. He ended your fear in one stroke, the only murder required. Fear takes many forms that share a common feature—is blocks intimacy."

"What does this have to do with either DNA or the *Om*?" I asked, taken aback by his critique of my masculinity.

"Om is the potent, living pulse," he said. "It is the *Pranava*, alive, the One that overflows into the many. *Aum* is *your Om*—it is absolute intimacy and grows out of your soul-fiber. So-called *DNA* is the label that science affixes to your soul-fiber. That miraculous helical crystal will always defy the human hunger to grasp its secrets. Why? Because it is *Om* expressing as *Aum*—it is the *Mind* of God becoming the *Voice* of God through your own substance. The dream pulls you toward a larger version of yourself. Pranava uses your own soul-language to help you through uncharted territory."

"I'm not consciously aware of the fears suggested by the dream," I said, attempting to mask the petty hurt inflicted by his dream analysis.

"It is natural, none-the-less," he said. "Fears and confrontations are required for growing-up and developing discipline. It is the human way. Animals are led by instinct; we humans have to take the bull by the horns, which is never an easy thing."

I had my shortcomings, for sure, but his disapproval pierced my thin skin. A flush of shame reddened my face as I packed up my things to leave his flat. I felt flawed. He stopped me.

"Ashty," he said in a voice that was firm and soft at once. "We are both men. Women are our bull. It's the wisdom of duality, the glory of *Pranava*. Reach out and hold the two horns; they are intimacy and boundary. The guru is feminine in these matters and we have no escape from her. This teaching has to be learned by every one of us. Believe me, the greatest danger is to avoid the match. I am here to tell you it took epic failures for me to tame the beast. I don't see such disasters in your future—you will not be gored. On the contrary, your dream tells us the challenge is already met. *Om* loves to become *Aum*. Your 'yes' to *Pranava* cannot fail you."

AH-OH-UM

"CAN YOU DESCRIBE EXPERIENCES you had when you said the sounds *Ah*, *Oh*, and *Um* at any time during the week?" he asked.

These were difficult to describe so I focused on obvious sensations, saying, "Each syllable was more like an intelligent space than a physical sound vibration. The syllables, *ah*, *oh*, and *um* take the character of unique beings. The sounds extend into my body like roots when I say them. Despite their intimacy, they are cool and detached."

"The expressions *Ah, Oh, and Um* seem aloof because there is no sentimentality in *Pranava*. Don't be deceived!—this entity *ah-oh-um* is your best-self and exists for you. Like any relationship, it takes time. Unlike other meetings, this one, begins as deeply intimate, and moves toward the surface, where you can meet it in the flesh. Let's invite our benefactress, before we forget why we are here.

> "She is the energy and brilliance of all phenomena. Our effective study is her presence. When she finds a seat here, in our minds and in our hearts—she leads us from darkness to light, from dullness to the eternal flame of awareness, from death to life-eternal.
>
> "In the world of objects, it is not what you know with the mind that can shed a ray of light on reality—but that which she gives, by which to know the mind and its objects—this is reality. Om."

Vishwamithra went on to describe how Cosmic-Om diffracted into Aum, and again into Ah-oh-um which moved in the body.

"Begin with what you have. Your mouth, the lips, soft upper pallet, the tongue, the length and density of your larynx, your mood, blood viscosity, what you had for dinner last night—all these give your *Aum* its quality as you say it. It is not a simulation of the sacred syllable—like it's a bad copy—it is the core of personal creativity. As such, it begins with intention, takes-on cosmic will, and finally erupts below the navel in a force that moves into consciousness as *Ah, Oh* and *Um*.

69

But we will stay with *Ah*. *Ah*! is spontaneous. Your expression of wonder and appreciation. It is the first sound in 'art' or 'awe.' *Ah!* Say it with relish. *Ah!* Here you are, listening to *Ah!* It is the active agent in the word 'father,' ff--*Ah*--thur."

Speaking the syllables, his pitch rose to a mild crescendo then would settle back to a mellower tone. As an unbroken flow it was a rapturous pattern of inspired sound that would have struck me as affected in a different setting. Instead, it integrated the syllables of *Ah, Oh,* and *Um* with such force that it carried me.

"This is the true big bang—not some speculative explosion dreamed-up by deluded scientists. Ha!—the Big Bang must be 'out there' somewhere! Don't waste your time with the ghosts that haunt the scary universe of grant-seeking scientists!—settle down and listen to *Aum*. Here, inside our own galactic wonder, the sound erupts in the depths of the body. Feel it move in your chest. It forms like a universe, sheltered within the rib cage. Who gave it to us and how do we deserve it? Fall silent. Stop and appreciate 'Who.' The *Unknowable One* gives your intention to you as an act of grace. That One encourages us, begs us to take his *Pranava* in our mouth to announce, to sing *Ah!*"

A WAVE OF STILLNESS COVERED Vishwamithra. He would not resist the overarching spirit which perpetually extended an open hand. His eyelids dropped and for a few seconds a veil passed between us.

My eyes swam. It was *appreciation*. Seeing the moment as it was, unburdened by ideas or expectations, was enough for him. Theories promoted by genetic science formed a dense skin over the spiritual nature of flesh and blood. His mystical mood stirred my emotions. The exalted state blended into the next part of his discourse.

"*Ah* is followed by *Oh*, yet another gift, hard-wired and inherited through consciousness. *Oh* is the sound of realization and sympathy. '*Oh*, I heard the news. *Oh*, what did he say? *Oh* yes!'

"The second sound is child of the first, the father is *Ah*. *Oh* plays off the soft pallet and echoes inside the chamber of the mouth, projecting forward into space. It is like whispers in a cavern or thunder rolling down canyon walls, resonant, full, but not fully-formed. *Ah* carries inspiration into creation. *Oh* names that spirit before it becomes a specific thought. *Oh* is creativity that moves—not static and conceptual. Thinking comes later. *Om* refines reason, but there is no reason in it. Say *Oh* and let its intelligence speak to you."

The second syllable formed in my mind as a hollow. Even without physical sound it appeared, full and round. Verbal meanings raced

70

around it but could not adhere. Thoughts about these primal sounds were inadequate. *Oh* was specific—more so than words could express.

He paused between each discreet sound-idea, spontaneously lapsing into brief meditations while they percolated.

STIRRING FROM THAT INTERLUDE, his speech at first was barely audible. He gazed abstractly toward the floor between us and resumed the explanation of *Aum*.

"Apa-Uma, father-mother—these are names that focus on the personal aspect of duality. The term 'opposites' is misleading—there are only boundaries we draw like lines in the sand. These distinctions are as meaningful as a stick dividing a river. One is certainly free to talk about one side of the stick versus the other—the water does not care about the difference. Black-white describes light or color. The *sum* of all pigments is black. The *sum* of the spectrum is white. *Ah*-father and *Um*-mother describes one being as two aspects. There is no first or last. *Being* starts in fiery inspiration—the father. It ends in enclosure, creation, and the womb—the mother. Father and mother are a cycle—one cannot exist without the other. They form the audible framework of *Ah-Um* and have nothing to do with time. They are not bookends or the start and finish of a race."

At last his voice returned to full-throttle, saying, "Endings are the stuff of every sad tale and yet a life without forgetting, sleep, or death would be living hell. *Um* resolves *Aum*. The mouth closes around the *Pranava* in embrace. Pursing the lips amplifies the sound and drives it inward. Its vibrant quality moves the jaw, enlivens the sinuses, enters cranial bones and engulfs the brain. It reaches all of the flesh. A person says 'umm, yumm, or mmm' as a spontaneous sound of enjoyment or assimilation. In speech it is the noise that buys time until the next idea forms. Dynamic silence is the shadow cast by endings and the sound *Um*."

He said, "Stillness after each repetition of *Aum* is the vital basis from which it emerged at the start—it came out of silence, the fertile void—and finds its home again in silence."

OUR CONVERSATION CYCLED INTO quiet. The emptiness held three simple sounds. They were vibrating strands, alive in my body, tones and meanings at once, sounded by my voice, or soundless within my cells. They were awake and gentle, ceaselessly moving yet having no agitated motion. They waited, content in themselves. I didn't assign meanings to them—they held meaning itself. The mysterious *Om* and subconscious, pre-birth destinies formed my body in every moment. How could anyone be lonely when they were held tightly by those vast streams?

"Some people simply begin with *Oh* when repeating the Pranava," he inserted, almost as an afterthought. "*Om* they say. Then *Ah* is only implied. A wakeful, conscious and aware *Om* is *Ah-Oh-Um,* the sounds merging. Know them as living symbols for discovery, appreciation, and assimilation. Subtle concentration develops by attending to dozens of mediating syllables—the *shruti* that connect *AUM. Shruti* are microtones, too fleeting to be actual notes. These are like minor deities, the entourage of the main sounds."

The ideas turned in my head as symmetrical patterns of meaning. My attention diffused into the room around me. Stillness within this bounded space was welcome, terra firma after navigating the deep.

Fine dust in the air drifted into an invisible ray of light from the window, making it visible. The particles wandered like microscopic planets delineating the edges of the sun's light. Passing through it, they glowed "on" careening end over end—and then "off" as they disappeared beyond the luminous shaft. Others, smaller, were pin dots that popped into view or vanished against the shadowed backdrop of Vishwamithra's wall.

With the quiet, smells became more intense. It was familiar, aged, but not old. There were traces of paper and hints of incense that mixed with cool dampness from outside.

Against a static scene, shadows, luminous dust, and aromas combined into a non-verbal portrait of Vishwamithra. The impression was learning and tradition—openness infused with levity and comfort. His voice broke into the ephemeral painting, making no ripple across the miniature worlds that swirled in the air around us.

"Vigilance for the shifting motions and effects of *Om* leads to meditation." he said. "Your awareness follows the mantra as it proceeds—vibrating up from below, seating itself in the center, pulling on the physical sheath like a glove and informing the heart. In the heart it is born new and emerges in the next *Aum.* Your actions move *Pranava* into the living world like leavening into dough." We ended.

THEY SAY THE WORLD will play out in cold demise—that it began as a fiery wad, a hot, formless soup of elements in waiting. Then there's the idea of the big bang—the singularity, which according to some law became too pregnant with itself. A seamless, dimensionless ball exploded into silent radiation; stuff out of nothing. For some supposedly logical yet unknown reason it expanded, all wrinkled with clumps of different sizes, shapes and distances. The whole mess fell into order like a stack of cards thrown into the wind, only to arrange itself according to numbers and suits.

The mythology of my schooling was desolate—"Primal, infantile life began accidentally and violently. It matured into survival strategies and will end in cold emptiness. Hydrogen groped and staggered in random steps toward increasingly complex bio-chemical reactions that turned into *dance, poetry, and love*. It will ultimately collapse into itself, frigid and pointless."

I pedaled my bicycle toward the artificially illuminated shed with slow, deliberate pushes against the pedals, savoring the likelihood it was a lie—scientists did not know what they were talking about.

I knew. I knew my father and my mother. They were present in my own body. I knew I was conceived in quiet mystery, not an explosion—in fact I was born into fluids and the comfort of warm flesh, not the cold reaches of abstract space.

The end would arrive as an act of creation and a smile—a dancer, swirling, drifting to laws of inner gravity, defining the edges of light. We creatures of earth were beloved children, born of our universe which was a song, an embrace.

I loved my parents.

Guru Gayatri *by Ashty Hozan*

Eight-sounds times three-lines
Maps clear mind void—
no thought,
free.

Many roomed mansion-home mother and
Comfort-father firm—
Be not alone,
Friend.

The way of the Rishi was a path slow to go
So Ma Gayatri showed him—
Her face like the
Dawn.

Natural, incremental, subtler than sense—
The light of awareness rises above
Small mind with such
Attractive wonder,

You can easily
forget to
notice.

DEITIES

"SHE IS THE ENERGY AND BRILLIANCE of all phenomena. Our effective study is her presence. When she finds a seat here, among us, in our minds and in our hearts—she leads us from darkness to light, from dullness to the eternal flame of awareness, from death to life-eternal," we said in our opening prayers. *Ma Gayatri* was also called the five-faced goddess, her faces being each line of the full mantra. I held her in a mythological light. It was unclear to me how Vishwamithra conceived of the world of deities he referred to with some frequency. On this day he erupted with hardly an introduction.

He said, "*Nirguna Brahman* exclaims *ah, oh, um!* That God who has no attributes becomes *Saguna Brahman*, the God with form. Your sense of being aware is proof of the Presence. Awareness, awareness, awareness—wake up! Allow the illusions of what you think you are to become true vehicles for wisdom into the world. What are we waiting for? Repeat *Om Pranava* while we still have breath. Witness and reflect on its living effects."

We commenced intoning *Aum* as he had presented it. I felt currents, one from the lowest tip of my spine crossing one from the top of my skull. Thoughts in my head about *Pranava* crossed the sound of *Aum* emanating from my lips. Meaning rubbed against sensation, creating a healing bath of friction.

"Understand this," he said, and took a long breath. "The central axis of the body does three things—it discovers, assimilates and integrates—sounded as *ah-oh-um*.

"Ah—think of the spinal chord as a network that reaches out to discover and bring back news from worlds beyond.

"Oh—the digestive tube is an alchemist that can assimilate foods from the animal, vegetable and mineral kingdoms into living tissue.

"Um—bones, muscles and tendons frame space to separate outside from inside and allow room for physical expression.

"Yet the origin of those three came when wholeness mysteriously decided to split—imagine that. At every step of creation *Pranava* is full and complete—yet it seems to crave the split, the birth of something new, as though perfect containment also includes expansion.

"The embryo begins as a flash of transformation—*Ah*. The first act of creation splits wholeness into two—*Oh*. These two expand and expand and expand to multiply the first act into four, eight, sixteen, thirty-two, on into the billions—*Um*. Creation is a vibrant hum that strives toward resolution.

"Say *Om* in the mind or under the breath to feel wrapped in the original wholeness.

"Express *Aum* as 'ah-oh-um' in audible repetitions. Sense the three chords—they lead naturally into Gayatri Mantra.

ॐ

Om (Aum) > Ah-Oh-Um

"The sound of *Aum* is the actual experience, a practice that rubs the body. Contemplate *Ah, Oh,* and *Um* to understand *Om*. Those sounds reflect your core experiences. Duality forms a bridge between the *Unity of All* and personal, physical, particular experiences. These are your *narratives*." And he added to the hierarchy he already began.

ॐ

Om (Aum) > Story, personal experiences > Ah-Oh-Um

"Your entire life is one story—an epic narrative with major themes. Each chapter poses a critical question. You propose answers and test them. Characters are there to sharpen the urgency or help out. They come and go. Some stay longer than others. The body tells you how the story is progressing through feelings. The mind speaks through peace, turmoil, fixation or boredom. That is how you harmonize the three chords: nervous, digestive and skeletal. Your life is a question. The life you live is an answer."

Framing my troubles as an epic fable was poetic, but details of the daily grind still seemed mundane and accidental. What I had for breakfast, what happened at work or who said what to whom rarely had any apparent value. My experiences were a hodge-podge when it came down to it. I listened anyway.

"Mystery and meaning meet as the universal tale," he continued, "You can know it in your own story. You are the drama, the discourse of divinity expressing itself as both the profound 'One' and the fragmented 'three.' When a whole people tell stories about themselves—to educate, enlighten, and unify—they talk about 'the gods.' Who are the gods? They are grand representatives of individual realities, called *archetypes*. Larger-than-life stories shed light on day to day themes that turn into mental clutter, an incoherent mess"

He was right to a certain extent. Even petty events had a plot of sorts, characters, and outcomes. Altogether, the History of Ashty Hozan was a series of sketchy vignettes, cobbled together by calendars or clocks. Tracing my personal and sometimes confused narrative to its start was impossible because the story started before I was there to watch it. No part of the tale was void of discoveries, realizations, and conclusions, whether or not I consciously participated.

On the graph, epic stories occurred between *Om* and *Ah-Oh-Um*. It implied that Om itself contained every potential story and that every story was a conscious record of people's urge to discover meaning— the human need to harmonize the core sounds: ah, oh, and um.

"BRAHMA IS THE PRIEST WHO initiates creation, corresponding with the sound, *Ah*. He conducts auspicious rituals. His wife, or *shakti*, is *Saraswati,* the goddess of wisdom and learning. Remember her name and leave her out for the moment. The function of the female energies is complementary and opposite to formal male aspects.

"VISHNU, THE PRESERVER, IS related to *Oh*, the glue of Om. What is he preserving?—the center, the story, and sacred meaning. Wearing a crown and royal adornments, he is a regal figure, integral to culture, the warp and woof of history. By his side, *Lakshmi* embodies beauty, sensuality, and wealth. She forever accompanies him on his missions to planet Earth or tends him lovingly in Heaven as his shakti.

"SHIVA IS A SHAMAN-MYSTIC, covered in ash, adorned with snakes, the one who presides over endings that are always beginnings. The sound *Um* dissolves Om into silence and resolves the cycle, preparing it for a new creation. His shakti is *Uma* or *Durgha*. She is a force to be reckoned with, armed to the teeth and fiercely protective of her children.

"DURGA, LAKSHMI AND SARASWATI are female aspects of the trinity; announced in an order opposite to the male gods. This is yet another detail that should be contemplated. Ask why—pull at the tradition and find out the purpose for invoking the female deities differently than the male aspects. Notice the anomaly and put it to the test—then decide. The difference isn't random.

"Males are listed top to bottom as *Brahma, Vishnu, Shiva* to make clear that the *form aspect* of reality begins in sacred initiation, an abstract, conceptual realm. Then it accumulates a meaningful place in culture and tradition. These institutions require maintenance. Finally, cultural content is transformed by endings and new beginnings.

"Females are listed from bottom to top as *Durga, Lakshmi*, and *Saraswati* to illustrate that the ultimate purpose for human life is experience—individual, internal processes collect and form institutions. Female aspects are the juice, the fruit of abstract ideals— and these erupt from below. They are the dramatic power of the world play—forceful and full. New creations take birth in heroism— boldness at the gut—love and passion in the heart—culture and learning from the head.

SOUND	AH	OH	UM
PHYSICAL SYSTEM	nervous	digestive	skeletal
CONSCIOUS STATE	discover	understand	integrate
MALE DEITY	Brahma >	Vishnu >	Shiva
ACTION	create	preserve	begin/end
FEMALE DEITY	Saraswati <	Lakshmi <	Dhurga
ACTION	learn	enjoy	protect
FIELD OF ACTION	the mind	culture	the soul

"*What is this all about?*—you might ask."

Exactly, tracking parallel groups of three was an interesting logic exercise—inter-relating them was beyond me. "If Om was a sphere," I said, "a closer look would reveal it was a ball of string. Following the single strand along its length are like experiences that connect one to the other. I must confess that you lost me—the meaning of it got too tangled to follow, somewhere around *Vishnu*."

"There is no end to the yarns that pull-on heart-strings. The stuff of life: songs, poetry, and drama force your participation. Their stories are your map and the human experience causes their actions. Relationships with deities and mythic tales are there to enrich your experience by shedding light on the meaning of mundane existence.

"Beyond the main three and their shaktis, *Shruti's* are transitional entities that reside between the main sound-deities. These are as infinite as you are sensitive, impossible to pin down. And they carry the meditation into pure awareness. They are like the elements in the periodic table that exist for microseconds and are gone. You can find them yourself by noticing that there are an infinite number of sounds between *Ah* and *Oh*, and again from *Oh* to *Um*. They continue as a subtle chorus in the silence—resonant singing that rejoices in your awareness, also called *Ghandarvas*. Their ecstatic praise across this ever-expanding universe is audible as galactic white noise."

He led me through the simple process of listening to the sounds, imagining the attendant deities and sensing the *shruti*. I did hear what he called *Ghandarvas*, subtle vocal overtones in the silence. He said they were a barometer of the clarity and emotional outpouring present in the practice.

An interplay of male and female drove the mythic structures he described—but gender had been downplayed in the name of equality—even demonized in media and culture at large. While musing on the meaning of opposites and their purpose, a lingering memory of village street performers came to mind.

A dozen or so bedraggled tribals arrived in my town. It was their seasonal migration and the journey left their clothes shabby and their children unwashed. I watched with curiosity as the troupe arranged themselves in a half circle, inviting uncomfortable spectators to fill-in gaps on the other side. A fiddler played slowly and mournfully while individuals made stylized movements with dignified airs in a well-rehearsed choreography. Women began the performance with three generations stepping lightly, kicking delicately at a grassless dance-floor. Children clapped in time, while forming a circle that orbited around them. The tension mounted.

The violin picked up the pace and introduced sharp strains as a handful of men strutted in front to displace the ladies' pirouettes. Shouts, rhythmic claps, athletic thrusts, and squats were a sharp contrast to the women. They pin-wheeled and leaped long past what seemed possible, defying not so much gravity as the limits of the flesh.

My body twitched in synch with their gymnastic frenzy. They

stopped and surrendered the floor to the unimpressed ladies who again tempered the mood with energetic gestures that were smaller and more precise. Back and forth they went, female to male and back again, eventually mixing geometry and physical power in a demonstration that caused a rush in me. Looking around, it was plain that the beaming audience was similarly entranced. Spectators barely held themselves in check. To our delight, the small group invited us in. They guided us in vigorous patterns that worked inside their confident arrangements. By the time it ended we were well-winded.

The thrall dissipated when they doffed their caps and passed a leather boot for donations. We emptied our pockets for them as though we could pay enough to keep the spell intact. The tribal clan shrank again to the margin and walked away, counting bills and coins.

Vishwamithra pierced my reverie, saying, "Indeed, procreation, like DNA, is only an expression of the vast power released when *Om* splits itself into a *this* and a *that*. Cleaving of the active from the passive is just an apparent split. There is only Presence. Your observation about male and female must come from some experience."

I related the scene with the dancers and how the audience was drawn in, almost against their will. A spirit of unity rose among us and diffused again into nothing, like a zephyr-wind. I asked him about the nature of a thing like that, which had the ability to possess a large group from no apparent center. A mutual, self-organizing entity enhanced the lives of each one there, individually.

"Things take up space," he said, "and that forces inwardness and outwardness. True creativity is never one directional, it requires those tensions you described, the foreign band, the homefolk, giving over, resistance, abandon and reserve. Trace the creation to the center and you seem to find the old, like it's a journey back in time—that is tradition. When you follow the course of development to an edge, an unknown fringe, you seem to move into a future. Dynamism is never familiar, always new."

He raised a hand as though supporting an invisible orb for our inspection. Testing the real weight of an object I could not see, he said, "The flux between origins and frontiers will never stop, neither in time or space, nor within the heart." His eyes narrowed below arched brows as he broadcast into the imaginary object, "Ah, but the mind— the mind can fix the impossibly small instant when the outer becomes the inner! Witness the Presence in all this. "

He continued the explanation with theatrical airs, saying, "Day to day tedium and tragedy happens on a stage. The entertainment has a purpose you can't control. You can appreciate the show when you become aware that it has meaning, one way or another." He had flattened his hand into a platform where he arranged other invisible pieces. "Puppets sing, dance, gather, disperse and beg for rewards, dangling from cosmic strings that go unnoticed. Their highest joy is to finally witness the skill of the one that moves them here and there. One who believes it is free remains a marionette—the puppet that sees the strings as they are becomes free."

"There is a deceiver who encourages mannequins to cut their chords, accept their austere loneliness, and exercise their independent powers; all an illusion." Speaking this way he slowly, forcefully squeezed his fingers together and the stage clumped into a fist.

The old street performers drew their power to enchant us from maleness and femaleness. Modern society intentionally blurred gender. Contemporary urban gods were not men, women, or even heroic— they were technocratic solutions—protocols built out of ones and zeros with no flaring signatures or intrusive phrases.

Vishwamithra backed away from urban innovations, to a time before gray sameness and garish diversions crept over human culture. It frightened me to think that out of this metropolis, beyond the established paths of "civilization," I might be the only one following him. What good was a culture of two?

Unwanted Vow *by Ashty Hozan*

Time has lost its tolerance for virtue.
Heroes are clunky furniture
Too valuable to toss
And useless for anything else.

What to do with the cherished heirloom,
Overstuffed, claw-footed, well-crafted
And completely obnoxious object
Venerated and avoided by all?

No one else will have it so
Burn it and earn their hatred or
Worship it and gain their pity.
Reupholstered heroes remain uncomfortable.

BHISHMA

"THINK OF GOD AS a beautiful horizon that calls you out of hiding, out from your small self. The conceptual mind loves that horizon and dreams about what might be there. On the other hand the nature of flesh is beastly and fantasizes nothing of the kind. Visions are born in fantasy while commitments thrive on passions and urges." He said after our opening. I had come to expect some explanations when his introductions were poetic.

He thought for a moment, head tilted forward with lips resting lightly on his forefinger. "There are beings with intense passion and there are visionaries. Body and mind is not enough—there has to be soul. Unwavering commitment can only appear when intent is pure; then soulful resolve taps the physical power innate in all of creation.

"Bhishma was a virtuous hero who attained the heights of angels on the power of his love of truth. Yet, his story had been woven into the warp and woof of dreadful human frailty."

"HIS HUMAN LIFE SHONE, radiant as the noonday sun, stripped of ambition and brimming with life-giving wisdom. What does the sun hope to gain? What does it have to show for its tireless efforts?—nothing. Seen rightly, Bhishma, though a man, was even greater. Heavenly bodies enjoy the rhythm of celestial pulses, freedom in space, the powerful simplicity of arcing paths, nuclear fire, and unencumbered expression. The warrior in consciousness has no such allies." That was how Vishwamithra introduced a story whose point I could not try to guess.

He continued, "From the beginning, he appeared as a bright star in an epic story called *Mahabharatha*. The tome is immense, a leviathan of stories—that great fish would be indigestible without radical trimming. To save time we'll remove the head, tail, bones and innards, to sample only a taste of the fillet."

"Bhishma was the central hub of epic clan rivalry," Vishwamithra said, "the hinge pin that allowed conflicting interests to push and pull in radically different directions while remaining locked together. His own chest contained a battle between natural affections for the whole extended family, and to live the truth, regardless of consequences. In all of this he was the beloved elder patriarch who discharged every critical action justly, with dispassion. Each decision was a gesture of exacting wisdom that frustrated the lesser desires of people who looked to him for their particular special interests. Bhishma's dilemma of duty against feeling is the essence of the inspired epic *Mahabharatha*. He was the epitome of integrity and stately dignity—*what* he did is far less important that *who* he was and *how* he acted."

He said, "I've given the head, tail and bare bones of the situation. Before we throw those aside, what have you heard?"

"Bhishma was a place where two conflicted families uneasily joined. A joint is an empty space that serves to keep two things connected," I said. "In a similar way, Bhishma was important as an empty space—he allowed each group to act freely, while holding them together."

He completed my thought saying, "And more unobstructed the space in a hinge is, the less friction is created. He did not assert himself, though he could have. The clan-chief's innocence and purity lubricated the evil ones to complete their dance of death with no illusions of goodness. Ironically he did it by being good, judging no one, not forcing his authority on others. Bhishma saw ignorance, passion, and attachment on both sides of the hinge and still allowed the gate to swing as it would. Lives lost, hearts broken, and illusions of virtue evaporated—all to protect a seed of unalloyed goodness. Truth has to be absolutely free."

Spreading his arms wide, making sweeping gestures he said, "In battle, both sides watched as Bhishma cut through armies of virtuous men like a sharp lathe scattering wood chips. These were cherished youngsters to him. He loved them and hated the war he participated in by the fates. Doomed soldiers worshipped him even while he harvested their lives like Death's impartial scythe. This was his last act in a conflict he rejected at every turn, and one that he had brought forward by every decision he made. This was the day his role would finally end. Truly, words, entitlements, ambitions and sentimentality brought clouds of murder the world had never seen."

Vishwamithra painted sad conclusions in a voice full of reverence, saying, "He would not harm a woman, and yet by design, a woman would bring his demise. Driven forward, lifetime after lifetime to get misplaced revenge, she appeared as one of the throng on the last battlefield—she would be the purposeful tool to bring him down. In that moment of crystallization, his guard laid aside, his mission finished, arrows by the thousands found their mark in his flesh. He fell, but would not touch the ground because of the many shafts that prevented his body from contacting the earth."

The story-teller returned to our room, sunlight creeping across the floor as morning grew older. Looking at me he said, "Embrace the scene. Don't let it skirt by, as do so many old yarns, archaic pictures of irrelevant bygone days. Here is leadership, pure and sober, with real authority and matchless skill—perforated by hundreds of lethal darts, hurled by the ones he had served for decades. His life was utterly just, as was his death. Warriors on every side wasted this paragon of goodness by following what they believed to be righteous paths. There were no guilty parties; so how do you explain the tragedy?"

Thinking for a moment, I conceded, "I don't know why these things happen. I don't know why good deeds might be rewarded by murder or worse yet, infamy. I don't know how it is possible that illustrious and true intentions could result in pain and tragedy."

"We began with a thought about God," he said. "It's still here. Put on Bhishma's skin and say what you find."

The image invaded me before I exercised my imagination. Arrows pressing deeply through flesh, piercing muscles, bones, and organs should have created a complete field of pain over every inch of the body. Instead, all was total stillness. Any slight motion would bring intense agony at the point of entry so my will-to-move divorced from movement. I was paralyzed—arrows were vectors driving me into myself, as far from the surface as possible. My head dangled, neck muscles straining and the weight pulled excruciatingly onto metal barbs digging into my shoulders.

"My head dangles," I said, opening my eyes and coming back to the room.

"So did Bhishma's," the sage told me. "He requested a support for his head that *befitted a warrior*. The one who showered him with so many deadly shafts devised such a 'cushion'—he released three arrow points as a tripod for the skull to rest on. Then the lion-hearted elder said he was thirsty—the bowman plunged a shot into the earth that sprang a refreshing stream right into his mouth. None of this gives a hint of Bhishma's grandeur. The waste of war continues through the present day, until humility cushions us like his mattress of arrows."

He adjusted his position and asked me to find a posture that was comfortable. I pulled a thin floor pillow under my tail bone which tilted me forward slightly, enough to feel almost weightless.

"Follow me in this," he said. "We want to push past the amazing image of a human pin-cushion and allow Bhishma to give his teaching. He told those around him he would give such counsel. How might he advise us on the essential questions? *What meaning is there when a pure, radiant life has to work for an unjust system? Is it ever justified to sever blood-bonds? Can the ties of blood or spirit ever allow for the murder of a brother?*—and further—*how does it happen that a few evil people are able to manipulate the virtuous masses into self-destructive war?* These conundrums are the substance of everyday existence," Vishwamithra said, and paused.

"If Bhishma could speak to us, he might make these four statements." The sage held up a palm and forcefully grasped counting fingers as he spoke in the mood of the elder-warrior.

> *"First, my death is living instruction from a servant of the absolute truth to those who want to escape the slavery of relative ideals. See my bed of arrows as an ironic negative image of radiant light rays.*
>
> *Second; the only reward possible for a radiant life in such dark times is irony. Misguided kings of corruption grab holiness for their utility. They wield virtuous heroes like hammers to pound down a universe of nails.*
>
> *Third; in those evil circumstances I killed the millions who had come for a warrior's blessing—death at the hand of a holy man fulfills lives, wasted in unholy wars.*
>
> *Fourth; the Era of brutality is from God and should not be resisted— instead you participate by becoming transparent—an empty space at the hub of events, turning."*

Finishing his discourse as Bhishma, he reclined with regal airs to parody a king resting on a royal divan. Bhishma might have said something like that, lying peacefully on a couch of arrows."

I asked, "Why did Bhishma or the virtuous brothers participate at all if they hated what their duty demanded? Why could they not exclude themselves from the drama?"

"That's the question for *our* era," he said, "Bhishma's death happened in another time with other rules. Indeed, why do we betray the heart, again and again? Do we follow Bhishma's path, duty-bound to the undeserving, or is there some other way?

"Rigid rules bring frustration and pain. Arbitrary boundaries cause anxieties and doubts. And when guidelines are altogether absent, people go crazy. Bhishma understood his place as an orienting polestar for his clan—the axis around which two very different families rotated. He knew the warring groups wouldn't say, *look at the grandsire—he refuses to fight—let's follow his example and lay down our arms.* He gave them that chance many times. But there is a thick skin of ignorance surrounding the sweet fruit of consciousness as it awakens. Forms require a protective covering while they mature and ripen. He spoke the only language they understood—valor.

"The elder taught them, 'Here's how you fight—here's how you die!' In that process he was like stained glass, an intricate play of deep reds, pale amber and clear cut crystal, beautiful to behold. If he had avoided his place in the conflict it would be like a broken window—distracted by the jagged shards, one can't see the light. And if he had kept his hands clean of the violence, he might be like one simple pane, invisible to the eye, letting in a maximum of light, but without beauty."

I told Vishwamithra, "How can his tragic end speak to me? Tell me in your own words what I should do with my life if I heard Bhishm'a discourse."

The sage said, "Gayatri gives her advice—worship the Creator of ironies and paradoxes, stop to meditate on the play of consciousness in form, and become a transparent vehicle that places your life in the hands of that greater One; *Om* by so many names. That's the voice of timeless wisdom—here is mine."

He examined the bare dregs at the bottom of his cup that had dried during the span of our morning session. Wrapping his hands around it he said matter-of-factly, "When this world system finally riddles you full of holes, winds of change can whistle right through—then resistance and problems come to an end."

The room continued in its quiet. Vishwamithra lifted the tea pot to pour again. Apparently it was empty as well.

Learning to Ride *by Ashty Hozan*

My first bicycle was
huge for short legs.
Father strapped wood blocks—
So pedals could meet straining toes.

He said, "I'll hold you up,"
I pumped the sprocket on his guarantee
To keep me upright—
I knew balance was impossible.

"I have the hang of it,"
I said to my support—
and turned around to see him
far away, laughing.

PRAYER

"IT IS NOT MAGIC. It is relationship," he said, waving the tea pot as he spoke. "Even though the repetitive nature of mantra practice may be machine-like, the power is in the real presence of another. The *bright* within you is conscious intelligence. It is your ability to be aware of anything. It is a person."

He popped open the lid on the small stainless steel container and comically peered inside as though the last of the tea might be hiding in some corner. Then he pointed a question at me. "Tell me—how do you coax a response from true God, *Om*, The Infinite Presence, the Wholly Other? How do you engage It in relationship?"

"Is it through my awareness—contemplating what I see and hear?" I asked.

"Those are only effects of the greater presence," he replied. "Relate to the cause, not the effect! Go back further. We discussed the root source of all decisions once before."

I grabbed at straws. "I see and hear what I *decide* to see and hear? What I *expect* to perceive?" If I imagined God, it followed that the formless would meet me per my specifications. The words came out and fell flat; that idea was pure fantasy.

"Vah—you've gone back to delusion number one. A body-mind can't *do* anything!" he complained. "Think. What is *will*? Who is the perceiver? Before the beast runs and hides, turn around and grab it!"

"Umm...intention belongs to...," this was groping, "*my* will...which is a false perception—I can only intend to be or to do something. The only will is...*Pranava*, the *Om*. It is all in Om. *Pranava* is the doer that I can intend to know in some way. There is nothing else," I said, not sure what it meant.

"Yes," he said, trailing the word into silence like air escaping from a tire. There was the moment to allow the exchanges to percolate.

His teaching could descend like a cloudburst and my ability to absorb was like baked clay. A flood of words built up, roiling on top of me. He would sense the glut and cease the rain. The ideas could find places to sink in. At those times the quiet was clean, like the air after a thunderstorm. He waited, watched, and inevitably, I softened and understood. The spate of concepts moistened my mind and enlivened my tissue. He spoke into the calm aftermath.

"When you look in a mirror, you see your face reflected back to you, reversed. You say, 'That is what I look like,' even though it is flipped from what everyone else sees as your face. In a similar way, when you conjure an image of God's face—your ideal Reality—it is like a *mirror image*. It is the reflection of your *idea* of God, which appears to you inversed, a negation of what your personal God actually is. It happens because each person juggles three Gods. The first one is the absolute reality completely beyond perception; the next is the true personal God which reveals itself in every one of your experiences, filtered by cultural conditioning; and the third is the one most people think of as 'God,' it is their psychological and emotional needs projected outward—it is like a working model for their highest sense of purpose.

"Take an atheist. You ask them for an image of God and they might protest, saying, 'An old man with a beard is absurd,' or, 'God is a projection, it's more accurate to hold the beauty of nature as God.' It depends on what they've learned, what they have been exposed to. But in practice, the deity they worship is likely a system, the medical or banking establishment, high technology or their computer—their God is an ordering power, sold to them by their culture. It makes sense; someone who rejects any possibility for a transcendent authority has to find security through a system.

"Then again, a devotee of Shiva imagines the surly god, pounding out the *Tandava Dance* at world's end or steeped in meditation on *Mount Kailasha*. Yet, their highest functioning ideal may be glamour, a movie star, or cryogenic magic to allow the skin bag to go on for eternity.

"In another case, a tradition forbids any human-like form at all and instead uses glyphs, calligraphy, or symbols to replace the bodily conceptions of the divine. These same people often grovel at the feet of very human 'gods' who can connect them to wealth, fame, or power. Their hypocrisy is ironic as they say; *it's not what you know, but who you know*. They may consider their *own* face as their greatest asset.

"Contradiction is the rule rather than exception when it comes to ideas about God. A Christian who embraces loving forms of Jesus may also dislike children or be a sworn carnivore. Our image of absolute divinity appears as in a dream to teach us rather than reinforce us. It vanishes when we awaken."

"What?" I said, astonished. "Now you sound like the atheist, implying that we dream-up gods based on conditioning and culture! Is there no absolute Truth? Are creatures free-falling according to laws of perception, culture and chance? Surely you don't mean to condemn us to random fate. Capitalizing on our gullibility, well-resourced individuals would plant so-called gods and heroes in our heads as they wish, to lead us by our unsuspecting noses."

He spoke reassuringly, "God is one—and it is Good. Evil simulates good to attract the natural goodness in human nature—in that sense it has no independent existence except as a parasite. Evil attacks good in an infinite variety of ways. All roads lead to the ultimate good, which is the absolute God. But listen closely—truth is awake. It is aware. The creator, the source, has such power in the deepest longings and fears of human creatures that the *God-concept* was stolen for use as the first *meme* by controllers. Remember, a *meme* substitutes for thought and yet seems like real content. Systems use every concept to coerce certain behaviors, in health, religion, or civil obedience."

I asked, "So tell me, how is it possible to sort the true from the false? A sleeping dreamer thinks they are awake. How can anyone be sure they are awake or only dreaming?"

"You must pinch yourself—often and hard—to be sure you are awake," he said. "If you feel anger evidenced by a flush in your face and hands when one of your cherished ideals is attacked, you are asleep. You have been brain-washed by a meme. It is not truly your thought, but something you adopted uncritically. Test your ideas; they should have reliable evidence."

By his definition, I was brain-washed. The 'sting' he described was familiar. It happened when Vishwamithra poked fun at science. I'm not a scientist; why would I be offended when he criticized it? My belief in science was strong. In a way I was an armchair chemist and took pride in the scientific method. All of it reinforced progressive ideas about human destiny as well as my technical preferences. Whether or not science served my ultimate well-being was irrelevant. The suggestion that education itself was a form of brain-washing caused another sting. And saying that emotional reactions might indicate brain-washing caused emotional reactions, more stings!

"Sage," I began, "The things that trigger me are almost infinite. Isn't it normal to react when your value system is attacked?"

"Beliefs function as deities—they receive your worship when you adopt them uncritically," he said. "Qualities of *whatever* god are

91

manufactured and sold to you as reality, *based on how aware you are of your intention.* Most gods are not of the religious type, though they are definitely *religions* with attendant rituals and compulsions. It is a convincing Maya-illusion that can as easily pawn off the money-god, the Vishnu-god, the fitness and health-god or the Jehovah-god as 'God.' Evil itself can be framed as 'God'—such is the freedom and power of implanted intentions. Absolute truth, the 'True God' is the engine behind this consciousness-technology. It is the water in waves, the sand in sand castles. There are gods of various stripes and there is *Pranava.* Those are the options according to your disposition. Primal Will relates to you through your personal illusions. All this begs one profound question. What is it?"

I stated, spontaneously, "Out of a world of so many people, entitled drifters, oppressed day-slaves or seekers of all kinds, I am here—they are not. What stirred me—muddied my mind in this way? What happened to patience and committed effort to accept the paths suggested all along the way by parents and authorities? Who is to blame for my mixed-up, wayward path? What whim in me chose your posting against more obvious, conventional paths? "

He replied, "*Grace* is an easy answer that does not help. The convenience store solves hunger quickly, and the price is marked-up. Yes, *grace* is there, right alongside *karma, destiny,* and *you think too much.* A while back you told me how you got here. Now go inside that answer and look for what moved in you *before motivation.* Look for the fertile ground that incubated motivation, which told you, 'Go to the old man, maybe he'll shake things up."

The old man, he said it in such a familiar way. Grace...karma and fate were dice thrown on the gambler's table. Who loaded the dice so that they rolled-up with *see the old man?* Out of all action-paths, how did I arrive at what I assumed was my choice?

Om was the only torch. With no light to see the true longings that resonated in my core, I said *Aum* and reached in the dark.

The objects and people in my life had simply appeared. Childhood just happened. I tumbled into adolescence which morphed into young adulthood. Today there is this sense of *now.* The mantra called all this *bhur*—the things that were no more my choice than skin color.

My motives and reactions were always the result of a current understanding of things—*bhuvah* flowed at me and out of me as right or wrong reactions, intentional, or unintended choices.

The idea of controlling *bhur-bhuvah,* the objects and the energies of the *river of life* was deluded at best. There was no proof for a solid ability to choose differently. Such speculations were always hindsight.

My laziness was at least sincere, based on temperament. My distracted modes usually got pinched-awake by something else, like an angel that kept the worst results away from me. Why I did or did not do this or that, while others did something else was a circular mystery. The *suvaha* of me coaxed and dragged at my attention until the whole of *me* arrived here, leaving a trail that staggered with flaws.

He sat there like it had always been like this. When I stripped-off ideas about *who* he was or what *I* was or *what we were doing* in these meetings—I loved *the old man*. I would never tell him because the thought frightened me. It was embarrassing to my illusion of control. There was no science to explain any of the things that drew me from a farm to a factory and now to a room and *an old man*.

Sidestepping sentimentality I said, "I might as well be a block of wood. I'm here, I move, thoughts go through my head, feelings happen on their own. Who moves me?—the mover, one that I don't know, who seems to know me perfectly. No matter how I try to find the motive behind any action, there is nothing there. And yet whatever it is, it happens in perfect order, regardless of complaints."

He said, "The key to the one and only God is in you—lost, hidden, or found in your particular experience. You are the scripture you must read every minute of every day. Your looking *is* the finding."

The question remained, *how to coax an answer from God*, or was the effort delusional? I presented my disorganized concerns to him, saying, "I never answered your question and you have not rescued me from being a half-hearted agnostic. If you have the answer, rescue me."

He seemed to transform in front of me, becoming mother, father, and guide in one. I sensed eagerness and at the same time, restraint. He bowed his head slightly, extended his palm toward me, and placed his left hand over the center of his chest. The leathered skin of his hand found contact with my forehead. The fit was as natural as the gesture was strange to my experience.

"Ashty Hozan, repeat with me.

Om—

bhur—bhuvah—suvaha—
tat—savitur—varenyum—
bhargo—devasya—dhimahi—
dhiyo—yonah—prachodayat."

My repetitions trailed after each syllable he pronounced.

He said, "Surrender and prayer are the posture of humility. They begin with self-honesty. Drop bravado. Admit what you feel. Your choices have fled, the hands grow weak, and your pockets are empty. Now prostrate—press your face into the dust—feel damp breath mingle with dry earth. Only then, fill your nostrils with the sweet aroma of rich soil, solid ground, your strength that will never fail."

He continued speaking toward the floor between us and brought both hands to his lap.

"This is prayer," he said. "*Ask, and I will answer you. Stay with me and hear my reply. Leave and know there is no beginning or ending to our bond.* This is *kaivalya*."

The room and its contents came back to me like waking from a dream. Checking my watch, we were within the hour.

THE WALL

"THE WORLD WE SEE is like a shadow, cast by living spirit. Earthly shadows suggest outlines of an object—we can discover a lot about the spiritual world by examining earthly life as analogies of spirit. Take sight for instance. *Light* is real, it lets us *see*. *Seeing* brings things from outside of us into our *mind's eye*. It is a type of touching—the body's grasp of the world is extended by an ability to see."

Vishwamithra stopped abruptly. Making our invocation to Gayatri, he said, "Before we race ahead of ourselves, bow inside. Recognize— *she is Shakti-ma, the energy and brilliance of all phenomena. Our effective study, made of warm breath, words and meanings, is her presence. When she finds a seat among us, in our minds and in our hearts—she leads us from darkness to light, from dullness to the eternal flame of awareness, from death to life-eternal.*

"It is for us, not her that I call on her each time we meet. As Shakti, she even lives in the electric intentions of our thoughts. These are various topics to bring matter into awareness. It has warmth and intelligence we can discover." He returned to the subject of light and shadow.

"Consider visible light as a symbol for *consciousness*," he began again. "Consciousness illuminates the mind—it is spiritual light. When we know something that we did not know before, it is like a light shined on our thinking. We have become aware of something that had been dark. The brain is like a shadow of the mind. Thinking is head-oriented and earth-bound. Conscious awareness brings spiritual light into the brain's activity.

He continued, "Sense-perception is the dim cousin of spiritual sight, or awareness. Eyes require light to see—and to understand a thing it must be true. *Meaning*, on earth, shadows spiritual Truth.

The metaphor of light went on, "Climb the ladder to spiritual reality this way: photon-light points to conscious awareness, understanding, meaning, and upwards to spiritual Truth. The point of this ladder is to know, as Gayatri clearly says, that the light of consciousness is worthy of worship as the bringer of intellect's dawn.

"*Meaning* is understood differently in each human mind. One particular interpretation is like one ray of truth. Taken together, all the billions of interpretations of meaning still do not define the Truth which is infinite. Human consciousness seems like a flux of changing meaning and partial truths—in fact it is only the singular Truth like the one sun, shining dappled light through leaves, shifting in the breeze."

He could see that the subtle point was lost on me. He motioned toward my billfold which lay on the floor near my leg.

"What's that?" he asked.

"My wallet." I said, "It's uncomfortable to sit on."

He said, "What does a wallet mean?"

What a question—answering would definitely be *a work in progress*.

"It holds identification and paper money," I said.

"That's what it does, its *function*. What does it mean? Surely it's not without meaning," he said. "Doesn't everything have a meaning?"

"A wallet is a container for personal effects, licenses, cash and maybe photos. Things a person uses to prove their identity," I said.

"That's a *definition*, not a *meaning*," he bounced back. "Is it only for authorities, clerks, or bureaucrats? What would happen if you lost it?"

I did lose it once. I didn't discover the loss until hours later. I was on a bus, hundreds of miles away from where I absent-mindedly left it on a counter. My frustration was excruciating until the bus finally got to a station and I could backtrack. Lucky for me the clerk put it aside in case I remembered. My relief was immense, despite the wasted time.

I told it to the sage, adding, "It was like losing myself, as though a very real part of me got left behind and I would be incomplete, a non-person until the contents of the wallet were back in my possession."

"The meaning of your billfold is becoming clearer," he said. "You and the society you live in believe that your practical, useful self is statistical and registered, a fragmentary substitute for the being called *Ashty Hozan*. It means your essence is irrelevant and functionless in the system. You also believe this. There is no objection to being carved into pieces that serve the state machinery."

"But this is necessary for any complex society," I complained. "How else could thousands of people share services and all the rest? Talking about it this way implies there is an option—there is none!"

"Of course not," he said. "At least the idea of meaning is clearer. Functions are not meaningful, though they can be clues. A definition is a handle provided for practical communications. It does nothing to provide meaning or purpose—those are of a higher, spiritual order."

He had not completed his point when my defensive reaction sent us in another direction. He asked, "Do you know the Ramayana?" I had only heard of it. "Take the time to understand how wonderful it is that an epic, so full of truth and practical guidance, even exists. It has to be proof of all-illuminating effulgence from far beyond our senses. Explore it as another metaphor that comes to shine rays of new understanding into the heart—if you let it."

He began, "The *Ram-avatar*, the seventh incarnation of the god *Vishnu*, came to restore the means to live correctly. The Ramayana epic is a trove of Indian culture—each part of the saga is a key to right relationship in all its forms. This episode begins with the kidnapping of a princess named *Sita*. She was neither a tiara-ballroom debutant, nor a diamond-in-the-rough wall-flower. She was subtle, the daughter of a saint-king, renowned for his ability to deal with the kingdom without losing the spirit of a renunciate-sage. As the wife of Rama she was also of divine origin, the goddess of wealth. Due to a sequence of tragic events, she was stolen by the king of demons, *Ravana*.

"The demons were a non-human race with extraordinary abilities, deceptive arts, spells and the like. They had profound affection and respect for Ravana. He had been a brilliant leader, charismatic and accomplished in every aspect of religion, art, and war—who developed a massive ego in the process. This narcissist had come to believe that the world and all its habitants were his playthings.

"He saw beautiful Sita and took her. The theft of Rama's wife is central to the *Ramayana*. She spent a year in the demon's royal court-yard, and refused his palace and bed. She wasted from longing for her tardy husband while fending off demonic seductions. Meanwhile, her warrior-spouse searched the continent with no inkling as to what happened to Sita. The drama of *Sita-Ram* illustrates the relationship of Rama as *Soul*, and Sita as the *knower* of the soul."

He changed tone and said, "Hear the story as your own. Don't let exotic settings turn you into a spectator. She was more than a desirable woman—she was desire itself. *Desire*, the motivation behind human action, was pilfered by egoistical craving, embodied in the demon-king. The theft of Sita describes the fate of moderns who have lost heart-longing and accept material gain as a substitute. Societal busyness has stolen the life of feeling. Without inspiration, all beings become hungry ghosts, going from place to place as joyless consumers.

"The adept prince was sick at heart. His loss was not an ordinary one because, as you know, your loss is never ordinary. Every loss is a loss of heart, until the light of awareness dawns to reveal Truth."

He paused and offered me a side comment, "These archetypal titans play for impossibly high stakes to make an impression on the dull wits that need the instruction." The comment found its mark. I resolved to shore-up my attention span when it started to flag.

"There is more to it than lost love. The stolen maiden—the eclipse of joyful union—was necessary to allow new relationships that could not happen otherwise. The prince allied with an ape-shaman named *Hanuman*. The Ram-Hanuman friendship expresses the unique love generated between *servant* and *served*. See them again as human-integrity bonded with animal-virility. Your physical vitality truly loves you—the affection can only be discovered when you long to reclaim the soul that is stolen by so many arid goals. Hanuman's heart beat with the sound *Sita-Ram*. This signaled a new chapter—self-consciousness had sheared away from instinct—*Ram-Hanuman* was a model for animal vitality to bond with reason, fueled by integrity. True heroism is sober, accepts the facts at hand—among those are a call to truth, integrity, and interdependence with others who can share the sober vocation. Heroism is reluctant and vulnerable—brave heroes don't score victories; they sacrifice immediate comforts to restore truth and integrity. Heroism is also a lonely act, often lost or buried in victory narratives. So you can know that *Ram and Hanuman* are written in you. You write the story of their friendship through your intention."

Vishwamithra sketched-in a small vignette from the long saga. Rama's armies located the maiden, who was captive hundreds of miles from the beach where they stood. The exiled warrior-prince led them to the vast sea which looked to be impassable, a dead end.

The story-teller challenged me, saying, "See the throngs of forest dwelling simians, arranged in rows and columns, waiting for orders to attack. Generals, military order, willingness to fight and die, to win the maiden, to serve Ram with every fiber of strength—all this was arrayed along a beach, waves lapping their feet. They stared, motionless, at a flat horizon of deep blue that hid the woman, their soul. With no way to cross, they laid all their hopes on Rama.

"Before meeting the avatar their days were spent bickering with one another or foraging for fruits. Now, invested with full faith in Rama, their lives had been animated by an ultimate good, the restoration of Ram and his languishing wife. They seethed while imagining her plight as a hostage, unable to exact revenge.

"See them pacing along the gulf, pent-up and anxious to begin. All the while they looked to their leader who they hoped must know. The animals gazed across another kind gulf, the unbridgeable gap between their impulsive enthusiasm and Ram's reluctant moodiness. Every twitch of muscle, every ounce of their devotion was in his hands to keep meaning and purpose alive. And yet he waited."

Vishwamithra went forward in the unfolding plot. "The divinity was on Earth to fully grasp the pregnant moment in calm awareness. He adopted a meditative posture there on the sand, surrounded by phalanxes of ape armies, all of them locked in rapt witness. Breathing slowed to stillness, inner eye opened, the yogi-warrior communed within himself to find passage. He felt a mysterious confluence of time and destiny. The way was not clear—and yet reclaiming his wife and defeating the abductor was a foregone conclusion. His sadhana would reveal the simple twist they required to hurl unbridled force at the distant palace—so he thought."

So many expectations weighed on this one person who had roused them, given them reason, mission, and purpose. It had arrived at a critical point, one that contained no solutions. A miracle would be insincere and unsatisfying. Pedantic lessons about failure would be worse. There was nothing to do but sit with Ram and watch.

The sage went on, saying, "The scene took-on the character of a strange wake with the yogi, still as death. He became an object study, not in decay, but in *tapas*, heat. His skin took on an orange cast, deepening as the sun marched across the sky. At night his silhouetted form was like a cut out against the star-studded heavens.

"Waves slapped rhythmically. After the first day, the sound was a challenge against a warrior's will—Ram remained motionless. With the second sunset, the sound seemed to mock their aspiration to prevail over the elements—Ram was stone. By day three Ram sat drenched in sweat, glowing like hot magma—the lapping water was flatly derisive.

"There would be no passage," the sage continued. "This Ram would gain no special favor from the natural order, even if he sat like a statue for a thousand years! It might as well have been sung by the gulls, written across the sky. It was certainly obvious to all gathered that their cause did not move forward a speck. In fact, it was thrown back to the opposite horizon, the jungle, confusion, an age before light. Ram was exposed as a mere man. His clay feet would not skim over the waves. His passion for justice could not crack a coconut; much less defeat the powerful, lusty demon." The Sage's tone was a difficult mixture of disdain and sympathy.

"Any reaction by the troops would be a blow to a grand purposeful design—they stood breathless. Hanuman was like a rib protecting Ram's own heart. He sank with him into the void at the austere vigil by the sea. Failure would mean apocalypse, the end of days. Hanuman would shatter into pieces before allowing any reaction that might explode the bubble of their warrior-resolve.

"Instead he looked at his master, eyes red as if to say, 'Reach past the impossible! I am the glove for your hand. Show me life has a meaning beyond abject misery and loss. Rise! I did once—my only power was in you. Rise, so we can all stand up again!' He said that with his look, wounded and expectant.

"Ram leapt up in righteous indignation at the sea, spun on his heel and addressed it saying, 'You have met your destroyer! I have been kind and compliant, now you will die for your stubborn ignorance.' He pointed his formidable bow and directed bright, hot energy born of three days cooking with focused intent right into the water to burn it, explode it to steam and make the sea bed dry as bricks for their walk to save the woman. The apes would see the human blossom as an avenging power beyond nature."

Vishwamithra wove a tale of all-or-nothing stakes, where total destruction made sense—given Ram's situation. Nature should help with the good cause. If the ocean colluded with demons to keep archetypal lovers apart, it was right for Ram to vaporize the problem. I had been on that beach before, trapped between ambition and the deep blue sea. Truly, what hope was there if nature made no allowances for virtue in the face of evil? The story commenced.

"Reduced to impotence by the insentient sea, Ram would end the world. This was neither wise nor ignorant. It had nothing to do with intelligence or reason. The elemental force in the warrior pitted itself spontaneously against the intractable elements. The meeting of matter and anti-matter would end any dramas or narratives, to be sure.

"The saving turn of plot is what they call *deus ex machina*, Latin for 'god out of the machine.' It means the only way out is to drag something in. In this case, the ocean deity appeared and begged forgiveness, reminded Rama-as-Vishnu that he made the elements to work in a certain unchangeable way. The god offered a discourse on the wisdom of the created order and tells Ram how to solve his dilemma using available means. Twin brothers, architects no less, were among the apes. They had been cursed in childhood that any rock they touched would float! Well, there's a stone bridge right there. Read the story yourself if you want the full sequence of events."

Vishwamithra opened the story, promising that it would give a way to overcome unbeatable circumstances. The solutions offered in the epic were the usual fairy-tale endings, full of magical abilities, superhuman feats, and celestial intervention. It did not say how to deal with my fate, populated with bosses, agendas, bills, and no magic lamps. I had at least learned to hear-out the sage for his reasoning.

"Guru-Ram teaches. His actions at the sea give instructions on how to behave and what to expect when you meet an impasse. There are times when you have done all you can, and circumstances seem to conspire against you. Two words summarize his advice in such a situation, 'Take action.' Ah!—Study Rama before you jump to conclusions. What did Ram do?"

I said, "He became enraged enough to threaten a whole ecosystem, just to get to the other side. His actions and attitudes may be profound at some level, but it mostly looks like a temper tantrum."

"Yes indeed, he lost his cool as many of us do," he said. "That's not the starting point. He began with a passionate quest for lost love. He befriended unlikely beings that helped find his stolen wife. He led them on a quest despite unanswered questions. And he performed deep meditation on an insentient obstacle as a first step. I will unpack these events that show how Rama met a wall and passed through it."

Vishwamithra used *Om, bhur, bhuvah, suvaha* and *Gayatri Mantra* as a contemplative map that could lead through impossible obstacles. He said Rama's acts of meditation, attack and worship mirrored Gayatri.

"The Avatar behaved like many people do when they don't get their way," the sage said. "He assumed that the ocean was the problem and invested in solving something he did not fully understand. His conclusion was natural, but sitting down to meditate was inconsistent with war—the move sent a mixed-message that confused the troops. Rama teaches the human race at its level. He doesn't suggest lofty detachment. People assume they understand their problem and then try to solve it; sometimes ignoring the facts at hand."

Then Vishwamithra combed-through Rama's threat, saying, "He was caught in a complex situation, felt betrayed, helpless, and angry enough to destroy the thing he claimed to appreciate. He lost face in front of his followers. They must have doubted the wisdom of miraculous intervention from the moment he sat down to meditate. He flexed his 'warrior-muscles' to regain the army's confidence— displaying wrath after a placid request was no improvement. Over-reacting is common when people misjudge circumstances at the start. They try regaining lost ground. The army, having sworn an oath of loyalty to Rama's just cause, now wondered about how the impasse could possibly resolve itself. It went from bad to worse."

The sage briefly mentioned the third action at the beach, when

Rama decided to worship and dedicate that place to Shiva. "When the ocean god manifested out of the turbid water, Rama regained their trust, as well as his own equilibrium. The miraculous appearance re-established Rama's special status. Thanks to the ocean god, there was now a clear strategy. Pacified, reinstalled as an effective leader, and inspired, Rama dedicated a permanent religious icon to Shiva, on the spot. The ritual would endear Rama to the powerful deity and secure blessings through the coming events."

Vishwamithra summarized, saying, "In order, Rama did these three: supplication, reaction, and worship. Said another way he performed the actions prescribed by Gayatri of *worship, meditation and prayer* in reverse order. Rama showed the painful outcome of reversal so that we may correct the common tendency in our own situation."

He was giving me a way to confront my obstacles by contemplating Rama's teachings in light of Gayatri Mantra.

"*Meeting the wall* is a term used by athletes to describe the absolute limit of the body. Strength, stamina, intelligence, emotional stability—all these have set limits, regardless of preparation or training. Meeting that edge means that *trying harder* is over. There is nowhere to go. The first impulse is to blame the thing that stops you—the hamstring, the knee, the boss, the ocean."

At that point Vishwamithra told me to write as he enumerated the things to do when limits stare one in the face. "Write this heading he said, "Rama's Tips for Meeting the Wall.

"Number one—be good, then act. If you are not good, do not take any action."

I interrupted, "How can anyone know they are good? Everyone thinks they are being good, don't they? This step would make action difficult or even impossible."

Vishwamithra replied, "We discussed this earlier. Being good means discipline, the desire to relate to the other, to understand. Rama had trouble at the beach because he did not do this and yet, his whole life was sensitivity to the other. It turned out well because Rama was good; he sought out relationship through discipline in every instance.

"Number two—commit, be bold, take action that suits *who* you are—your dharma."

This list would not be as clear as I hoped. "Excuse me again," I said, "Not knowing who or what I am, the truth of my actions is uncertain. I don't know who I am, so I don't know what to do."

"This is precisely why Guru-Rama violated number two by meditating at the beach. Warriors don't meditate unless it is to penetrate the weaknesses of their foe. Worse yet, Rama's action might have looked desperate to the troops, hungry for action. If he makes mistakes it is to tell you something. He shows that the good cause will provoke answers whether you are doing it right or not. The Ocean-god set him straight by telling him who he was and what he had."

"Number three—avoid reactivity. Hold fast to what you know about yourself through introspection to prevent useless, wasteful actions—but err to the side of boldness—do not procrastinate."

The avatar literally shot arrows into the water. I could hardly imagine a more useless action. To Rama's credit, he did act boldly as a warrior should. I doubted that some god of wealth, hearth, or home would magically appear and give me concrete directions to undo mistakes. I could not resist a side comment.

Under my breath I said, "I should be so lucky for God to appear, to redirect my strategy for handling dead-ends."

"You think He doesn't? Every event in your life is a word from the generator of that life to instruct you precisely and directly. If God were Martian, you might be inspired to learn the Martian language to understand the wisdom he gave. Fortunately, the creator is not Martian—the only language you have to learn is your own moods and feelings, your intuitions, the scripture of your life you must read every day. Discipline, step one, requires all this before one begins.

"Number four—assess the result of your bold action. Pray that the results of your bold action are carried forward and bear the fruit you hoped for. Know that your actions were not wasted on an insentient field—all actions enter the field according to their qualities, and fructify according to those qualities."

At last the episode at the shore seemed to catch up to steps listed by the Vishwamithra. I said, "Rama finally offered thanks and backed away from his destructive threat against nature. That much is clear."

The sage countered, "Nothing the avatar did is clear. He drew from depths that transcended time and space, let alone immediate circumstances. An observer might wonder what Shiva had to do with his success—no ritual gratitude was offered to the Ocean-god. Rama speaks to us from ten-thousand years ago, saying 'There are gods and again there is God. God alone receives worship. My life has been a puja-ritual offering to the One. This is the One who saved me from my ignorance. This is the One who will bring success. This One alone is sure to right the scales of creation. If my intention is true, this God saves me from my untruth."

After his talk, I mused about Rama's temper tantrum, divine intervention and the list of "sure-fire" actions. Several things became clear and made me happy—I wrote my own list.

How to Behave at a Wall

1. BE GOOD—ask these questions: *Who has the problem? Who holds the key to the problem? Do I know the best outcome? Who am I helping by solving this problem?* Ocean, role, goal, status and available means formed a whole environment that Rama considered before acting—*Om*.

2. COMMIT TO THE BEST IDEA to succeed. Practice brutal self-honesty. *If commitment is weak, partial, or conditional, find out why—propose a better idea.* Ram meditated at the gulf because he knew that there was an intelligent effulgence behind the appearance of water—*Bhur*.

3. HOLD TO THE VISION of your best idea for action by not changing it in the face of resistance. *It is not a fight—you are expressing your current awareness of who you are, what the problem is, and who benefits from success.* Rama communed with the obstacle and himself according to laws of relationship—he was a bellicose warrior, it was behaving like a dumb object—he demanded a good faith response and got it—*bhuvah*.

4. ASSUME SUCCESS AND BE VIGILANT for the form it takes. *Be grateful and proceed in this process until the wall is no longer a wall.* Finally, Rama gave a creative testimony to the source of his success. He erected a tribute to the God who he intended to serve all along. He chose the deity that transcended social forms, the one that bridged elemental creation and destruction rather than a particular minor god—*suvaha*.

5. THE UNYIELDING WALL IS A LOVE LETTER to help you understand what is important, what is not important, and who you really are. Rama did all this *as worship, meditation, and prayer—the three tasks of the mantra*.

SUVAHA

"THE ELEMENTS ARE OBLIVIOUS to your problems and therefore, immune to persuasion," the sage said, almost as though a week had not passed since our study of Rama's dilemma. "In the same way that Rama attacked the insentient sea, threaten your bored acceptance of ruts and habits. The habitual trek from feed-trough to bathroom to bed might as well be wooden. It can only respond to force. But what is force? It is *Shakti*. And what is that? It is she—but note the irony and laugh at the joke! She is both the obstacle and the force to crack it. She is the motivation and the brain that ruminates on it. What is her game?" He went spontaneously into our invocation, saying:

The energy and brilliance of all phenomena is the gift of life, and has no reason in it. It is Reason itself so that God can know God through the language of human substance. May we unmask the veil of sense-perception to reveal the truth beyond. When she finds a seat in our minds and in our hearts—she leads from darkness to light, from dullness to the eternal flame of awareness, from death to life-eternal. As such, it is all Aum."

He opened his eyes toward me and asked, "What moves the story of Ramayana? If we know that, we know every true motivation."

"Love—Ram wants to get his wife back," I said.

Vishwamithra winced, "Obvious answers miss the point. Yes, Ram and his wife belong together. They are the essence of love, expressed in the ideal forms of those times. Clear your mind and tell me, is there a difference between your actions and the things you want to act on—your desire and the thing you desire? Which came first, the chicken or the egg? "

They cycled into each other. Leading, following—one pulled while the other got pulled. The woman got stolen. No one led her. She was taken against her will. Hanuman followed Ram, the god-man who pulled up short—the physically powerful ape chased the effectively powerless human—but Ram led none-the-less. An egg had no will—it existed. The chicken had a will, if you could call it that—and it resulted in an egg. Strictly speaking, the chicken *followed* the egg—which placed the egg first. The egg did not *follow* chickens or anything else. The hen's instinct made it chase the reproductive cycle—eggs.

"The egg came first," I said, grasping at a straw.

"Yes," he said. "Convince me it wasn't a lucky guess. Tell me again, what drives the story."

"The woman Sita," I responded, "the one who *does* nothing but *embodies* everything is the engine." I vaguely sensed a pattern.

"Tell me about it. We are discussing *bhur, bhuvah, and suvaha*. If you understand this, the Gayatri Mantra unleashes its potency."

I said, "Sita leads no one. Yet, Ram, his demon-adversary and the army of apes all follow her. Therefore she has primacy. There is the phrase, *chase a dream*. A dream is inert, it wants nothing, yet the bromide invites anyone to follow that dream-entity, whatever it is."

My analysis continued, "The story is full of pairings. Ram-Hanuman is a *complementary* pairing, like the colors blue and orange intensify each other but make gray when they mix.

"Sita-Ram is an *ideal* pair. The helpless damsel, Sita, brings out the hero in Ram. She has humanness and beauty that tempers his truth and clarity. She gives Ram a cause for heroism by her presence alone.

"And Sita-Hanuman is an unlikely couple that catalyzed the actions by all. So I would say they are an *effective* pair. Without the lost wife, Hanuman would remain only a devotee. He needs Sita in order to release his skills through service to Ram.

"In every case it is the helpless Sita who stimulates actions. Her inactivity seems to generate energy."

"Yes," he nodded. "Where can we find the three primal worlds, *bhur, bhuvah*, and *suvaha* in all this drama?" He waited, visibly enthused.

This was beyond me. We had not reviewed the meanings of the syllables. I had only heard them, so felt my way.

I said, "There are four characters, the warrior, the devotee, the woman, and the demon. Ram may be *bhur*, the whole set-up, the basis for the story. *Bhur* and Rama are complete in themselves. Hanuman, despite his power, is Ram's dependent so he must be the second word, *bhuvaha*. His heroic actions only make sense when they attach to Rama. Either the woman or her captor inherits the last idea, *suvaha*, motive engines behind all the action. That is as far as I can go."

"Your deductions are on the mark," he said. "These four—the warrior-exile, the stolen woman, the strong helper, and the demon-adversary—live and breathe in an archetypal world that you visit in dreams and fantasies. Names like *Ram* or *Sita* are cultural labels—the characters are qualities, named differently in every culture. Dwell on the qualities, not the names. See how they can inform *bhur, bhuvah, and suvaha*. Names obstruct the essence of things because the mind loves labels, handles to grab and possess. An archetype can never be fully understood or possessed, neither can the *mahavyahriti*."

He turned toward me as though to find a better angle to deliver the idea. "Ram, for example," he said, "fits *bhu*, the Earth, the primary set.

"Dwell on Ram's soul loss and his thwarted effort to recover the kidnapped woman, Sita. Feel Ram's pain at separation, his wounded ego, his doubts and anxieties. Ask yourself, 'What ocean blocks me from confronting my demons? What is my adversary? Who are my helpers? What is my aspect of soul, held hostage? Why has this Ram come to me with his troubles and what has he come to tell me?' In this way, the story cultures the mind and heart. The archetypal tale infuses your flesh and blood with the deep meaning of *Bhur-loka*."

Sizing me up he said, "You have to insert yourself in this 'Ram vehicle.' Travel with him to find the meaning of your life. You can be Sita, wasting and waiting in a foreign land. You can be Hanuman, poised and ready for a direction when none is forthcoming. You can be the demon, consuming other people's resources, taking pleasure in false possessions while your true purpose wastes. The only satisfying role for you is the warrior, hitting a wall, throwing your best effort to no avail and going with him to find the next piece. You are *Om, bhur, bhuvah, and suvaha*. They do you no good *over there* in metaphysics!"

What he was doing did not make logical sense. They were connections only Vishwamithra could see. I expressed my difficulty, saying, "The words and phrases are clear enough—your deductions are beyond me. Myths are myths, philosophy is dry, and metaphysics confuses me. Combining them as psycho-therapy is a big stretch."

He said, "Then simplify. The story wasn't so complicated. You learned three syllables. They are as basic as *a set of things—the energy between those things—and their ultimate destinies*—or again, *stuff, dynamics and ideal outcome*. Use those to label the characters and see what it reveals."

This game did not require much effort. I said, "*Bhur* is in exile with his wife who is *suvaha*. That would be like *a set of things* and *their ultimate destinies*, in exile, cut off from the flow of life. A demon steals *suvaha*— some thief steals purpose and ideals away from the set of things. *Bhur* goes out to find what was stolen and meets *Bhuva*—that would be *stuff* partnering with a new kind of *energy*, or dynamic quality. Armies, enthusiasm and devotion are forms of help. *Bhur and bhuvah* as a team—find *suvaha*. In other words, the *set of things* had to find *new energy* in order to reclaim a sense of *purpose*. It was impossible for *the issues* to cross an ocean to reach the captive *purpose* or *destiny*. *Bhur* tries to find a way across, acting alone. This fails and he threatens to fry the ocean— trying to beat physical reality into submission. The ocean tells *bhur* of some talents or *energies* among his group that can be useful. Apes relate to *bhuvah*, animal vitality. I'd say it means that a situation can't solve itself—there has to be a new, maybe unlikely energy, one that is nearby, as yet unknown. Sometimes it seems like a game of words."

He stated flatly, "Ram and his problems are a field of objective issues—*bhur*. Sita is the vital purpose you are missing—*suvaha*—stolen by society's false promises. The field of possibilities as Rama, lost its natural bond with meaning, as Sita. When the lovers are parted, true creation is impossible. In the absence of true creativity, you begin fabricating illusions of heaven on earth—the cynical effort to create meaning through consuming and doing. That is the demon.

"Loss of meaning causes spiritual lethargy. It results in random values based on convenience. Evil is a patchwork of gray zones where decisions are motivated by lust and fear—always with an eye-out for ease. The demon is a type of *wrong bhur* grasping at a *false suvaha*. When the basis called *bhur* is deluded, alliances and motivations will be warped. The well-endowed demon-king saw himself as *good*. For him it followed that his desires and decisions were as good as he—quite the opposite of self-esteem. Self-esteem has to include humility—proper proportion—or it is grandiose, no matter the talent involved. Truth is the actor in any good deed, which is seen as good because it reflects *truth*, not plans, strategies, skills or even heroism. Evil deeds are always a misinterpretation of the facts. The play of life originates far beyond earthbound creatures. The demon's intentions were warped by delusions of power. The *false will* interprets pain as pleasure; crooked appears to be true; and yours seems to be rightfully mine."

He sorted further through the core of demonic ambitions, saying, "Creatures can witness and then reflect Good—they cannot truly *be* good. *Being good* is a way of saying, *turn toward the ultimate good.* Rama met an impasse at the sea because he saw himself as good. Unlike his demon-shadow on the other side, he accepted counsel from nature which told him, 'No one is good enough to pervert natural laws—the good is all around you, find it.' He listened and benefitted."

Troubled by the potential for error I said, "I thought my intentions for leaving home were good. Now I am afraid I only hurt people that I love. They had to take over my chores which must have created a hardship. Given your discourse, it seems I could have deluded myself with lofty intentions, only to justify faulty actions. What do you say? Should I go back?"

He looked at me kindly and for a moment I was afraid he would agree. He said, "The things we call mistakes are part of consciousness. They are mental assessments, not real. There can be tragedies, cruelties and missed opportunities, but technically, in the eyes of God, there are no mistakes. Hindsight and self-criticism can help you wake-up. It's good to discern motivations and the rest. Should you go back? Should you stay? The questions are the same—neither affects this moment.

"Something moved you to leave. Your actions were based on a mix of intelligence, reactivity, and ignorance. Now you are different; so are the ones you left. Time travel is not possible—don't flog yourself with thoughts of how it might be different. Yet, healing the past is possible—by understanding the thing that moved you at the start. Even now, you are not separate from your family. Before deciding about burning or rebuilding bridges, find the one that inspires all of it: hopes for a better life, leaving the familiar, regrets, and this conversation now. See how all your activities swirl like winds around the eye of a storm."

Thinking out loud I said, "Deadness had already crept over me, even before the decision to go. I resisted. Sri Vishwamithra, all the dreams of success and helping others has come to nothing. Returning empty-handed seems worse. The idea of doing any good for my family now seems ridiculous. I wanted to lift us all, and now feel useless."

He said, "How can you recover the missing thing, the lost paradise that slipped away by degrees? There were no alarms. There are so many trials and relationships to help solve the troubles. Healing the past is another matter—it begins immediately, as soon as you start looking for Sita. "

Gayatri Mantra   *by Ashty Hozan*

Om—Reality
The unified field contains heaven, hell, angels, and archons.
The gift from God is to see worlds where there is only Om.

Bhur, Bhuvah, Suvaha—The universe extends infinitely
Below as our foundation, above as our ceiling and
We live among walls called experiences.
Every moment has content, relationship, and purpose.
Everything draws toward Om.

"Tat Savitur Varenyum—our portion is to worship
The hidden source of all the worlds we experience.

"Bhargo Devasya Dhimahi—our task is to meditate
Through the gods' bright veils that enchant the mind.

"Dhiyo Yonah Prachodayat—pray in each moment
To the One who receives thought and quickens insight.

We are compelled always and forever
toward truth, purpose and beauty.

INSTINCT

THE SAGE TRIED TO cut through my fog in various ways. He went back to themes in the Ramayana that might be strategies for me to find a glimmer of passion. I functioned, moment to moment with the dull, anxious peace of a terminal patient, awaiting test results.

He said, "Hanuman, *bhuva*, brings the father and mother together again. He is animal strength, guided by devotion to the pure and the beautiful. The ape-shaman archetype appears when you gather your instincts and passions in the cause of truth. Whose truth? Is it relative to whatever you want? That is the demon, the false guide. Truth is the catalyst that makes the impossible possible.

"The domain of animals is physical application, persistence beyond reason, and ignoring barriers. They are not burdened by judgments; they pump with vitality. And their devotion, once established, is to the death. Instinct is the animal's original inheritance, their gift of grace. But humans have lost that grace and have to be led by the Truth or they are capable of terrible deeds. Gayatri Mantra is the true guide.

"Ram meets a vast gulf. Hanuman can leap over it. That is not the point. The point is *how do you, as consciousness, meet the wall and reclaim your soul. How do you address the impossible barrier?* In so many ways the story of Ram delineates right order as 'heaven brought down to earth.' Your Rama is the *soul*—Sita is *meaning* Your Hanuman hankers after *soul-satisfaction—its purpose is to find meaning.*"

The models he presented could not find a hook in me to animate powerful intention.

"Ultimately, the barriers have to inform you," he said, his voice developing heat, "They force you to mature. A satisfied soul is something you feel—it's Ram's way, really, the only way."

Ii was plain my reactions or understanding did not satisfy him. He continued angling to find a chink in my dull armor.

"Stand-up, wag weapons at the vast gulf and make demands! Let your eyes turn red with tears or rage. Glow! Let the blood rise to the surface of your skin—there is Hanuman. The animal in you is not blind or indifferent. In your vitals, your physical reality is the bona fide servant. It pants for a worthy master...*the* worthy master, worthy!" he barked and continued, annunciating distinctly, "Va-ray-nee-yum! Worthy of worship...your impassioned desire for Sita-wholeness is such a master. Meditate on her! You fight gravity to stand erect. Know your enemies and fight. Be upright. Stake your claim! If you ignore the archetypes they will destroy you. It may be a slow corrosion of morals, confused ethics that lead to deadly traps, dissipation, or tasty but poisonous traps. Human life is a journey in wakeful awareness. Contemplate the archetypes to wake-up the mind and avoid the way of death. Join them in their play or be trounced by them!"

As though he tested the wall in me and found its true density, he adopted a different vein in a measured tone. "Tell me more about your life, your interests, and your ambitions. That will pique your interest."

Maybe he didn't understand. Talking about *me* seemed even more fruitless than armchair speculation and mythology. Old warriors had their epic motivations—my reasons were shrouded in malaise.

I told him "Mine is a tale told by an idiot with very little sound and no fury. It signifies nothing." Shakespeare's tragic characters at least had red blood and ambition.

He said, "You think your story is not worth telling because of the idea that someone, somewhere, lives a fulfilling life. Listen, every story is the same. Here's a correction to your cliché, *a life that struts and frets its hour upon the stage is nothing but your average, unexamined self-entertainment.*"

Unexamined entertainment?—it made no sense. What would it look like to really examine my life, the things I did and felt? Obscure bit-parts, waiting for a lucky break while floating from scene to scene was my inevitable lot—I was an extra, not a main character. Decisions seemed empty and pointless. 'Real life' was someplace else, happening to someone else...and yet my melodramas were emotionally absorbing and struck me as very important when they happened.

HE PROPPED HIMSELF ON ONE ARM, raising a hand. "Stop," he said. "It takes intelligent application to penetrate walls or cross impassable oceans. Consciousness has to grasp the polar tendencies of its animal nature—either dullness or panic. Instinct is a sub-conscious force of nature that grants the animal powers, like strength, speed, endurance, persistence, and indomitable will.   that makes the animal create illusions so dense they can't be breached, also to pierce them with a power that seems divine. Ram, stopped cold at the beach, has a 'prequel,' a fable from before humans were created; when actions were all in the shadow of instinct."

Voice muted, he said, "Ah, Vishnu...he had to act and then paid the price. Every time he came down to help people it ended up a mess—an occupational hazard for saviors." The damp tone put me on alert.

The narrative continued with sardonic flair, "Vishnu is lush, regal, and spends his days on a couch provided by a massive coiled snake. Since the primal serpent known as *Adisesha* and the god *Vishnu* are counterparts, the couch is infinitely accommodating. It conforms to the god's body as the ultimate, ergonomic sofa. In addition, the goddess Lakshmi is there, massaging his legs for all time." He grinned through clenched teeth. "Epochs come and go and there is no variation in their bliss and comfort, floating on the milk-sea of awareness." This had the ring of sarcasm.

"The three—god, goddess and timeless serpent—live like happy cats in a sunny window seat until the cosmic order is threatened by some demon or another. Only then do they pounce down to earth and correct the matter as they did in the Ram story. It has happened ten times. Those are the ten avatars—each one is a form of Vishnu that leapt-off the serpentine perch to save the human race from demons and degradation."

Now he taught, "Their time is not measured in solar transits. They are not bound-up in hours and minutes. Their lives and actions are in a continuous stream of 'quality.' If you pretend you can live apart from *quality*, you will suffer."

It seemed obvious that it was very easy to live apart from *quality* as I knew it. Most of my choices slid toward mediocrity in spite of my higher motives. He answered the unasked question.

"*Quality* is the meaningful part that animates every seemingly mundane thing or event," he said. "Call it *spirit*. We discussed how each archetype is a particular quality—lengthy descriptions can't do justice. There is an ever-present *charge* or *spin* that gives events their vitality. Nothing can exist without it. Quality motivates feeling.

"*Boredom* is a charge—it means you are not engaged in the matter. *Excitement* means you have expectations. *Anger* means the matter is coming at you. They certainly change one into the other like a school of fish swimming one way and darting altogether in a different direction. You must realize and take seriously that *mood swings* and subtle feelings guide you, push you, and seduce you into all manner of decisions and behaviors. They are like deities; intelligent, mysterious, and potentially destructive—thus my earlier warning about qualities."

The sage resumed the narrative. "The Earth Mother, *Bhudevi*, was lost below the waves of the cosmic soup. She should be familiar to you by now." He paused and raised an eyebrow in my direction. I nodded, *bhu*, of course—the substantial aspect of all existence. He went on.

"She sank under the primordial waters. Call it depression, call it hiding, call it kidnapped by a demon...in any case the destiny of the earth was threatened by some thing that would cover her, hide and enslave her. See the blue pearl, alive with possibilities, whisked away by an alien agenda—a demonic force that dragged her down. And who plays the role of Earth?—none other than *Lakshmi. Sesha* is there as well, integrated with *Vishnu* as raw animal passion."

"In this tale, Vishnu appears as a gigantic, mountain-sized boar to restore mother-earth to her proper place above creation. Predictably, after defeating the demon, the boar swims to the bottom of oceanic murk, raises *Bhudevi* on his tusks and delivers her to the surface where she reigns—high, dry and sovereign over nature. This victory scene is where your painful worries about wasting a life actually begin."

"You see," he began, "Earth Mother fell in love with her deliverer, and the gargantuan beast was just as smitten by the beautiful planet-goddess. Avoid the distracting visuals of a bejeweled goddess taking on family life with a pig." I welcomed his clarifications.

He said, "There is bound to be drama when divinity appears as substance. The split between *perfection* and *works in progress* is the split between an object and its shadow. Divine love mutates toward passion. Primal unity casts a shadow of clinging. Confusion of levels is ignorance, native to earthly life. Even the most difficult worldly-stuff is a gleaming pearl when seen correctly. Likewise, pleasure and ease are earth shadows of divine beauty and awareness. Those shadows can rejuvenate the soul—they are not its purpose. The boar-savior's raw animal power attacked a specific danger—submersion under water, or *unconsciousness*. Awareness builds on animal passion—it does not negate it. The beasts are messengers for those who become human."

He went ahead, explaining, "Tusks are phallic. They penetrate, they protect. A boar is famous for its placid nature—unless provoked. *There is nothing angrier than an angry pig*, they say. This means animal-force protects terrestrial life, our land of divine shadows. You can't think your way out of the soup and into bright awareness. It requires a ferocious charge into the fray, fired by purpose."

"What happened then?" I asked. "You said they fell in love."

He said, "The story has been instructive and predictable until this point. Now it takes a poignant turn. Let's see the passion and beauty

114

of our lives in these events, described by ancient seers.

"We, you and I, have heard the cry of the beautiful damsel. She was stolen, raped by the demon who wanted her body for himself. We saw her soiled and became mad with rage. We plunged down, further and further. We would impale the fiend headlong. We did so. We do every time we gaze at the beautiful planet and say, 'Thank you, Ma. I love you. I will protect you with every ounce of my strength. You must always be the beautiful pearl, my goddess and partner.'" He paused—his eyes moist. He was not telling me mythology. This was his affair, his lost love. He spoke again.

"And we fall in love. We want to stay. We will stay—the bliss is so attractive—how can we leave? Well, truth be told, we can't. Affection expressed in brute power brought us here, and the only way out is to kill the beast. It is a human portion to live the story with gusto and experience the sticky-end with regret."

He said, "The gods finally came for Vishnu and warned him, 'You have forgotten who you are.' He only snorted and said, 'This is better. Leave me alone!' The great swine turned away, frolicking with earth goddess, begetting children and enjoying mud baths on sunny days. Tell me what could be better?" He stopped, staring at me.

"Nothing—nothing is better than this," he answered himself. "But the gods have their place. They set the pace for earthbound spirits. Heaven is not an idle playground. They answer to a higher authority—there are duties and responsibilities. They killed the pig and forcibly put Vishnu back on his heavenly throne." He sighed in the pause that followed.

Again I was caught in his blank stare. He said, "You, Ashty Hozan, have forgotten who you are."

I may have met my slayer. Hackles rose on the back of my neck.

Thoughts are Birds *notes by Ashty Hozan*

A thought has autonomy.
   and lives a life span as your creation—
   independent of your personal agenda—
   yet they feed on your responses to them.

See a thought as a bird that flies
   away from the original nest
   to eat, mingle and propagate.

Personal awareness can't keep up
   with thoughts and their ways
   of flocking, breeding, and migrating unhindered.

Categorical thinking will snare you—
   Fixed ideas may provide a sense of security—
   they also cage the bird of free thought.

CATEGORIES

I LIVED THROUGH THE week. The image of Vishnu enjoying life as a pig popped into mind often and unexpectedly at mundane incidents—giddy at new selections in the vending machine, peaceful repose in a toilet stall, ogling the courier from upstairs and the irrepressible urge to see what she looked like from the back. All around me, smooth factory finishes and proper behaviors hid the beastly from the beasts—we each protected our own precious truffles. Really, it was the mud baths, troughs of fresh slop and all those private comforts which made life tolerable, even lovely.

After settling into our seats at the dawn meeting, we convened in the room-like mood of Gayatri meditation. The first doorway always addressed Ma Gayatri as living-being, the mantra as her real skin and bone. He led us through a deeper portal by offering a slow, deliberate litany of the first words.

"Aum Bhur, Aum Bhuvah, Aum Suvaha," he sang, and then took long breaths. Our lesson began within the sheltering walls of sacred space.

"Words are always imprecise, shifting categories," he said. "*Bhur, bhuvah, suvaha* is the 'Great Utterance,' or *mahavyahrti*. These are alive and beg for relationship with you. Don't let them waste as empty sounds on a mental shelf. You experience each of them all the time. They are the material basis, the dynamic relationship, and the meaningful resolution. *Bhuvah* is made of two Sanskrit words, 'Bhu' plus 'Vah.' What happens when we add a dynamic quality to *Bhur*? We see relationality as *bhu-vah*. We see pulsations of attraction, repulsion, and neutrality that are forces in the stuff. The stuff has its own sovereign reality, but then again the stuff is only a puppet for energetic flux. Like matter-gravity as shiva-shakti, *bhuvah* reveals *the material—bhur* as interlocked with *experience—bhuvah*."

"How is a word a category?" I asked. "Aren't categories some kind of filing system? Is it that the idea of a 'cup' is a category that includes many possible cups? Or that the word 'bhuvah' includes many specific, similar things in a larger, inclusive set?"

I could almost hear his mind go into reverse. These detours, based on my questions, were usually edifying—yet, I felt anxiety because of throwing a wrench in the works. I should know enough not to ask.

He said, "It is important that you bring up any sticking points as we speak. The animal in me is set to proceed directly to the point—beasts, not humans, proceed from point to point, unstoppable on habitual tracks. Your questions humanize us, elevate us from simple barnyard creatures headed for the intellectual trough, to beings of conscious awareness—relating to each other and the world of ideas." The proofs multiplied that we shared something too subtle to identify. Time and again he addressed unstated concerns like he was seeing thoughts flash across my forehead.

He said, "Before we launch into a full description of *Mahavyahriti*, let's examine *bhur, bhuvah, and suvaha* as categories rather than simple labels. A category is more than a file for related ideas—it's like a regional transportation hub that connects other hubs in huge networks. Its structure allows a human mind almost infinite capacity."

He handed me a small metal figurine he took from his altar. It was a bronze of a kind of creature, dancing. It had an elephant head on a human body. One tusk was broken. It held an ax, a noose, a ball, and a pen. It seemed childlike.

"There is a deity that embodies the conundrums of categorical thinking." He gestured toward the statue in my hands. "Meet Ganesha, the *Lord of Obstacles*, who presents himself at every transition. His most benevolent form is a lucky solution to a problem. His least desirable message could be an accident, injury, or sickness. He may throw such temper tantrums because the victim refused to ask the question, hear the answer, or were too dull to notice. He throws a wrench in the works so beasts can shed their habits to become human beings."

He gestured toward the image in my hands, saying, "*Gana-Isha* is the lord—*isha*, of the group or category—*gana*. Each of your thoughts has autonomy. They live out their life span as creatures, independent of your personal agenda, yet they feed on your responses to them. See a thought as a bird that flies away from the original nest to eat, connect, and propagate. It mates with other thought-birds and can form whole flocks—guided more by the nature of the thought than your intentions. Your personal awareness can't possibly keep up with the effects or ways that your thoughts breed and cluster into groups— you can't take full responsibility for these flocks of thoughts. That is the domain of the elephant-headed god who represents knowledge of the habits and tendencies native to the beast of thought."

Vishwamithra cautioned me, "Watch thoughts in their patterns, be sharply aware of which ones you feed, and notice your reactions. Do not be quick to cage them or shoot them for control's sake. Thoughts are effects, not causes. Applied-intellect can find their roosts and breeding places. This is discriminative intelligence or *Ganesha*"

He continued, "A *category* is an essential group-type used by the mind. It files every aspect of every thing into clusters of qualities. Spontaneously, the intelligence in you sorts every possible idea into overlapping and yet clearly defined categories. Every idea is cross-referenced and catalogued in so many ways."

He held up his cup and demonstrated. "You see this and say, 'tea cup.' It seems so simple and there is where the trouble starts. The mind is not simple. It is infinitely subtle and has conceived this tea cup—as a vessel, *my* possession as opposed to *yours*, an aesthetic object with form and style, a material thing of porcelain, as similar or different than other cups, or as a reminder of some event. These interrelate in too many ways to count. Another example is that you might say to yourself, 'I am going to work,' and yet you perceive a prison there, and tell yourself you are trapped. Tying work and prison together might not be your idea, likely it came from somewhere else, like a social critic or a parent. This is a tiny instance of something that extends to every aspect of life. *Ganesha* is the symbol-archetype that guides us as we try to navigate through blind-spots and pre-conceptions that result from the vast weaving of thought forms."

Vishwamithra then stated somberly, "This issue of categories is not part of nature—it is only in the realm of mind. This quality of human consciousness makes it vulnerable to illusions. Discriminating the real from the unreal has to be a full time occupation, without such spiritual efforts one is sure to meet disappointment, if not shocking hints of addiction to novelty—the darkness which often passes for grace." Grace is grounded. A wise man said, *God would not appear as other than food to a starving person.*" That declaration led us into a fable.

"ONCE THERE WAS AN average village called *Nah-yeev*—it was nothing special," he said. "They were happy in their unremarkable lives because they had each other. Mothers, daughters, fathers, old people, strange people, the smart ones and the not so smart ones all had their unremarkable place in their average world and it was good.

"A black magician named *Faldiraka* inevitably came to *Nah-yeev* town. He had been systematically kicked out of so many villages that

119

he knew they would eventually learn of his unseemly character. Weary of rebranding himself time after time, he resolved to design a way to accumulate the simple folks' wealth through control over their every habit—by stealth rather than theft. It had to be that way because his reputation, by this time, would precede him.

"One night just beyond the city gate, under cover of a dark moon, he fabricated his most ambitious deception; a beautiful, well-planned *Illusory City* that exceeded *Nah-yeev* in every way—only he concocted it upside down—this was no mistake. Watch and learn his devious cleverness in concocting a world on its head.

"Nearby farmers saw it first, nosed around and did not loiter since they had their endless chores to attend. Rumors of the miraculous setting fired through the community proper and they all wanted to see. First in small groups, and eventually, en masse, the town made their pilgrimage. Within hours, the entire population milled around this topsy-turvy habitat, and *they were* duly impressed to linger.

"They promenaded the central square with its fountain which sprayed gentle arcs of water that tantalizingly returned to the elaborately hewn marble base that hung from above. Stamped pavers interlocked in fabulous geometries—thwarted by gravity, the villagers could not tread there. By design, beauty and frustration met them in every detail of 'Faldiraka's folly.' They could not experience the pleasures that invited them, given that it all hung from above—or were they the ones doomed to dangle upside-down? They no longer could tell the difference. The ground they apparently walked on had an azure luminosity that mocked the sky, completing the illusion. Food was no problem. Their lush reward for attempting to unravel unnatural mysteries was to enjoy fruits like Eden's garden, hanging down to them in a seductive feast of gravity and magic.

"The people of *Nah-yeev* very soon found themselves entangled in the city of illusions crafted by the black magician, who, by the way, congratulated himself for his success and the glowing rewards it brought him, all hidden from the clueless townsfolk. The once idyllic village of *Nah-yeev*, by the by, had become an abandoned waste with dust accumulating in every corner. The citizens' once tidy-town had become home to spiders, bugs, and mice.

"Those farmers and craftsmen that earned a livelihood by the sweat of their brow had no place to sell their wares and soon began to suffer terribly. They went into the empty town and sought audience with the righteous priest who had been the godly glue of their former, average lives. But his services had been altogether abandoned as well.

Marriages, rituals, wise counsel, or even a casual game of darts were forgotten. Every man, woman, and child was spellbound by *Illusory City*—held captive by the fabulous life it promised in every last detail."

Vishwamithra stopped abruptly. I had the sense of hurling forward in the tale, myself perplexed by how I would function in such a distorted place. He asked, "How on earth do you suppose they can get out of this one?" The momentum continued to pull at me even as his question was like a brake on the illusion he wove.

Anchoring myself in the present I said, "The work of the magician has to be destroyed and his disruptive role must be exposed."

"You know they would hang the one that *rained on their parade*," he told me with a hint of a smirk. "But you are right. Somebody has to *pull the plug*. Now if the black magician had wanted to help the people of *Nah-yeev* develop soul sense and meaningful purpose by inventing a world of that sort, their self-satisfied routines might be uprooted and they could be saved. Our little upside-down tale would have a different outcome. This is not the case. In fact, that task of a happier illusion to undo the destructive delusion would be *the thorn to remove a thorn*. And that was precisely the treatment they obtained."

Beginning again he said, "The farmers were dismayed when they found the old priest. Unshaven, bleary-eyed and tearful he was surrounded by all his icons and deities, burning holy smoke and wailing to God for an answer to the terrible vacuum that had cursed what had been such an ordinary life but was now nothing at all.

"They said, 'You have been our wise-guide. Finding you like this, tormented by the bizarre fate God has dealt us, doubles our trouble. We will go to that hellish *Illusory City* and destroy it ourselves.'

"The priest, concerned for all their safety, startled back to a shred of his former sanity on hearing their plan. He knew that destroying an illusion was a tricky business. The upside-down townsfolk would sink into depression, erupt in rage, and come after the truth-tellers with revenge for destroying their intoxicating world. He had another idea.

'You right-minded folk are grounded in the good earth. I could not bear to have you become the targets of the poor, deluded waifs of our fair town who now busy themselves with gravity boots, headstands, and suspension cables to try and reinvent the blessed pull of natural soil that they have forgotten. I know of a shaman-fakir who has some special knowledge—he disdains city-dwellers but may offer help, out of compassion. Let me go to him before we take this difficult task into our own hands and risk disaster.'

"So saying, he went into the hills to find the reclusive mystic. An austere shaman appeared from the depths of a cave. Soot and ash were his clothes while dung from the high pasture lands smeared his head to form a cap. The desperate priest had to remind himself of the import of his mission and stammered, 'I beg your indulgence...' The ghostly seer stopped him.

'Let's get on with it,' he said flatly. 'I know your situation and the charlatan who has spun all your troubles. You need not explain your predictable fate. 'Let's go.' And off they went—the weary and doubtful priest with the ill-tempered hermit who spared all chit-chat. The recluse held his energy in reserve to dispense with the proximate evil. No one would believe or understand his methods in any case.

"Wasting no motion, they stood at the gate of the *Illusory City* and beheld the wonders of human gullibility, run-amok. There were people dangling here and there from terraces and lawns, feigning to extract enjoyment as the blood rushed to their ruby faces. There were women, fighting nature and gravity to unsuccessfully hold their skirts in a modest repose. Some children laughed and sang while suspended *right side up* on tree limbs, or crawling along ceilings. Some men had engineered scaffolds, steins, and seating so they could enjoy leisurely pursuits of croquet while sipping their favorite lagers, affixed to lawns sky-hooked to the clouds.

"The dust-clothed mystic bent to the earth, kissed it and addressed the priest, slowly wagging his head from side to side. He said, 'This is the work of *Faldiraka*, a cheap magician who was once a brilliant wonder-worker. His half-baked attainments have seduced him into a bane on the simple, unwitting, and trusting souls who still *believe in worlds of wonders* rather than *wonder at worlds of beliefs*. Go enjoy this aberration while you can, or better yet, watch and learn the character of your people.' So saying, he vanished.

"The priest wandered into the main plaza, dumbstruck, standing among 'clouds,' looking at his fellows who hung like colorful fruits from varied urban props that furnished *Illusory City*. Many of the former faithful waved to him enthusiastically, 'Ah reverend, you are walking in God's airy canopy. Come down and visit us.'

"Just then a figure dashed into the main square, turning cart wheels and nearly screaming in a shrill voice. It was a black-clad wraith of a man with pointy black beard and spiky hair jetting out from his head like twisted wire handles.

"He cried out, 'Fools, I am the great *Faldiraka,* creator of this wonderland and I deign to destroy it!' As though he were weightless, the madman clutched an absurd down-turned torch and went from point to point setting the upside-down city ablaze. The shocked citizens cried out as one, 'No...someone stop him!'

"But it was too late. Dream stuff is very volatile. It snapped and popped, bubbling and melting like the sappy veneer it was made of. People had to cut loose, drop, fall, roll, and hope for the best as their world tumbled into large burnt cinders that bounced aimless along the ground in the slightest breeze. The angry, disentitled folk of *Nah-yeev* became a wave of revenge and surged after the arsonist who high-tailed it, pell-mell out of town.

"Just over a hill they were stopped, amazed to face the gaunt figure in a robe like midnight who flailed his arms in imposing gestures. His spiked locks pointed fiendishly in the cardinal directions out from his otherwise bald head and he nearly screamed, 'I am *Faldiraka*! Who has destroyed my wonderland? Who wants to receive my fiercest punishment?' And he cocked a gnarled staff at each of them in turn.

'Faldiraka, you are indeed mad!' they shouted, 'This miracle was a gift from the gods. Now you have to pay!' And they flung themselves on him as one writhing mass of hands, arms, fists and teeth ripping at whatever piece of clothing, hair, or flesh they could find.

"The display of blind, wanton violence made the priest sick at the stomach and heart. Heaving and bent toward the ground, he had not quite recovered when the calloused feet of the sky-clad shaman came before his bleary, downcast eyes—how was this the helper he had given up for dead? Grasping the *Nah-yeev* priest firmly at the shoulders, the mystic said, 'There, tend your flock. The thorn removes the thorn. Their disturbed minds will require your ministration. I suggest you say the Gayatri Mantra one-hundred eight times and call on me in a fortnight.' And that is our morality tale about false realities and the danger of trusting your categorical thinking." Vishwamithra concluded the yarn and our session.

Was my life any less absurd than the delusional folk of *Nah-yeev*? Craving connection, I did not love anything around me. Longing for purposeful occupation, my days were spent moving sand piles. Now I grasped for something meaningful by dallying with esoteric spiritual traditions. Was Vishwamithra a force of gravity pulling me back to earth?—or maybe I was hypnotized by a madman who would burn my world to ashes.

Part III / Practice

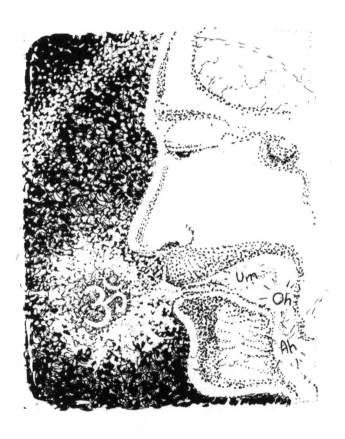

The Wonder *notes from Vishwamithra*

Gayatri Mantra sound energy teaches Om
to the aware and to the dull alike.

Take those sounds on your lips,
then create and become sharp .

Sound and Heat are the two great streams.
Sound must be true—heat must be personal.

Om plays the body like a harp,
Then it is true—be celestial sound.

Tapas heat friction forms you.
Grind mountains of sin—reveal creation.

Gayatri path is sound and heat—
true and personal—sharp and creative.

The wondrous Gayatri is the Sound of God.

KRIYA YOGA

"She—understand 'she'—the intelligent, pliant partner to the Immutable Spirit. She leads us as 'the bright' within all flesh, out of our darkness, into the 'bright' hidden inside our own flesh. Again she veils our sight with light and eye-flesh so our hidden spirit strains for her vision. Laughing, she stops her dance and we are blinded to this world by the brilliant vision of hers. Finally, a human-being walks and talks like a pompous mannequin until she reveals her art—it collapses to know every sound and movement was hers. She was Aum from the start." After Vishwmithra completed the invocation there was a subtle shift into the topic which was not apparent until after we were far along.

"IN SPRITUAL PRACTICE YOU must choose the painful-pleasure of correcting course over the pleasant-pain of habit." he said, once we got to the meat of the session. "Be honest with yourself and realize it is necessary. Avoid misery and accept you are the owner's man—captain of the ship, as well as the chief mate— responsible for all it holds. I can offer lore about the islands and oceans in the Self—but navigating stormy seas, doldrums and restless crew can be a lonely business that require your wily, bright participation. In the early days my spiritual efforts were more dramatic than they are now."

He glanced here and there, squinting, maybe looking for something, and began again. "For years at a time in those days I was alone in myself, steeped in the mantra," he said. "Journeying on foot in ages past I fixed attention to the movement of weight shifting leg to leg and heel to toe. Those paces took me from Mt. Kailasha, across the Deccan plateau and down the Eastern Ghats to Arunachala. One stride could take from sunrise to sundown. My very cells excited in waves when gravity pressed bare callous to stone, spread across the foot, upward toward the skin of my leg and transferred into my shin bones. Sensation traced from the point of contact, flowed through the center of my spine and washed over my skull, sometimes like ants crawling, other times like a cool shower. Senses were lashed to every footfall; such was my concentration. Other times I discovered myself running barefoot on ice or baked clay, chanting with each heave of my chest. In those days there was little need for food or drink. Such austerities are beneficial and not necessary. Mindful awareness leads to meditation, whether sitting, walking, or reclining."

He smiled while rummaging in his memory vault, saying, "I would walk in deep woods, listen closely for the sound of growing trees, and observe the seasons as they rolled one into the next. It was a rapture to see forests as fully conscious and alive. There were no trees there, only stoic populations of saints, branching in all directions. They cherished the earth with longing feet and held the sky with upraised limbs. So many creatures made their homes and found food in their foliage and woody skin. I could wrap my arms around a trunk or place a blossom to my forehead and understand their wordless speech. Every moment was a new opportunity to waken."

Something moved in me as he spoke. Those things were possible. My body craved those rigors. His way of speaking gave the feel of rough bark against my chest, ice biting the soles of my feet, and my lungs burning with charged Himalayan air. Vivid images formed while he described his world, a landscape that fired his resolve like a kiln.

He continued, "Specific practices are infinite. In any case, the mind is busy and nearly tireless. The body wearies quickly in comparison. Don't fight the natural tendencies of either. Laziness, the lack of discipline, is the enemy of both. Intending discipline vanquishes sloth.

"The Gayatri itself is the only practice required. It is unique among any spiritual disciplines because it is inclusive. The instructions, contents, and criteria for success are within the lines themselves. It is intelligent. It instructs. Enter the mantra as living beings."

Vishwamithra recomposed himself, saying, "Patanjali's first line of the second chapter of his Yoga Sutra gives the components of the *Yoga of Action* as a triad. The three elements are *tapas* or inner heat from intense application of effort, *svadhyaya* or self-knowledge gained in that effort, and *ishvara pranidhana* or offering the friction, the efforts, and the knowledge into the fire of mystery, the personal God. *Tapah-svadhyay-ishvara pranidanani kriya yogaha."* He announced the Sanskrit syllables again and again, at varying speeds. He asked me to repeat after him until I mastered the pronunciation, assuming an explanation would follow.

Instead he said, "Let's approach the yoga of action, through action. Take a deep breath and hold it as long as you can.

Expecting more discourse, the aerobic drills were a surprise. Doing as instructed I pulled in a lungful of air and held. There was the question how long was "as long as possible" and the fleeting concern about suicide through breath retention also lingered strangely. In a way this was a game of chicken with the ultimate stake as death by oxygen deprivation. Did my body know what I was up to or did it perceive the threat? There was nothing to fear, but physiologically was "I" afraid? Was that what pushed at my chest within seconds? Suppressing the urge to breathe, an internal check told me there was no pressing need for air—but the body dealt with a lot of things and had to know better than me about who needs what and how much. I struggled and now felt it in my head; something was rising within, taking over. Strategies like fighting it, holding hard, and pumping-in false breaths all quickly succumbed. Oxygen-depleted air forced out in a gasp, all on its own, followed by a rush of fresh inhales. It was maybe a minute.

"Who breathed?" he asked. "I assume you were trying not to, and fighting another 'you' that wanted to breathe. So who did? But before you answer, note the rush you feel, the energy and freedom."

I said, "There's exuberance and release, but it's not emotional. It feels good to breathe, very pleasant. You could call it happy but there are no concepts or thoughts."

"But you are defeated. You lost by taking a breath before you intended it. How could you feel good about that? Were you lying to yourself? Did you not make a sincere effort? Go after this unseen adversary and hold your breath as long as you want to. How long do you want to hold? I measured forty seconds, that time."

Forty seconds! When I was a kid I could hold for a minute without a lot of trouble. "I want to hold my breath ninety seconds," I said.

"Prepare yourself. Take some practice breaths and then do as the pearl divers; they hyperventilate and then relax their lungs. They fill their blood stream with oxygen and then plunge for as long as five minutes."

I did rapid inhales and exhales until feeling woozy. After one last deep inhale I let out about thirty percent and held. It was comfortable for a long spell. By relaxing I stretched it some more and then worked through the first convulsions to breathe. Pretending there was lots of air cheated a few more seconds. The convulsive urge came back, strong and insistent. Jacking the tight volume of depleted air in my lungs didn't help much. It was over. Nearly faint, something forced my throat open to gasp in and out, followed by uncontrollable panting. "What was it?" I asked between ventilations. It had to be close to two minutes.

"One minute and eleven seconds. Good enough, but nothing to gloat about. Go home and practice if you want to dive for pearls. You made a decent showing but lost again! Tell me, who did you lose to, and why do you feel good about it?"

There was no one to look for; whatever it was, overlapped "me" and at the same time remained a mute stranger.

"It doesn't feel like I've been beaten by an antagonist. It's more like a partner I wrestled with and we are both stronger. This thing that won't let me suffocate thrives on these contests. It likes friction."

"You said it—I didn't." Vishwamitra smiled. "That is *tapasya*, friction that benefits both of you. The term 'both' implies union of two things—that is yoga. Did you notice anything else?"

"With practice, five minutes might be doable," I said with a twinge of revenge. "Pointless, since it's not a matter of livelihood or survival. Someone willing to swim down fifty feet looking for oysters and pearls has real motivation. I also know it's impossible to kill myself that way. The thing that forced my lungs to work has some kind of total superiority over me. Honestly, I don't think it is beatable."

"So *join it*, as they say. You have just explained to me the first line of the second chapter," he said.

"First is friction-as-friend. Your efforts, applied against the limits of your experience and ability, generated heat.

"Second, the heat had physical, psychological and emotional components. These told you things about yourself you could not know otherwise. That is self-study.

"And third, the whole exercise happened in the context of an invisible, immutable law. The ruler over the small self is the Teacher, the *Self*. Someone might call it the autonomic nervous system or etheric body, but ask yourself what it is. In my experience it is caring, intelligent and precise. It does not want simple obedience; it wants relationship. Pushing, pulling, and testing these implicit rules are yoga, the way to knowledge. You can just as well call it the mighty Hanuman who can carry you across an ocean—once you befriend it.

"You can't kill yourself this way because suicide relies on some thing that operates outside of your power—it requires more than a decision to die. The self-killer has to disable awareness by throwing the body into a mechanism, as it were; guns, gravity, chemicals, *et cetera*.

"Playing, working or striving in the natural world is safe, so long as you are aware. Obviously, you can play the daredevil, jump off a cliff, or pass out on the train tracks. A deluded mind can pull such tricks and short-circuit the sacred law of life—however—awareness will not let you end your life voluntarily. Whether it's your own hand, the hand of another, or ignorance—suicide requires a gap in awareness."

I mentioned Socrates, who drank the hemlock. That story had been told as a proof of his integrity, not his ignorance.

He said, "I think that was an execution. He was forced to drink the poison. In any case, the first and most powerful impulse of any organism is to preserve itself. Maybe, if the philosopher had Gayatri Mantra, the difficulties leading to that end would not have occurred. Endings are consistent with their beginnings and the deluded mind can disable survival instincts—pray it is not your karma."

LATER ON, I PRACTICED the breathing drill near a stream that ran not far from my flat. I found an isolated spot in the shade to sit and review the mechanics of breath. Was it even possible to catch the *rule-maker* at work?—there had to be a way to consciously observe the mechanism that forced me to breathe. Physiology was inflexible but benevolent, definitely wise. By contrast, political authorities were arbitrary. Who had the right or the ability to tell anyone else anything? Community leaders were often controlling personality-types or worse. At the same time, conventional wisdom carped on the need for external laws to keep social order and uphold the common good.

I tossed stones into the water. Pebbles formed an arc toward the water when they left my hand. When it hit the surface, ripples ringed-out in perfect circles at precise distances. What were *natural laws,* those intelligent rules that were also insentient? The soles of my feet, my rear end or fingertips responded to pressure and weight compulsively. The world was a webbing of laws and very few choices. Something or someone separated me from my breath. It was not mine to control, really. I had to breathe. There was no choice.

What was gravity? No one had any idea of the cause behind something so basic—a study to find out would be absurd. Was the virgin state of a body truly weightless and free? Of course not—every form was its own testimony to weight. Fleshy-tissues grew, shaping themselves, guided or dictated to by mysterious, invisible forces from down there, somewhere. Muscles, bones and organs bloomed out of internal laws that responded intimately to the external law of gravity. Who could say how that unknowable force of attraction worked on hormones, emotions, psychology and desires? Where was freedom?

Observing splash patterns, the swirling drift of a leaf as it snagged, spun, and whisked away on the flowing current was idyllic—something in the clearing beyond broke my reverie. Someone young, maybe ten years old inspected their surroundings. Glancing about they determined they were alone. I was under trees, in shadow.

They methodically cleared an area of grass and leaves, gathered sticks and crouched down for some minutes. I saw a wisp of smoke rising, a fire. Remaining low, continuously vigilant for trespassers, the child fed the small flame and stood back. They added small sticks, and then larger ones until the blaze was nearly a bon fire. It had grown to such a size that any kind of wind might whip it toward the dry grass and cause a brush fire. A stand of scrub and trees was all that separated the meadow from nearby buildings. They seemed mindful of the dangers. I sat quietly, observing my reactions: to reprimand, to judge the child, or to criticize myself for not doing anything.

A breeze pushed the blaze toward the ground. Hot tongues curled upward and then whipped down, scorching the dry grass outside the fire ring. As the flame grew, their movements became a frenzied dance to control the situation. Alert to every change, the child threw dust to that side, ran to another, stepped into the heat with some tolerance and stamped at the growing perimeter. Just when I might have jumped up, the kid ceased throwing on branches and the fire died down. A calmer wind also helped, as the child continued to pour dust, clean out risky areas and smother stray cinders. It burned low again. The fire-starter walked around the burn, completely absorbed, and oblivious to possible witnesses.

I was sure some law or another was broken. Whether the young scientist was aware of that was impossible to say. None-the-less, the drill was a statement of autonomy, away from authorities.

In the end, I approved. They satisfied an inner need to establish sovereignty toward maturity. The experiment was planned-out, required some skills and knowledge, and harmed nothing. It was a test, an exercise, a ritual of self-awareness and personal power.

On the other hand, very few ten year olds, or persons of any age, had enough self-responsibility to stretch lawful boundaries without causing harm. It took uncommon discipline to remain harmless to self, other, and environment with no guide but inner integrity. A world with no legal protection might be dangerous. But without learned-discipline, who could have the maturity to dictate behavior to others? There wasn't a single person I would trust to set just-laws except for my teacher. Paradoxically I obeyed hundreds of behavioral limits set by people I didn't know and whose motives might be questionable.

Such was the material I brought to our next session.

LAWS

"WHAT ABOUT THE RULES imposed by governments, parents, or authority in general? I asked. "Since inner guidance is more precise than imposed laws, is government helpful or even necessary to order a society where discipline is part of the culture?"

He said, "Earlier I told you that discipline was essential to 'how' as a *question.* That is equally true for 'how' as an *answer.'*

"Specified behavior for individuals and groups is what we call 'law.' A traffic sign, police uniform, or courthouse are *signs* of the presence of laws, authorities that enforce *how to behave. Discipline* is the precondition for asking or answering *how.* Your question—about rules, laws, implied issues of authority, trust, and wise guidance—is enormous. Let's spend a moment to taste it here.

He asked, "What is the ultimate law of life we all can agree on?"

"The cliché is death and taxes," I said, laughing. He did not notice the humor.

"Yes, physical limits and accountability to the system you believe in is fixed for everyone." He continued, "Death is the ultimate counsel for how you use your time. Taxation is the social contract, the public account. Man-made laws can be foolish, manipulative, or downright harmful. Ideas about death can be equally useless and damaging. Discipline requires inquiry into these matters," he said in a dry torrent.

"The universal social contract, written on the fabric of each being, appears as though from the outside. It is the basis for human community and has five aspects. They are: *non-harming, truthfulness,* and *non-stealing*—it also requires *continence* and *non-possession.* The order is meaningful; harmlessness or non-violence is an attitude that enfolds the rest. Truth has to be harmless and includes the others. It goes that way. Non-stealing is an obvious prohibition against taking what is not yours, but each of these has unfolding depth that can't be exhausted. These are the disciplines every human has to accept in relation to society. Continence, said simply, is self-control—but for what end?

And the most enigmatic of the five vows is non-possession. Even discussing the concept demands self-knowledge."

He waved a loose hand toward my notebook, and said, "You've been scribbling like mad. What do you understand by these? How can a person make them their own, not just words?" Being on the spot was not new. I cobbled a reply from the notes.

"NON-HARMING reminds me of your earliest advice about discipline. Functioning in the world requires curiosity and sensitivity toward the ways of others. Without such discipline, harm will occur. Each individual is like a species unto itself with unique habits and needs. Each has to *learn* right behavior with the other. I assume another person's ways are foreign to me. Harm comes from the wrong assumption that we are all alike." At work they gave a nod to differences by using three personality types. Their goal was not harmless. Efficiency, systems, machine processes; all that could be a violent cutting across the creative spirit of an individual—that insight could lead to a *Pandora's box* of anarchy.

He was pleased with my grasp of the matter. "That's it," he said. "Keep it in mind and relationships will be more fulfilling. Continue."

"TRUTH and fact bear some relationship," I said, "but they are not the same thing. It's impossible to know anything absolutely or make absolute statements—truth and facts each have a shadow—untruth and fabrications. Facts can mislead. Truth is always true. Facts can masquerade as *the truth* and cause harm or even violence, no matter how well-intentioned. I'm not sure where that leaves me—maybe it's better to not say anything at all."

I waited for more information from the sage. Under strictly enforced laws, the young scientist-arson could not have performed the fire-ritual and would never have learned what it taught them. Their real-world ability to control and influence a dangerous situation would remain undeveloped. Too much policing led to stunted, dependent individuals. A growing, maturing being required real tests—and to be true, something had to be harmless all around—to nature, society *and* the individual.

"You used the word *declare*," he said. "Protecting the unique way of another being is the intention. Truthfulness has to do with how you express that intention out the world—you instinctively related truth to speech and stopped yourself. The concept of *being true* includes self-containment for the sake of others. Someone said, *it's alright to make a mess as long as you can clean it up.* The true intent of non-harming sets speech as *communication.* When the intention includes the well-being of the other—facts and details aside—the communication will come out right." He motioned for me to go further.

"NON-STEALING sets the boundary between *me* and *not-me. Stealing* is ignoring the boundary set by harmlessness and truthfulness. Stealing is not possible when the intention is both harmless and true."

His eyes remained shut while he added, "You gave the essence. Stealing can include taking away opportunities or butting-in when someone needs their own time and space. Each of these categories is a profound meditation on who you are, who they are, what is known and unknown about every aspect of relationship." With a placid expression he motioned me ahead.

"CONTINENCE begs the question *is this body my own —is my energy my own?*" I asked, expecting no answer. With harmless, truthful intent and clear boundaries about what is mine, I had to wonder—in an interconnecting world of substance and energy—how much of my life was actually mine alone, to claim like it was a possession. The inquiry unfolded while I spoke to the sage.

Thinking out loud, I said, "Even though biochemical processes that involve food, air, and water are automatic, that does not mean they belong to me. This awareness leads to containment—truth requires the body-mind to act harmlessly by understanding what *non-injury* means, practically. A fourth law—*continence*—naturally follows the first three laws. There is an implicit duty to abstain from harmful indulgences and dedicate one's energy to the highest cause, as they understand it."

The sage quietly interrupted my connections. He said, "Continence, the fourth restriction, is *Brahmacharya* in Sanskrit, often interpreted as sexual control or celibacy. Taboos and commandments can dictate behavior to a point, but I want to be clear—the truth of these so-called restrictions is written on the heart. Find them there and effort falls away. They are spontaneous gestures of common interest when the intention is awareness. Please continue."

Contemplating these restrictions on behavior, I recognized they were not artificially-imposed chains against freedom; they were working descriptions of community. They were like the gift of fire, an invention that brought safety and comfort—vulnerable human creatures needed a mediating buffer in order to live among wild things. A controllable source of light and heat gave humans a niche within

135

nature; much like the five social contracts provided isolated individuals a comfortable fit inside supportive groups—collections of people that would otherwise be fragmented by conflict.

"My only real possession is my intention," I said. "Things placed in my charge and the materials I require for living are trusts, not possessions." The way a law implied the next one was unerring. The child created a rogue-fire so they could experience autonomy and to stretch their potential. It was a paradox. How could there be a law to allow breaking the law? On the one hand, over-bearing rules can ruin individual initiatives while flaccid laws can breed crime and insecurity. The solution was in the five laws.

NON-POSSESSION came naturally out of the first four laws. "Finally there is a refusal of *acquiring*," I said. "Reality is the commons, the shared experience that negates the idea of ownership. I own nothing in truth—how can I hope to possess more of it?"

I thought to myself that society would have to provide the child flexible laws based on natural laws that encouraged personal growth. That would be a wise society. When a system lacked such foresight, laws would either break people or be broken. Individuals would ignore social contracts in order to keep personal integrity—the first internal urge for creatures is to grow and thrive, regardless of consequences. Laws have to consider growth and evolving awareness or they harm the ones they supposedly protect—rules can become weapons.

The sage spoke, "Let me summarize your explanation of the five guiding lights.

"The great injunction is to *do no harm*. It allows for freedom.

"Understand that *truth is a quest*, taken in relationship to other beings and the world.

"It requires clarity of meanings which are *boundaries*.

"Violating boundaries is harmful and not true. Boundaries-respected lead to *self-control for the good of all*, the God-vehicle of a people.

"The cap and conclusion of the harmless way is *refusing to accumulate* anything. That is an expression of contentment, the highest happiness available for a created being."

His explanation was succinct. It all seemed so far afield of Gayatri Mantra, yet, the holes in my understanding had to be addressed or Gayatri itself would be misunderstood. My questions took us away from the third *mahavyahriti* yet again.

"As you can see our path on the ground meanders around obstacles and goes toward scenic vistas. This is natural. There is wisdom in it. The straight flight of the crow is not for us. When we fly it is more like a bee seeking nectar. The crow's direct flight seems full of purpose, however when they land they eat every manner of garbage imaginable and then strut as though they owned the world. Let them have their methodology for now. We are bees. The golden honey of truth can feed the world that has gone mad with hunger for meaning."

He looked at me and said, "What do you think—are we on the right path?"

Who could say? His questions were usually a subtle message so I answered with caution. "It's my fault that we strayed from *suvaha*. Your thought on this still hasn't surfaced even though you marked it as most important and difficult."

He sat upright, saying, "The profound presence of *suvaha*— 'sweetness in motion,' and the movement of all creation into perfect resolution—guides all our deviations. A study of our byways would reveal the face of perfection. We can't escape it. Next time, our wise drifting will continue with the five attitudes to free vital air, or *prana*. You said *we own nothing*. Extend that to our body and mind and you realize that the five ways enable us to be stewards of ourselves. Then we can approach a gravity that pulls us heavenward—*suvaha*."

I was thankful for my notebook and the thing that compelled me to keep some shorthand scribbles. We repeated the mantra for some time and concluded.

I walked to my flat through the mid morning activities along the block: vendors selling fruit, racks of clothing for sale, women sweeping the dust from concrete stoops and children chasing one another, laughing. None of this was mine to accept or reject. It was a gift on loan. The sense of responsibility for a world of perception, placed mysteriously in my care, all unasked for, seemed to enliven my legs with power from the dirt itself. Steps became stronger, firmer. I would not cling. That, too, was a gift I could never have known enough to ask for.

The Bee and the Crow

by Ashty Hozan

Straight flight of the crow is direct.
Then he struts and pecks
At garbage.
O
Bees fly loopy,
Restless for nectar humming,
Clueless that fruits grow after they go

VITAL AIR

I LIVED, SURROUNDED BY AIR—a gas that is four parts nitrogen and one part oxygen—something we eat twenty-thousand lungs full every day. Without the invisible, untouchable stuff, the body panics within minutes, even seconds. After the breath holding drill I spent more time trying to understand what I was, physically.

There was something called *Five Element Theory* that explained the composition of our world—before modern science. Basic blocks called *earth, air, fire, and water* got thrown out in favor of the periodic table of a hundred plus elements. For sure, elements like nitrogen or oxygen were abstract ghosts to my actual experience. On the other hand, air and water were so common I never gave them a thought.

Chemistry said my body craved oxygen and nitrogen. Yet, I only noticed my attraction to air when it was not there. Somehow, breathing and my body was the same thing. My body was breath, as it was the other elements of *earth, fire, water* and the mysterious fifth, *ether*—these could be experienced, not nitrogen. Vishwamithra's discourse on the breath-holding exercise created questions—not just about my breathy, watery, earthy, fiery composition, but about thought, consciousness—and the strange *ether* that held it all.

Ether had to be an awake-thing, the bright part of consciousness— my breath was the vital messenger, refreshing the bright aspect with constant circulation, penetration, and absorption by fire, water and earth. It was a dance of relationship between the elements, each of which was a world unto itself, but *who* was dancing?

After our opening prayers, I described these things to the sage and said, "Sri Vishwamithra, it shames me to think how I ride my body like a dumb beast and flog it senselessly with demands and criticisms. Something in me, an intimate partner, causes me to breathe and I have no clue *who* this is. It certainly is not me. I don't know of a good way to truly meet this entity or at least not take it for granted."

"Your energetic self is a subtle sleeve that holds you completely.

This living planet has a similar envelope. Those two interpenetrate each other in a constant pulse of *vital air*. It is your servant, pure and simple. And it is a gift—the quality of your consciousness and work in the world are all you can give in return for its selfless service. *Ether* or *Akash* is intelligent and conscious, even aloof, but it loves the servant, vital air. And vital air rides not only the breath, in and out, but your intentions, your desire to align with *Pranava*. Vital air is Hanuman to your Rama, the perpetual partner, never lowly and never abused. Like Rama, you will benefit by friendship with this other in conscious awareness—but how? There are five practical actions that accomplish the tasks of rejuvenating your vital air while nurturing friendship with this dynamic companion. Tell me, what were the laws we described?"

Notes were not necessary. I had studied all that we covered in the previous time together. "*Non-harming, truthfulness, non-stealing, self-containment, and non-clinging*," I said. "Those laws allow civil society."

He nodded, saying, "Now, take the *kriya yoga* triad and add *refinement and contentment*. Those are five ways to strengthen the *vital air* necessary to those bodies and minds in social relationship. They complement the laws we discussed and are categories of action—they might better be labeled *attitudes* rather than specific activities. Similar to the laws, they proceed from the most inclusive to the most subtle. Realizing that your energies are critical for how you interact with the world around you, think about the role of refinement."

"REFINEMENT strains away the unwanted," I said. "It happens routinely in cleaning. Some people measure it as a state of purity, which can't be absolute. I see the vital air as operating at its best when there are no impurities in it—that would be anything inside or out that does not belong. One would refine the mind, creating clean and direct thought. Bathing and hygiene are direct ways to refresh vital air."

I continued, "There is an immediate problem with it. Clothing or certain diets for example, block the circulation and clog the digestion, yet these are considered necessary and normal. True refinement would throw a person out of society altogether in order to live in pristine purity and innocence. They might be naked, fasting on herbs, bathing in rain and sunshine, or sleeping on bare earth!"

"Purpose drives the action," he said, "Remember Sita! She is the soul which defines purpose and organizes every activity. Refinement that ignores meaning, purpose and relationship is no refinement at all. What about contentment?"

"CONTENTMENT is being satisfied with what you have," I said. The cliché clogged my ability to receive a fresh insight. He did not rush me. Frustration rose-up in me at my lack of anything to contribute. That passed. We were still outside of words and he did not rescue me. I was about to say anything to break the silence. He abruptly stood, went to the kitchen and left me to my thoughts.

I mused in the space provided; *contentment has to go deeper than being satisfied with one's lot in life.* The most satisfying experiences always resulted in contentment. My thoughts were like coins down a well, sinking to the bottom. Vishwamithra returned to his usual seat.

I said, "*Contentment* means that the content of the present moment is sufficient." It was a new concept for me.

The sage picked up the idea and said, "*Contentment* is a moment by moment awareness that the current situation, as it presents itself, is complete. It is refinement applied to moods and mental states. *Tapas* or inner heat follows—by practicing *contentment,* one tempers various urges and that causes friction. It leads to an internal *cooking* that strengthens the energy body. A strong core is a clean stabile energy that can stay firm in the face of cravings, fear, or anger. Are *tapas, svadhyaya,* and *ishvara pranidhana* any different in this context? Why do you suppose the ancient sage recycled *heat, self knowledge* and *surrender* in this way? "

"INNER HEAT would be a purifier as well as allowing contentment," I told him. "*The refiner's fire* is the phrase for purifying gold. It's clear that heat is energy, kin to the vital air. It seems natural that generating subtle heat would be a better environment to free-up energy and increase vital air. At this middle point, the subtle pulls hard from the bottom of the list. May I continue with the last two?" With a tilt of the head he waved me forward.

"SELF-STUDY implies the three above it," I said. "*Refinement* through *self-knowledge* requires *being contented* with the object of attention—one's self—so the observer can be still enough to make observations. Stillness and focus are part of discipline and inner heat."

The sage added, "Vital air is as diverse as you are. There are many shades to your energy. Observing and then understanding these aspects of energy make them increase and purify. Continue."

"SURRENDERING TO GOD is the subtlest of all five," I began, "an inevitable outcome of the first four attitudes. One might call it

141

alignment with *Pranava*. I think the ancient yogic-sage was stating that the *yoga of action* or *purification* is not some kind of spiritual endgame—a healthy body and clear mind are essential for living with others."

He said, "Imagine a campfire. A ring of stones and a clearing separate your fire from the vast woods. It's for control. To attend the fire it has to be contained. The ring keeps it from spreading into the woods, causing a disastrous blaze. The buffer allows you to focus the fuel and heat in one place—refinement and contentment are such simple firewalls, creating an orderly setting for relationships in the outside world. Containment is critical for living with others. It includes more than just space, but fuel, smoke and fumes as well."

The fire scenario was still a paradox. I wondered, *can man-made laws be broken for the good of the whole?"* The idea of laws and the risks of punishment reminded me of something from years before.

MY UNCLE AND I went fishing every so-often when I was grammar school age. For reasons hidden in the past, he was a black sheep among his virtuous siblings. My mother was maybe the best-behaved of the lot. He was my favorite relative despite a tarnished reputation. He looked at me when he spoke and did not take on parental airs. He quietly accepted his place as was one of the fallen. He had been in the most brutal battle of the Big War. When pressed he would say, "People who go on about bloodshed didn't see any action. If they did, they wouldn't want to talk about it." I linked his tarnished place among my other aunts and uncles with those painful experiences, though there may have been no connection. All I knew was that he took me to the lake and had an immense tackle box full of intriguing lures, hooks, reels, bottles, and plastic line.

Once he instructed me on baiting a hook. We were using worms. He pinched a wriggler in his fingers. It flailed wildly to get free. He punctured it with the hook, turning the writhing, ringed crawler back on itself in folds until the barbs were hidden. He tossed the baited line into the lake and I waited. Quickly the bobber danced on the surface and was still again. "They got your bait," he told me with a smile. "Let's try it again."

"Can I use a lure?" I asked him. There was a beautiful bug-eyed thing with tassels and treble hooks in his gear that attracted me.

He said, "That won't work out here. Live-bait's the best," and handed me the empty hook, pointing to the earthy box of worms. This was a moment of initiation. Of course such a concept was alien at the time—but it was definitely a cross-roads. I would hold the hook and press the living creature onto it—or I would complain. The option was to remain a child and embarrass myself, requesting, "You do it." That would be too humiliating. Despite my fears, there was no backing down. Any way to discuss life, pain, or reservations about such a simple act of murder was out of the question. This was my moment for manning-up to the grisly task.

Left hand grasped the curved barbs and leader. The fingers of my right felt into the loam and found the taut, elusive body of a worm. They were stronger than they looked and violently resisted their fate. Something like aggression rose in me to hold onto it. Thumb and forefinger clamped tight. When the steel barb touched its ribbed skin, the invertebrate doubled its fight, begging my smooth, pudgy fingers to dig in tighter. The surface tension of rubbery flesh punctured and the hook threaded easily through its body. Repeating the motion as my uncle demonstrated, I managed about three holes in the beast. When a palm sized Bluegill happened onto the hook a few minutes later, the success was hollow. Relief that the deed was done over-shadowed any sense of accomplishment.

That same uncle gave words of advice that stayed with me. It may have been my softness. He may have seen the pietistic morality that carried over from my mother. Maybe he talked to his younger self who would need some way to carry a heavy reputation. Lowering his voice he said, "Sometimes you have to break somebody else's laws to keep your own. Don't advertise it—just keep it to yourself."

On solo outings, skewering live bait never got easier. Plopping plastic lures in the lake from a shady spot was good enough. Every once in a while a Bluegill would actually hit my glittering hula-skirted contraption out of curiosity—but there were no takers.

The teacher must have noticed the mood wash over me and commented. "Instinct works for animals. Humans have to find something else—they are shaped by discovering the sacred character of inner laws. A story comes to mind."

And so, once again we began a journey to another time and place to talk about our own.

Three Words *by Ashty Hozan*

No—Stop—and Go Back
Words that defend the timid
and temper the brave.

No
can be the greatest yes.
Stop
can be a joyous start.
Go Back
can be the surest progress.

The mind, the body and soul
Feel *your "no."*
The fortress, womb and heart
Crave *their "Stop."*
The sage, the child and feet
Demand *"Go Back."*

Without No,
"yes" is a sham.
Without Stop,
"beginnings" are tragic.
Without Go Back,
"progress" is hell bound.

Fences protect gardens
Brakes save lives.
Memories shine like mirrors.

"Erasers, paint and graveyards
deliver me from sin."

DAKSHA

"THERE ARE WORLDS WITHIN WORLDS," he began, "all the way up and much farther down than you would want to know about. Each one has rules, and if you don't follow them, things don't go well—assuming you would even *want* to get along in a place that's alien to your make-up. Mostly you are built for the one you are in, which works well most of the time. Then you get the itch to step out of a rut and try something different, which increases the chance of bumping into a strange realm with its requirements. Good intentions are not good enough—if you want things to work out for you, the rules are there to follow. Frankly, it's not possible to know every critical guideline, and you don't want to find out by breaking them. The role of a *mediator* is to know the rules, how to keep them, and ways to avoid the penalty for violating them. Even gods need the service of a mediator to keep from stepping on important toes—and that priest's name is *Daksha*."

I prepared for an illustrative journey into laws and vital attitudes. Each story had a pattern—there was at least one glaring anomaly which contained the essence of the story. Aside from obvious plotlines, paradox was the key to the message.

"We usually think of the gods and their escapades on a human scale. We picture bodies in motion, clothed in different ways. They may have hair, ornaments or mannerisms of our own invention. Those are our ways of understanding the action. Before we begin this drama, recognize that the players are not human egos; they are *principles of reality*. They are not small personalities in the usual sense. Their distant actions create blueprints for our earthly stories—so we pay attention."

I pictured the worlds he talked about so often, *Bhu-loka, Bhuva-loka, and Suvah-loka*, and wondered about their inhabitants, rules, and penalties. Kneading the heel of his palm he began.

"Here was *Daksha*, planning a great ritual," he said, "a *yagna* that would harmonize these divine actors within their multi-dimensional universe. The function of ritual is to balances the scales between your personal actions and the host of invisible factors all around. It was their discipline to recognize inherent limits before taking action. Daksha's task was to set everything in order—what they do, for good or ill, inevitably trickles down to the planet we occupy now.

"To that end he decided to exclude one guest, *Shiva Mahadeva*. This *Shiva*, whose name literally means auspicious, cared nothing about their activities. This *Great-Yogi* found his pleasure meditating among corpses in burial grounds that all others avoided. Immersed in the twilight between life and death, his world was heavy, musky, populated with scavengers and birds of prey. He was absolute purity, adorned with sacred snakes beings, clothed only with the ashen remains of the god of desire—he was detached from conventions of any kind.

"Daksha decided that such a guest would detract from the perfect ritual offering. You can imagine the smells, the appearance, not to mention the unruly entourage accompanying Shiva which would ruffle the fine feathers of such divine birds. So *Mahadev* was not informed. There were *beautiful people* even in heaven, so it seems; *la crème de la crème*. The itinerary unfolded perfectly except for one detail—*Sati*—Daksha's daughter wanted to attend. She happened to be Shiva's adoring wife and spiritual companion."

He continued, "There's always a hitch isn't there? Of course there is. It may look like a rock in the road or a wheel in the ditch, but it is the *Lord of Obstacles* throwing his weight around—this is how *Ganesha* sorts out the true from the irrelevant." Vishwamithra took a sip of tea, signaling a segue to highlight his point.

"The elements at this point are clear. What are they?" he asked.

I said. "Daksha, a priest, is going to conduct a grand harmonizing ritual. His daughter, of course, wants to attend—her husband, Shiva, had not been invited. It definitely seems like a complicating factor."

"Storms brew over the holy gathering," he said. "Given what you know, how do you suppose this can resolve itself?"

I cobbled my reply, saying, "Potentially there's a common family squabble between a father and daughter... She wants to exert herself and a headstrong patriarch might stand in the way. Shiva is aloof by constitution. Someone has to either accept the situation or change it."

He said, "The story tells about a subtle conflict, doing what is *truly* right as opposed to doing what truly *seems* right. Entertain the story along those lines. We will see what can animate the unmovable Shiva into fierce action—why and how he balances the scales."

After another slow sip, he placed the cup on the floor and leaned back on one arm. He reached across with the free hand and grasped the opposite shoulder joint. Looking toward the window he massaged absent-mindedly while speaking.

"Sati told Shiva she planned to attend, regardless. He reminded her that he had been nixed from the affair," the sage said. "She was pinned between opposing principles. Her lover was the incomprehensible yogi of yogis and her esteemed father was the highest adept in ritual form—here we see spiritual essence, pitted against religious method.

"A storm brewed—she was torn between her own mystical nature and an inherited respect for lawful precision. It was internal realization versus the common good, content versus form, the shock of the real as opposed to mere aesthetics—an epic battle on the stage of *truth*."

He continued the narration, saying, "She took the first and most predictable step and complained to her father."

"*You have to invite my husband*, she insisted. Of course he refused. Was it possible for him to miscalculate? Was there any detail or outcome he had not anticipated? No, he was the divine functionary and at that level, there are no mistakes. Leaving Shiva off the guest list was not an oversight. It was a statement of *status-quo* reality. Assume his decision is correct to understand the truth of what happened next."

The sage gazed skyward, his face highlighted by ambient light, speaking as though to himself. "What could Sati do?" he said, shrugging casually, "She attended the yagna-ritual anyway, churned up by Shiva's warnings and irritated by her father's pig-headed insistence on protocol. What did her divided mind see when she arrived? It looked upon beautiful people, refined, intent, and pious. There was not one iota wanting. All was perfect and accurately attuned to harmonizing the world— except for the obscene absence of Shiva.

"Distant, removed, unconcerned, he was full and complete in himself. His lungs pulled in the stench of decay and exhaled a gentle bouquet. Nothing could enter his body and escape without becoming pure. Every breath of Mahadeva was ritual beauty. The steady beat of his heart was the rhythm of worlds manifesting and dissolving in turn. Shiva did not require the *yagna*. He *was* every yagna.

"*Shiva, shiva, shiva*, Sati repeated, sinking into herself to herself, bonding with the absent *Lord of Hosts*." Her split attitudes rubbed against one another and created yogic heat. Sati and Shiva merged in her dispassionate realization of blazing *Truth*. She glowed, radiated. The gods gasped. Daksha's daughter had become a hot ember, bliss, on fire, a perfect fuel, ignited in Shiva's ocean of calm intensity."

Vishwamithra paused, staring at me.

"Understand this," he told me. "Being truth, and knowing her spouse, she herself became Mahadeva. Without an iota of false social propriety, she converted into what the yagna lacked—Shiva, the great uninvited, the sacred core. No one can resonate one-to-one with Shiva and maintain form. Her body ignited and reverted to dust. Ash is the basic, radical expression of human flesh. Her ash, purified in the heat of her discipline, was Shiva-manifest. It showered those gathered and thus purified them. They could not survive the causal communion of Shiva and Sati. They shook for fear of Shiva's wrath and waited.

"In a trice it happened. Shiva's lover, Sati, had been liquidated in fire. Shiva responded with a mere hair's worth of correction that they received as a storm of destruction. The True Offering was flung at Daksha's empty rightness and would demolish it.

"Why is Shiva so still?" Vishwamithra asked, looking at me, "because his silent dynamism is the source of nuclear radiance. The created worlds, *bhur, bhuvah, and suvaha*, have to fall flaming into *Om* when Shiva moves. A splinter of him ripped through the gathering of deities as an avenging warrior and dispensed with them all, beheading Daksha."

He offered me this aside, "Daksha learned the hard way, *Clear your plans with Ganesha and be sure to invite Shiva!* Meaning, be aware! Completeness is impossible in a dynamic reality, so be humble—holiness cannot be earned. You can't bargain for heaven. Relationship is not economics."

I asked, "Is that how it ended? There is this picture of a bloody mess. Sati burned up, Daksha, bleeding and headless, and the gods all in fearful disarray."

"That is one ending worth holding onto," he replied. "This is the end of the world, the apocalypse. Rites and rituals in ruin, boundaries and meanings dissolved, truth and auspiciousness exploded to the ethers as the nebulous beginning of something new. There is no happy ending when forms outlive their useful purpose. It breaks. It ends."

I complained, "But it's too much. Such a dark ending doesn't satisfy. It leaves frustration and sadness in its wake. Sati and Shiva are parted. The gods' righteous ambitions spell Creation's destruction. The high priest who would bring a shattered world together is himself mutilated. It may be instructional, but I want to look away."

"Do not!" he ordered. "Hold your gaze on the scene. Behold the macabre resolution of the repugnant old way and the difficulty of the new. This teaching is true. Don't waste it! Feel the discomfort as it works your body. Know that it announces auspiciousness, prying apart your sinews to make space. This is Shiva. His ways are always strange because the original freshness is always rudimentary. Generate affection for the impeccable Sati whose body became pure white ash. Rub it on your skin. There is her communion with Mahadeva. It's no maudlin sentimentality. Truth gives itself so thoroughly to auspiciousness that no form can hold it. Ritual bathing, anointing, and remembering is all you have. Accept it. Let it make you whole in all your incompleteness."

He offered me a dish of ash from his fire. "Take her now. Let her touch your head, eyes, and lips." The gray dust had small bits of charred wood and smelled subtly of incense. I applied them as he suggested and waited. "Now I will finish," he said.

"The gods appeared before Shiva like pilgrims coming to the holy mountain. He received them placidly. Shiva, the one who was 'easy to please' asked what their hearts desired."

The sage folded his hands, bowed his head and adopted a sufficiently penitent tone, "*By your grace, our decadent schemes are obliterated. Deliver us again, oh Mahadeva, into a fresh beginning.* They always resorted to Shiva and he always responded.

"He went to the site of the carnage, took the head from a decapitated goat and fused it to the body of Daksha, restoring him to life. Everyone was grateful to Shiva, as is the usual happy ending for such stories."

He was about to explain the relevance of Daksha's sacrifice. I took the opportunity to express alarm over the bizarre concluding scene.

I said, "The head of a goat!—there are so many problems with this. Shiva had the power to restore his life any way he wanted. Daksha may have been proud, but this final solution seems like an insult at best— even mean-spirited. And then I'm told Daksha is satisfied with the outcome. Fairy tales often have idealized endings. This one is irrational and impossible to accept."

He said, "Observe the spike in your reactions, notice where they occur. Contemplate those places. The body is a physical gage for your invisible spirit. Dissonance, moods, emotional hot spots, all these are little red needles telling you something. You have to figure out which dial goes to what important feature of the spiritual vehicle and what the indicators are telling you." He smiled at me and said, "So you don't like the head of a goat?"

My complaint was toothless but I made it anyway.

"It's unnatural," I said. "There is nothing happy or conclusive about it. Sati is burned up and her father has been turned into a freak. The plot really hooked me and then this grotesque act by Shiva seemed to get thrown in for shock-value." My urge was to discount the whole story on the basis of one, gross decapitation.

"The gods do not dance to your tune," he said. "And the rishis of old did not set upon thousand-year meditations to fabricate truffles so that you might feel good."

I did not expect them to—and yet, there should be cognitive glue for the listener to understand the ancient insight. He went on examining the cryptic myth, as well as my reaction to it.

"These stories were perhaps written a millennium ago, but they describe a critical, even frightening transition during an era before time had any measurement. Humans once knew animals and were not so condescending—the inner language of beasts spoke to them clearly. Two-legged creatures, after all, had burdens they shared with four-legged brethren. The web of life had not yet been shattered into the abstract labels imposed by human thinking. All was acceptance, simplicity, and innocence, before modern interpretation invented the idea of a *fight for survival*. They felt no such struggle. They were like children, awed and blessed by the abundance around them." He held a long glance at a mockingbird that landed on his sill as if to listen and test his conclusions.

"They intuitively sensed the mind of a goat or ram," he said. "The decision to sacrifice any animal was not brutish ignorance. As human brains added conceptualization, anxiety increased. Mysticism, magic, and neurotic solutions multiplied as well.

"They put on the skin or horns of the one they ritually killed, to imbibe its powers. Picture a wild mountain goat scurrying in high forbidding places, sure-footed, living on bare rock at the dome of sky. Lonely stone canyons echoed with their cries or the crack of horns as they bashed each other in rut. Humans laid their fears on the animal and killed it, sent it to realms beyond the billowing white clouds to mediate for them. This was science. Do not laugh—science is no better today."

I jumped ahead and asked, "Are you saying that Shiva bestowed a power on Daksha when he put the animal head on his shoulders?"

"Yes," he nodded. "This is subtle, maybe ungraspable. These are archetypes. The *priest* is an urban innovation—the power to mediate between earth and heaven through ritual forms was created by society. Shiva corrected what Sati protested—separated from nature, priestly power was ineffective. Mahadeva declared that the priest has to *be* the sacrifice, or the role would be empty. The goat head signified this. The priest Daksha could no longer be aloof from nature, which contained every benevolent thing. The priest must place the urban invention of priesthood on the altar and symbolically kill it. Consciousness requires such a bloodless sacrifice—to free animal nature for communion with the divine. The modern mind is cynical and wary—it can't meet God in that state and needs to be led by the innocent animal.

"Shiva is even now called *Pashupati*, or 'Lord of Beasts.' This ancient title places Shiva apart from other deities. Daksha's refusal to invite him to the ritual gathering expressed this difference. Let's stop that one there and focus on your twitches."

I said, "Details are easy enough to understand. What I don't grasp is why you brought me this particular tale?"

"We were discussing laws," he reminded me, "the restrictions that allow various kinds of people to function together peacefully and productively. These are the qualities I wanted to demonstrate as elements in a fable rather than academic talking points.

"First—laws are lethal when they remain mechanical, constricting true creative expression. They must be auspicious. Take non-harming for example. Non-harming is a mantle you take on yourself like ancients climbed into the hide of an animal to receive power. There is no virtue in refusing to kill, simply as a moralistic stance. Cloak yourself in harmlessness and look onto the world with those eyes. Likewise any of the other 'laws' we enumerated.

"Second—always invite Shiva which means *auspicious* or fortunate, as though the stars aligned favorably. Invite true benefit. It may be out of line with what you judge to be good taste—but here is the point—it cuts to the root. *Rudra* is the old name for Shiva, as in *rude, rudiments*, 'first principles.' Do not make aesthetics a god. Strip back to core fundamentals. People might play *tasteful games* and achieve the look of holiness. Auspiciousness is not there. Beware if *Sati* does show up.

"And third—rules of any kind, good or bad, are social rituals. They are empty trappings, conventions whose only truth is in a spirit that protects and nurtures culture. If your so-called sacrifices are really *ritual for ritual's sake*, monstrosity and pain will result. The human race can lift their eyes to heaven and try to win favor. If their appeal is machine-like, a social convention, and does not return to essential, humbling truths of the human condition, there will be a correction. Learn from Daksha's experience."

Vishwamithra, *by Ashty Hozan*

Vishwamithra was not a prophet,
reading time currents.

Neither was he an alchemist,
mixing lives and events
into the philosopher's stone.

He was a carpenter,
touching the latent beauty of a wooden plank,
running an experienced hand along nuanced grain
honing palaces for souls according to silent dictates.

He was that savitur
which ferried vision out of radiant darkness
and tied random stars into constellations.

By his example I abided in the mantra,
followed stellar movements
and resisted final destinations
that would stifle the breeze at dawn
with its secrets.

LIFE CYCLE

COLLEGE COURSES AND TEXTBOOKS didn't mention these kinds of laws. Forget topics like magic, moral boundaries, or the inherent nature of a human being. Such topics might as well not exist. The idea of aliens or trans-dimensional influences still did not set well with me. In any case, the sage pulled such matters into the center of almost every talk. According to what he had said, those areas, at least, provided the meaningful basis for the rest—if I could avoid derailing into literal, fundamentalist arguments. His conversation on triads, right behavior, laws, observances, and the role of personal narrative convinced me that they needed serious study. He presented a new orientation in the world, in ways that shook my familiar assumptions.

An inner schism formed between my personal *narrative* and the truth of what I was *as a being*. I perceived an *essence* guided by a subtle purpose, with power that was displacing old priorities. The meetings had been a lark at the beginning. Now they took on critical mass, disrupting the trajectory of my life—vague thing that it was. My prior attitudes were accidental and anemic. When I reviewed the current situation it was apparent that despite my renegade delusions, popular tide dragged me along. The amazing thing was that the widening gap between my old life patterns and this compelling direction caused no trouble for me. It was pleasant, and at times, beautiful.

More like feelings than words, those things colored my mind while pedaling to our morning meeting. I leaned the bike against a stucco sidewall in the entrance court, approached his doorway and pushed it open. Diffuse morning light penetrated the vestibule. He was standing just inside.

At the sight of him, I fell at his feet. It was unexpected, a reaction on my part with no prior thought of doing such a thing. Touching flesh, sinew and bone I watched myself, dreamlike, and pressed my head to his toes, aware of my hands alongside his bare ankles. I wept. "Who was this doing these things?" half of me wondered—the other half immersed in colorless joy. It was the glad reassurance of a mooring, solid land. It was the peace of safety, even invulnerability. None-the-less, it was a surprise and after less than ten seconds I stood up, restraining a compulsion to apologize. He ignored the event—rather, he accepted it indifferently. We went to the cushions in front of the waxed-wood altar plank, highlighted by a single candle flame. He led us in the invocation and chants before opening a new topic. My sense of time was diffused after the scene at his front door. My knees buckled with no choices involved. But someone acted—who?

"HOMO SAPIENS IS AN animal that develops in five stages: physical formation in the womb, emotional formation at the breast, mental formation in nature, spiritual transformation in the will, and integral transformation in Spirit. These correspond to the *Five Personal Practices*. Please remind us what those are, as background." I only referred to my open notebook as required.

"Cleanliness, contentment, internal heat, self-study, and surrender to the source-presence," I said. "These are forms of subtle hygiene that keep the body and mind in tune with the energies around us."

"I'm glad you did your homework," he said, "A certain amount of memorization is necessary to allow mental freedom. The implication of those five is that the human entity is in continuous, dynamic-relationship with an energetic sea. It appears as the web of life, the geometries of living structures and all the natural laws. These express the innate intelligence that is *the ocean of consciousness*."

Vishwamithra expounded on the vital-airs which knitted the fabric of a human-being. He said, "*Cleanliness* becomes purity in the womb. The child enters physical life as non-dual awareness, sealed-off from the world. The mother is a surrogate cosmos, a creation-matrix in the manner that all primal life required the pristine isolation of mangrove and reef edging vast salt seas. The mother's enveloping womb is truly a cosmic portal straddling pure consciousness and elemental earth.

"*Contentment* manifests as emotional peace, satisfaction learned at the mother's breast. Birth initiates the child into a world which the womb-matrix held-back. Oceanic oneness splits in two. The child clings to the mother who becomes an emotional mirror. Dual awareness requires grounded contentment that can mature into love.

"*Internal heat* is physical friction as the child weans away from absolute dualism at the breast. The mobile body is ripe for mental challenges posed in a dual world full of increased uncertainty. Tests do not overwhelm when the being has been prepared physically and

154

emotionally in the womb and at breast. The child gains teeth, strength, and skill that it applies in an expanding matrix of possibilities.

"*Self-study* continues the journey into full awareness. Choice enters as the first step into spiritual being. The prior stages form a foundation for inquiry. *Who am I?—Where am I from?—What is this life?—and Why am I here?* An unseen hand guided our human journey through the womb, from the breast and into mobility and seems to let go, allowing freedom and choice. Many humans do not accept the freeing burden of asking meaningful questions. They remain reactive and dependent. Like children, their minds are putty in the hands of others.

"*Surrender to God* is the transformative final stage of maturity. The questions have been asked. The answers are received as an ultimate mystery—a love without sentimentality which again takes the human by the hand into places beyond logic or reason. The embryo was alone at the start, immune to loneliness. It was surrounded by the unfaltering presence, a brightness which was air, water, food and warm pulsation at once. Fully aware, a simulation of divinity returns to the source."

My birth and early childhood had complications that made it less than ideal. Would I be able to complete the journey he described in five stages? I related how my development might be compromised beyond repair. He swatted my suggestion like an imaginary gnat.

"It's the human dilemma," he said. "Grace does not bypass any creature, regardless of hellish or distorted circumstances. Each phase has its quota of grace that levels the playing field. Call it faith that the child of God can emerge. It has to emerge—that is *meaning*."

He continued, "The mystery of karma is too great to explore here. Suffice to say that becoming human is not an action film or suspense-drama—it is grace, faith, and creative acts of intention. All doubts and troubles can be addressed in the last two phases of human development: self-study called *svadhyaya*, and the divine pull from the front known as surrender to God—*ishvara pranidhana*."

Still slightly inebriated from the scene at his vestibule, I received his talk on human development in a pleasant fugue. What jumped-out at me was the indictment of most adults, implied by his statement that, by and large, society is a populous of children.

"People are burdened by schedules, even simple survival," I said. "What you said implies that the planet is run almost entirely by adults who are functionally *children*."

"So goes the state of the world," he said. "Guaranteed graces have to end. After the stage where friction and heat are sure to teach and temper the child, maturity is an active quest. Clearly, *becoming conscious, generating intentions and asking questions* are adult tasks. Kindness is built into the journey—the inhale sounds *So* and the exhale responds *Hum*. It tells the truth of who you are, thousands of times each day.

"The vulnerable body, the field, the dark unknowable, repeats *sohum* with every breath, saying, *I am the Self-Supreme!* Birds fledge and tadpoles lose their tails—humans must become conscious—the nature of being conscious is expanding awareness. A human-being must accept responsibility for their thinking mind to become mature—it is not automatic!"

He laughed, "Ah—'*So-what?*' is the mantra for cynics. Most people are ignorant of their cosmic entitlements even though they would shrivel without life's womb, contented relationships, and the beauty of physical form—all day these three are the ship they sail toward their best hope of *a good life*, whether or not they make true choices. The deep foundation of life is a free gift, proof against the atheist. Yet, they cling to misery and ignorance like shipwrecked waifs hanging onto lottery tickets. This condition begs the question, 'Why?' Lives wasted in waiting and wondering must be the result of a magician's trick or hypnotic conditioning.

"Most human creatures are distracted away from the fourth stage of development. It is the dawn of maturity. Dare to ask the question, *Who am I?*" His mouth suppressed mirth waiting for my answer we both knew would fall flat. He said "Go ahead, take a shot at it."

"I am Ashty Hozan, a clerk working at the Bureau of Package Deliveries. I am unmarried, of Eastern descent, height of one hundred seventy-three centimeters with a weight of twelve stone. I am twenty-eight years old and enjoy reading and philosophy." A more substantial reply would have been nice. His corrections were inevitable.

"Of course your package description would work well in the classified section if we were fishing for offers. They would have to come and check your teeth, maybe kick your tires before buying."

Again he challenged me, "Ashty Hozan, cleric of twelve stone and philosophical bent—who are you?"

Resigned to find the broadest category I said, "I am a human being—an animal who uses reason instead of instinct." He backed away from more interrogation and moved-on to philosophy.

"WHAT GAVE WINGS TO A BIRD or fangs to a wolf? Think it through," he prodded. "*Nature* is too easy to say, and doesn't mean anything. Think. There is a form-giver that bestows diverse shapes on minds and bodies. Assume that the form giver is real, that it lives somewhere, has some shape or other. It saw a rising quality in ancient humanoids, be they apes or aliens and bestowed an innate direction. You aren't a bird, wolf or chimpanzee; what is your essential nature? In the human context—arms, legs, thoughts, jobs, distractions—who are you?"

If breathing—the autonomic nervous system—knew something about me that eluded conscious awareness then I could ask the breath why it says *I am He*, over and over again. If only there was an ability to communicate with that presence.

I answered aloud, "I am a thing that has to determine what I am by going inside, a thing that becomes outwardly aware by finding the internal essence. That would be a natural law. The key must be in the breath, as you have said all along."

He asked, "Is it possible to know why a bird flies or a wolf has fangs? They can't know because they live the answer—but you can find out! Sink into the inner experience of a bird or wolf to hear a wordless answer about your own reality. Make it your business to plumb the existence of wings and fangs; they are your urge to either fly away or stake your claim. Tell me what you find."

His command drove me into myself, alert. An image rose, the crossroads again. When a defined picture formed it had a verbal tag and dragged into details which stopped the free expansion of thought. There was a tendency to lock onto a fixed idea. That urge had to be resisted. The process was precise, like a particular aroma is exact, and yet impossible to describe in words.

Birds' wings were an answer to fangs. They were a thing of lifting. They merged bodies with air currents to become light. They quickened themselves away from predators by an inner urge. My thought did that now. It went up, staying open, and not locking down on a definite idea. Thought hovered over the fishing trip that flashed in my mind earlier. An image of my uncle and me appeared on the mind-screen. I experienced that situation again silently, as a witness.

There was urgency in the center of me when I actually baited the hook—inner listening and crafting myself, growing up. Choosing to impale the worm allowed me to avoid *losing face* with this man I admired. I abandoned myself to unfolding events. He did not like himself going to war—I did not like myself slaughtering a worm. He accepted the patriotic role as a son of society, its protector and an heir to its methods. In my way, I did the same. We were both creatures of conscience and then again, beasts of conformity.

There was a possible future when my uncle and I would stand facing each other to commune in consciousness and not conform to abstract ideas or images that pressed onto us. We could *intend*, choosing truly. Together we could fly in a blue sky, aware of the ideas at play—or pursue the meat of matters hidden in practical realities. The fang rips into the *other*, driven to discover and succeed. The wing responds to currents, swimming in space. Wings sprang-forth from freedom to find overview—fangs confronted the other directly. Only consciousness could save a worm on a hook or a man in gunfire. Awareness brought freedom and knowledge, beyond fight or flight.

He asked again, "Then, who are you?"

My eyes opened and saw the room around me. It was new and a thousand years old. The books, altar, and rays of morning light shimmered in stable sameness. Objects, shadows, the play of solid and void, the intelligent placement of things, and even the sage were waiting for me—for *me*. He waited, as did his question. And I waited for me, patient in my ignorance. Freedom's wings and successful fangs waited. Urgency could be picked up or placed down while moments ripened. My mouth opened and I answered, breaking the spell.

"I am at a crossroads every second, choosing either freedom or success. I am ambiguous and precise."

He said, "You are the witness *of* the crossroads—that is the bench mark of consciousness. That is *svadhyaya*. Birds take wing and embody freedom. Wolves bite and eat their way, urging toward success. A human being studies choices and informs them in spite of restrictions and failure. Can you finish this line of thought for me?"

"I think so," I said. We were still exploring stages of life. The thought he wanted me to complete had to go further than simple definitions, to the essence of *ishvara pranidhana*—how to actually make contact with the intelligent resident inside the highest good. It was the end goal of human consciousness. "Our conversation comes down to these: knowledge and wisdom," I said. "Binding and releasing confront my every waking breath and they are mine to observe. The witness requires all the available facts—the most critical is *information and logic is never enough*—any actions, based solely on information and logic, have to fail—they will certainly fail. The play of my life, any life, is deeper than facts and reasons. One has to finally admit there is something beyond this visible presentation. A transcendent principle, a being, an unseen hand leads to the highest good."

I mused silently—the witness is at the crossroads again. Does the witness choose to fly past hard conclusions? Does it hunker-down to accept the fates? Can the witness find a third way?

"*Suvaha* is here," I said, "the third *mahavyahriti* behind this practice.

Urges toward freedom and success are allowed as creature strategies—and the transcendent third leads both of those, with no judgment. And yet, choosing perfectly is not possible. I don't know."

In that moment it was clear he was an eagle—the wing, the fang and the aloof witness all at once. I was prey, a rabbit behind a rock, nibbling greens in unprotected meadows. A question arose, what was this hunt all about?

Vishwamithra resumed the point saying, "Wisdom is latent in every circumstance—*ishvara pranidhana*. Observe the richness and symmetry of dilemmas to witness *Ishvara's* existence. Resorting to *Ishvara*, or God, completes the circle of *choice* in the same way that wings complete the urge for freedom and fangs complete the urge for success. Mature awareness leads to aware reliance. The human, a thing of consciousness, has to seek refuge and fulfillment in the Mysterious-Source of consciousness." He paused, smiled at me and continued.

"People's fates and destinies are offerings in the eternal flame of unknowable reality. The human creature formed of physical abilities and mental tendencies cannot be whole. It stands at the edge of a deep ocean, casting prayers and dreams into the unfathomable. It inevitably comes to know that the distant, unknowable presence is intimate, nurturing every cell, informing every fleeting thought and action. The human creature has come in order to know itself as *the unknowable*."

LIKE A RABBIT, MY nose sniffed the ground for my versions of sweet grass and places to hide. Meanwhile, a bird of prey circled far above and saw a creature—*Ashty*—distracted by simple things to nibble in the web of life. Wise rabbits enjoy every tender, succulent bite because, in a flash, without warning, they might be flooded by soaring-visions of lush green— while gripped in the talons of a god.

LIFE STAGES *Ashty Hozan's notes*

5 FACED GAYATRI	VITAL-AIR	LIFE-CYCLE

OM *cleanliness-womb* *embryo* feel
full and complete, nothing added, nothing to remove—state of one-ness

BHUR BHUVAH SUVAHA *contentment-breast* *neonate* accept
duality with meaning and purpose, reality pulses on and off—in a direction

TAT SAVITUR VARENYUM *inner fire-environs* *child* open
reality is to-be-discovered—appearances hide purpose behind form

BHARGO DEVASYA DHIMAHI *self-knowledge-mind* *adult* discern
body-mind is an interplay of bright motion—observe and take stock

DHIYO YONAH PRACHODAYAT *surrender to God* *elder* give-over
realize: complete self-responsibility, no autonomy—return to OM

The urge to escape and the impulse to attack are called the *wing* and the *fang*. They appear at the transitions between stages. Acting on either of them by fleeing or attacking will keep the cycle locked-in with no vertical movement. Maturity is to observe the two urges. This is the *transcendent third* which cultures the observer toward better decisions.

Every cycle begins as a feel, whole and complete, regardless of judgments—like a child in-utero.

The situation differentiates into a play of apparent opposites that have a direction—the dependent infant does not argue with reality and can only accept it.

Then the situation becomes a surface that hides purposeful meaning—a child opens to the discovery.

Then the situation reveals its blinding aspects—the adult takes responsibility by discerning hot and cool urges to act, without making hasty decisions.

Surrender is only appropriate for the elder—giving-over is the last act before returning to the beginning.

Pre-mature surrender means a full cycle is looping—when an infant, child, or adult become elders by giving up or giving over, something has to influence from the outside as grace or guidance to bring vertical movement.

THINGS & ENERGY

OM—WE ARE KIN to the Mother of the Universe—bearing the same intimate relationship with her as struck-sound bears to un-struck-sound. First there was soundless Pranava which came to be resonant Om. Pranava cherishes our Mother above all, holding her in infinite embrace. Every created thing is her child and we carry the Father's DNA as our awareness. *May the mother sustain us from dullness to awareness, from lethargy to brilliance, from inert matter to living substance, Om.*

"Begin with some object you can label," he said, to begin the start of our discussion. "A thing or collection of pieces—they could be emotional states like depression, rage, glee, boredom; ideas like moving away, getting married, meeting the king; or outcomes like failed plans, great successes, gaining or losing a friend. Lay them out as if they are on a table for inspection. Strain off judgments and opinions you might have about them. Feel the weight and stability of objective reality. It is a world called *Bhu-lokah*. It has gravity."

I stared at his half-full tea cup. It rested on the floor and was the simplest example of *bhur* nearby. He slowed the process and asked me to pay microscopic attention as we went to the next world called *Bhuva-lokah*.

He said, "Every object in our universe, from the dense to the most subtle, is bound up with all the rest. The binder is attraction-repulsion and everything in between. This 'glue' has the character of an energetic pulse, something charged with electricity that causes you to have feelings and opinions about the objects. An example is *anxiety* about meeting the king, *bitterness* over a failure, or unexpected *apathy* toward the death of someone close. A toggle switch in awareness allows you to switch from *Bhu-lokah* to *Bhuva-lokah*—that is, from awareness of the objects as objects, to awareness of the linkages between them. Do that; flip slowly, feeling the edge between stabile objectivity and dynamic relationship, back and forth and back again between inert stuff and the charged energy that surrounds it."

I did as he suggested, all the while staring at the cup. It was not possible to pay attention to both the cup as an object, and my feelings about the cup at the same time. The cup had its physical qualities, and those were very different from *his* cup, the one I associated with *his* habits. It was like moving between worlds that overlapped without touching. Optical illusions like *the young woman or crone* and *opposing faces or lamp* also revealed the mind's inability to hold both ideas at the same time. I flipped between the porcelain cup in sight and the narrative story about it in my mind. The first was mute phenomena, the second was a cascade of feelings and related images.

He asked me to stay in *Bhuva-lokah*, the world in motion, and listen to attractions and repulsions without attaching to either. I centered myself in the coming and goings of opinions and feelings about the cup. It had a floral pattern not to my liking. It was stained like it was unwashed. These aspects were also its charm, what made it part of the sage. As his artifact, the cup contributed to the mood of the room. It seemed breakable. What if it broke? What if I broke it intentionally? Why would that thought even occur to me? I liked the cup. I would be sad. Would he care one way or another?

"What do you find there?" he asked. "How would you tell others about your experience in *Bhuva-lokah*?"

I gave a summary account. "It is a world in continuous flux. Images, feelings, and moods wash one on top of the other with no order. There is an urge to hold on, and then push away. There are fears or excitement that seems to well up for no reason at all."

He said, "You must be familiar with the *Uncertainty Principle*."

They taught us factoids about particle dynamics in *physics 101*. A sub-atomic particle had location and momentum. It was not possible to know both quantities precisely. The more exactly one knew momentum; the position was less possible to determine and vice versa. I told him what I knew and added, "These qualities—location and momentum—seem to relate to *bhuh and bhuvah*."

He created a planetary spin on the subject, explaining, "*Bhuh* is the world of *What*—a place that is only concerned with chunks of stuff and the grain of their material. *Bhuvah* is the planet *Where*, also called *When*—on that world you can only see position in space or a location in time. The objects' bulk means nothing. Let's think of a real-world example. You buy a car because of price, functionality, and general appearance; it is perfect—then you are going to car-pool with all your upscale friends. Suddenly your car seems to be the wrong model, a symbol of your low ambitions—you bought the vehicle in a *Bhur* state

162

of mind and discover your friends judge you from the planet *Bhuvah*."

The sage continued comparing the two qualities in the *mahavyahriti* to particle science. "The physicist said uncertainty was built into reality. It wasn't a matter of flawed perception. One cannot know what something is about and grasp its movement at the same time. Please understand—this is fixed. It is not a limitation—it is an invitation." He stopped to let the idea sink in. It was like a puzzle created to temper the *human* animal. It had always seemed like a weakness. According to the man in front of me it was a developmental stage, essential for becoming a human-being by accepting 'the unknowable' as an intelligent partner.

His explanation continued. "The dualistic filter is purposefully fixed over our ability to know anything. The reason is this: reality is whole and complete—cognition is always partial and flawed."

He said, "This fantastic place of experiences is continuously conceived all at once. No perceiving mind of any capacity can have complete awareness. It is wisdom to know the beauty of that limit, folly to ignore it, and evil to sneak around it. Some people pretend to have inside information or cancel-out mysteries as irrelevant.

"Clear away the dynamic, electrical qualities of a situation to know what it is. That would be *Bhuh-loka*. Meditation on *bhur* requires austere concentration. It creates tapas, or heat. *Bhuvah-loka*, on the other hand, requires detachment from the objects themselves. You become the object of inquiry—in relation to the thing in question. It takes a kind of persistent purification to remove the stickiness and heaviness of objects. Their dynamic aspects are not other than your mental and emotional reactions. In physics, an object reveals itself as either a wave or a particle, in other words, a dynamic event or a fixed entity. They are distinct. *Bhur* is a particle and *bhuvah* is a wave."

A STICK OF FLORAL INCENSE burned on the altar. A plume of smoke rose from the glowing tip. Occasionally it was a still, vertical stream with no indication of movement. A draft might send it into wild gyrations, twisting like a snake or scattering into a barely visible haze. It would inevitably return to a coherent shape, rising up through rays of light to dissipate at the ceiling.

The thing began as solid substances rolled by hand into a flammable wick. A match ignited the rigid shape and turned it to ash, exposing a scent of flowers. Discreet particles of jasmine were too small to see, while the liberated masses of them became an aromatic cloud. Nasal sensors pulled in samples by rhythmic lung action. The thing called *incense* was all at once a stick, cloud, aroma, and mood.

Static form as *bhuh,* and dynamic change as *bhuvah,* were always present, everywhere—only one could dominate perception at a given time. Either, contemplate invisible particles-drifting in the vaporous smoke, or focus on ingredients-hidden in a stick of incense. Seen this way, the order of *bhuh and bhuvah* seemed arbitrary. It was not clear whether forms gave rise to dynamic relationships, or if subtle relationships birthed solid forms. One could argue that the dynamic nature of light as a wave came first, or that the pleasant smell was the reason for a stick of incense. Approaching it that way meant *bhuvah* could come before *bhur.* This challenged Vishwamithra's insistence on fixed order.

"Particles and waves are as different as rocks and rivers," I said. "There's no basis for saying one or the other has to be considered first. Who can determine formal order? It has to be a kind of convention, ultimately unimportant." The intertwining of matter and energy contradicted what he told me about the need for determining a solid basis before grasping the effects within that basis. I concluded, "Isn't it just as well to know the object by studying its behavior? In other words, *bhuvah* could be considered first and the knowledge of *bhuh* would follow."

"This is not only a good question—it may be the original and only important question of all possible questions." He spoke soberly and directly into the room as a void, chastening the world at large.

"You are tampering with the mind of God when you rearrange the primal template. It's not about word order or concept priority but Genesis and the inner coherence of reality itself! Relativists say, 'It is a matter of taste. Everything deserves equal consideration.' The fundamentalists say, 'There is only one way, the right way.' There is the middle position that says, 'One must be balanced. Some issues are relative, others are fundamental, blah, blah, blah.'

"The whole question is infernal, masquerading as playful experimentation, dragging us to hell all the while! The wave-particle paradox says, '*Both* have to be taken at once. *Bhu-loka* requires the objective quality of inquiry. That always comes first. *Bhuva-loka* calls for empathy and experience, which is second. But first and second is an accident of the dual filter—they have to be considered together.'"

He continued to clarify the point, saying, "Misunderstanding the nature of order causes every problem. A cow is a thing that eats grass all day, moves slowly, makes milk and cow-pies, all very useful and true enough as cow-dynamics. But this summary is not about the cow, it is about me and my limited understanding of the beast. The cow remains a mystery until I contemplate its mass of intelligent, roaming flesh as truly unknowable to my experience. My filters for the cow are secondary and irrelevant until I relate to the cow in bright awareness.

"In fact, cows have suffered interminably at the hands of those who only see the usefulness of a cow. I can tell you from experience that they are powerful and fast as lightning when they need to be. They are clever and witty. Those cow-eyes are windows into great souls that have chosen peace and harmony as a genetic disposition." He emphatically schooled me on the wonder of bovines, in a torrent.

He said again, "Did you know that cosmic forces enter the cow through the vortices of her horns? Did you know her milk and feces is so beneficial because that 'dumb-beast' transmutes cosmic rays into its own physical byproducts? Humans have a lot of work to do before they are as spontaneously giving and fruitful as a cow! That's why they rightly symbolize the grace of God. A person who has surveyed cows and invents hamburgers is only looking at his own paltry idea of life. Truly meditating on the essence of cow-ness could only produce a loving soul, one who constantly seeks to transform the stuff of the world into goodness." He gestured toward me, saying, "Now do you understand the nature of *bhuh and bhuvaha*? Do you see the error in determining the nature of reality by what you can find out about it? Reality always requires relationship."

"I want to compare it to two hands opening a jar," I said. "There is the stabile hand, usually the opposite or left hand. And the acting hand, often the right." His posture eased away from his earlier, taut disposition and he listened. I continued, "Once I sprained my left wrist and had to hold jars between my knees, under an arm, or in a clamp to open them. It was a surprise to learn how awkward it is, especially screwing the lid back on. Even the left hand is an active presence when the right seems to do the actions. The same could be inferred for the relationship between *bhuh and bhuvah*."

"The analogy is excellent," he said. "We call *bhuh* 'the basis' and *bhuvah* 'the motion.' The example of hands illustrates the quality of service in *bhuh* that anticipates *bhuvah*. The material basis 'loves' the dynamic expression. Their bond is emotional. One can sense it in all triads. The Father loves the Son which is expressed by the Holy Spirit—grammar loves logic, stated through rhetoric—and man loves technology which, at its best, extends nature through human ingenuity. Explore those paradigms. They shape the world we inhabit."

He continued, "Hands opening a jar also bring in the third, *suvaha*.

165

Why open or close a jar at all? The interplay of left and right ultimately serve a purpose. Notice the difference in the third place. It is a level up from the other two. *Suva-lokah* pulls from the front. Theology calls it teleological—the *Mind of God* determines all natural results. Suva-loka is realm of true meaning and leaves terms behind. Contemplate. Ask yourself, 'What is spirit, rhetoric, or nature?' Probing the answers reveals the interplay of matter and energy—*bhur* and *bhuvaha.*"

He went on in an animated tone, "Can you sense the obscene result of tying the essential third aspect down to definitions? Revelation!—a science that does not hold the *revealing ways* of the other as *sacred* is no science, but vandalism. Think of it as relationship; I have to accept the boundaries you impose that allow me to know you on your terms. All knowledge requires such basic kindness or it devolves into rape. Neither science nor relationship has the right to rip off the veil."

The sage fell into quiet reflection, looking toward the floor. In the gap I went back to the incense and did not see a burning thing that gave off fumes. It was a gift of fragrance. It did not begin in a stick, a cloud, a flower garden or a nose. It came from *The Good.* Good for eyes and nose, good for cottage industry and livelihood and it was good for the spirit that rose up with the beauty of a flower, a heaven-sent stream of smoke.

He caught my eyes and said, "Please indulge my telling a story."

Obviously, permission was not required. Each tale provided precious characters that lodged in the imagination to help remember his ideas and these moments.

PROTECTION

"THE LIFE-GIVING WATERS of the wisdom goddess flow between banks called *relationship* and *boundary*. She will not spill past those protective sentinels no matter how the arid scientific fields hanker to crack open her secrets. Hell is not hot; it is dry. Kindness, the sense of *kin* is an armor that will always frustrate even the boldest strokes of warriors or scientists. The binding power hidden in the blood is the unknowable goddess, flowing in the serum. True boundaries are wise—true relations are kinship. Recall how *Draupadi* bound wounds, families, and destinies like serum binds iron in the bloodstream."

I did not know of *Draupadi* and the sage's mystical introduction to her was ominous. "Who is she?" I asked.

"We can never know—we can only tell her story," he said, and began fleshing-out those strange references to blood and kinship.

"Once, there was a maiden who married all five of the brothers we have already mentioned elsewhere. She was no fonder of the idea of five husbands than any woman would be. There will always be something of the obscene when one woman must satisfy the emotions, longings and projections of more than one man. The one is trouble enough, especially considering the insistent feminine urge for closeness and intimacy. Of course it wasn't her big idea to hook five men, but fell accidentally from the lips of her...can you guess?" He paused.

I had no idea who might have devised a quintuple union all at once. It seemed absurd, as many of these stories seemed at first.

"...Mother-in-law," he finished. "Now, Draupadi's mother-in-law was a saint, having borne five demigods plus another we haven't met. She was just a little impetuous on this one occasion and when her son said, "Mother, I've found something very wonderful," without even looking she said, "You must share it with your brothers." That was that. Back then there was no haggling over parental suggestions and they had the odd wedding."

He made an aside before getting into the relevant part of the tale, saying, "I don't want to leave you distracted with such a bizarre sample of polyandry. Rather than five dandies fawning over one lady, think of these brothers as five elements that share a common energetic bond.

"There is the oldest brother, who was incapable of falsehood, absolutely true and integrated. That would be the element *ether*, an all-pervasive medium for the others. We would experience ether as *gravitational force* that mysteriously causes all things to fall together. It's true that forms eventually fall apart—things break, change, rot and all the rest—but the less obvious reason behind that process is unity—all things seek common ground. The decaying world rejoins the earth. The tired earth falls into the sun. The fading sun becomes stardust for other suns. This is *gravitational force* which unifies apparent fragments into one universe.

"Then there was the archer whose arrows were one with the *air* element. See how the bow and arrow symbolize *kinetic energy*—once the string is drawn, the arrow must fly. *Kinetic energy* releases out of gravity's perpetual winding-up. What clumps together cannot stay together.

"Twins represented *fire and water*, opposite phenomena that are so alike on closer inspection. Energetically they would be *radiation* and *electricity* both are phenomena of ions and the movement of electrons. The clumping power of gravity creates a kinetic urge for freedom which glows as *radiation* and flows as *electricity*.

"Finally, one brother was immensely strong so we'll associate him with the *earth element*, or the *magnetic* aspect of gravity. Notice that the five brothers *as elements* represent a looping spiral. It begins with all-pervasive *ether*—known as gravitational force, and cycles around to our felt experience of that cosmic binding power—magnetism that holds us to the planet and draws us to others. The magnetism we feel is similar in nature to stellar phenomena that pull all particles relentlessly together." Without exception, ancient dramas were teaching tools.

The lesson continued. Vishwamithra said, "Their bride has to be a goddess or she wouldn't be involved in such a confounding union. Draupadi, like Sita in another story, is *purpose*—the urging of all reality toward full consciousness.

"Some say our solar system revolves around a much larger central sun. When that elliptic distance is greatest, human access to wisdom suffers. Minds, thus deluded, reach depths of depravity, as we will see in the story. When it gets close to that polestar, human civilization reaches heights of virtue and knowledge—ultimately, every action is an urge toward that holy state.

Now listen to one small fragment from the vast tome. Draupadi's tale offers hope of protection."

"TRUTHFUL TO A FAULT, the eldest of five brothers was the catalyst for mind-numbing tragedy," he began. "Impeccable in virtue with unmatched adherence to absolute integrity, he was a standard by which all facts and falsehoods were measured. This was the one who first announced Draupadi to their mother. He also was addicted to dice games, gambling. It was uncontrollable. Like so many of the details it seems absurd. *What's the point? It doesn't make sense! I thought he was virtuous,* are the complaints anyone would make if they were paying attention. I'll clarify that fatal flaw before digging-in.

"Absolute virtue and adherence to the complete truth *is* absurd in a corrupt age. A truth-teller surrounded by lies and manipulation is like a fool at such times. He was a good man in an absolute sense. That's why Draupadi was attracted to him. His gambling addiction tells us something that has been said elsewhere, 'Be wise as serpents and gentle as doves.' He had to learn ways to protect his virtue and guard it from abuse. Depraved people see virtue as weakness and revel in taking advantage—but the truth-teller's mind was not in that gutter, so this brother's whole life in the world was a gamble. Until he learned the truth of the matter, every interaction was a crap shoot. He did learn hard, drawn-out lessons along with all his brothers through the course of the epic.

"This young patriarch, leader of the others, accepted an invitation to play dice. The game had been rigged against him on every throw. He lost it all: land, wealth, armies, down to the shirts off their backs. Everything went away. He even threw down his brothers and himself, offering them all as slaves in a hopeless bid to recoup his losses. He knew what was happening and proceeded anyway, as if to highlight the base intentions of his relatives who cheered, jeered, and cheated him toward utter degradation. That mad, virtuous man, wrapped in the passion of the sport finally offered the young wife of the five on the gambler's crooked table."

Vishwathra sighed and tossed me a forlorn glance, "*Truth is true* as they say. Truth will ultimately tell the terrible truth however gut-wrenching it may be. This public humiliation is our mirror. We must put-on the foolish gambler and learn the game or be ground into dirt."

"Now hear the poetic beauty of *Purpose* that shines in spite of such evil. God himself cherishes Draupadi's virtue and protects it using every natural means, inconceivable to linear thinking. In advance, let's

169

you and I praise *Holy Purpose*, the destiny of consciousness which God so loves that he twists and pulls physical laws like taffy to keep human purpose unsullied by the game. The light of awareness teeters into peril and then rights itself. Cling to that bulwark. It cannot fail!"

He closed his eyes and receded for a moment. For my part I was torn between his guarantees to hope and my fears that consciousness was doomed. Our world might be dragged down, like water dripping to the lowest level. He came back and started in an animated fashion.

"Evil cousins were the ones who rigged the match and forced that woman into their circle. They closed around her while the helpless brothers looked on, worthless really. She was alone, chattel, property for their use. And she was beautiful so they did not have to think long before proceeding to strip her naked. The beasts pulled and pulled at her long sari, the cloth that wrapped her body. The cloth fell onto the floor, an unlikely amount, like a whole bolt of fabric. They continued to pull, hungrily seeking the bare flesh under it all. Oh, such a goal fired them on, to see her shape, hips, thighs, breasts, available for their pleasure and they kept pulling. The sari filled the room and still she remained clothed. What's this?—a miracle? And they redoubled their efforts to pierce her veil until they fell down in complete exhaustion. Draupadi the chaste stood among the ravenous and now exhausted hyenas like a Holy Reserve. *This is mine and mine alone* a divine voice seemed to scoff. *She is not part of your game.*"

"But this is just a story," I argued. "There's really no protection in such a situation. She would be raped and shared like any spoils. No, in reality the gods don't spare anyone or anything." Holding onto such magical ideas made the sad truth seem even worse.

Vishwamithra surveyed me, while Draupadi and the awful blight of rape in so many forms dangled in the quiet.

He broke the pall saying, "Your observation is astute. This small ray of light comes in an epic full of woe, so you are right—a reasonable sequence would be more realistic. The more predictable turn of events would be pornographic, violent, and vile—as we have come to expect from current storytellers. It would provide graphic detail that would sear the brain, scar the mind and drain hope for humanity at large. Better still, it might be a bestseller instead of a mammoth sheaf of papers collecting dust on some shelf. Why, you'd have to keep the Mahabharatha heirloom under lock and key from curious children, hungry for a glimpse of horrible, titillating scenes. Instead, the holy work gets the same lukewarm attention of old photographs, sentimental mementos and the like." He was still weighing, still saying more in breaths than words.

"Do you love Draupadi?" he asked.

What a question, I thought to myself, of course not. She was third-hand character in an old story.

"I might have in those days," I said diplomatically. "It seems she was not only beautiful, but charming and graceful as well.

"Wake-up and listen!" he barked. "Do you love this woman? Your very life depends on the answer!"

Story time had ended. What was this now? What on earth did he want from me? I stalled. *When will you learn?* I asked myself. He wanted something deeper, something below my glib reactions. *Did I, could I love her? Love her? I don't even know her,* my hollow defense continued to chime. My reactions were superficial—that was frightening. Falling in the dark, finding the gut, it had to come from below.

This was no longer about fables. I held Draupadi in my mind, generated feeling, felt pain as they pulled her hair at the roots, as men laughed, her shame and confusion unfolding within arms reach of supposed hero-protectors. The gloating victors in the debacle were cousins! They jerked her limbs, sized her up for their pleasure. Or was it my pleasure? *She seemed to be good-looking, charming, graceful,* I told Vishwamithra. These were characteristics for fine female property.

I went down, away from old yarns and wanted to reach out to help the distressed woman who stood so close. My arms would not move. Like a paralytic, they dangled, impotent.

Spontaneously my mind cried, *Draupadi, beautiful Draupadi! Your men stand limp like eunuchs. They can't help and yet you are there, exposed to snarling mongrels!* What would I do? What could I do? Tears filled the corner of my left eye, welled-up and spilled down the outside of my cheek—and still I'm useless to her. *Draupadi, I'm sorry,* I said. *I love you. I love you.* The room fragmented into a watery blur.

I spoke out-loud to the floor, "I love her" and swore oaths silently to myself and the woman for a day when it could be righted.

His voice came into my ears, "You will have your chance."

My mouth opened, sore and awkward to speak, but the vocal chords froze. I forced them to croak, "Not soon enough..."

He said, "Heal her now, for the good of us all. Say your prayers. Find a hero for the tormented lady."

A lithe form came in my mind, a deft dancer, quicker than dark plots, humorous and as lethally precise as the arrow of an assassin or a lilting melody playing over a verdant pasture. I lightened, the knot of my guts released and I said, "Krishna."

Vishwamithra whispered, "Look! He has set aside his flute and is here—not to disembowel the evil ones—he comes to make a joke of us all!"

At those words I saw billows of colorful cloth like festoons over the dreadful situation. Relieved by his presence, cheered by the signature color, levity and desperate for a new vision, I bowed inside to the god-man. Then my view was hers; the humiliations and indignities were mine and the lips whispering, *"Krishna, Krishna, Krishna..."* were ours. My tears fell onto a room no longer visible for all the brightly patterned silks.

Sanity returned, but I clung to color and melody. Wiping at my face I asked the sage, "How can it be? I don't want the nightmare of realism. I am trapped between grim conclusions and dreamy longings."

"What is here?—purpose," he said. "Remember, Draupadi is what animates our limbs. She is purpose. The sad day comes when the very impetus of this fabulous, created-world gets splayed out on a table as chattel, gambled away, and she would be raped but for Krishna—*Krishna-suvaha, Krishna-prachodayat,* Krishna—the beautiful attractive thing that tempts beasts away from their rank fodder. Pray that he does not wait long. We don't know who or what he is—we only have his stories."

"Tell me more," I asked, unashamed that I had become a child who wanted legends of yellow and lilac, lovely scents and sounds. I craved a fixer, a helper, a lover, a Krishna. The sage obliged.

"Do you know how he saved the day?" Of course not! Not even Draupadi knew how Krishna played the cosmic weaver and spun infinite bolts of fabric to surround her. He has to tell it himself."

"I am ancient time, grown tired in experience.
I am new, a child ever curious,
Soaked in memory and knowing
the story complete before it began.

Warm, white milk from the wish-granting cow
splashed against black stone.
Nothing can stop the spectacle
unfolding and yet never begun.

Princess Draupadi tore her own garment
wrapping my bleeding finger.
From the start I knew her love

172

for a wounded boy, longing.

My blood laced her gauze and holds our gaze.
the touch of a mother
wrapping and again
wrapping and again.

Memory expands wrapping her love eternally.
I am always her child, wounded and waiting."

The sage seemed satisfied with his spontaneous verse and asked me, "What did you think of Krishna?"

"Are you saying that Krishna saved Draupadi?" I asked.

"I am saying that explanations are word-concoctions, bare shadows of *meaning*. Draupadi *as purpose* was never at risk. Krishna *as savior* was never apart from her. The best way to understand the mystery *beyond reason* is to know that Krishna's long memory is based on pure affection. Kinship has no reason in it, it is visceral, essential—bundle upon bundle of innate laws, latent with purpose, lost in the very beginnings of things. These tales have more science in them than any study or experiment can reveal. Purpose is not a nut to be cracked open and picked at. Purpose is whole. Purpose *is* Draupadi *is* kinship."

We had been talking of Suvaha which brought Vishwamithra to his telling of the sari. Wanting to anchor the story in the topic at hand, I commented, "If Draupadi is purpose, then Krishna is the *Divine Will* that protects purpose. I understand that much," I said. "And you suggested that even the elements, the five husbands, could fall away from their sacred reason for existence. In other words they gambled away their purpose. I have to ask, is there any protecting the life I cherish? Frankly, any sort of change frightens me."

Principles of divine intervention worked for mythic figures, but what about little people. Draupadi had Krishna's cosmic protection because her role as purpose was important to her husbands—and they were heroes. Why on earth would a cosmic hand reach out to protect the likes of me? My life situation, like most others, was surely expendable because of its triviality. I said, "I'm just a small player in the grand scheme of things. I ask again, is there any reason to expect divine help?"

He said, "When your intentions seek a purpose that is true, the protective shield surrounds you. When your intentions are mixed with lesser motives, only the sacred parts are saved. The rest gets stripped away, maybe painfully. Lives guided by chaos, blown by superficial aims will only have equally lukewarm security. That's why I advise that you cling tightly to the True Power that expresses as awakeness.

"Learn from Draupadi—eventually she lost everything, but *Pranava* preserved her spirit, a lamp that led the remnants of their clan through tragic episodes to come. Meaningless dross is doomed. At the same time, purposeful action inspired by *Pranava* is stainless, pristine, and guaranteed by Infinity." He adjusted his sitting position, the cue that the lesson was wrapping up. "Meet beings, things and processes in their own unique languages," he said. "Meditation is reality beyond labels, the presence inside of feelings."

The story had a lingering effect on my mood—my thoughts were melancholy. Maybe I had overestimated my ability to help others. And the mix of subjects confused me as well—blood contained kinship, somehow—but it was about wisdom, not tribal belonging. And yet family ties were elemental in Vishwamithra's discourse. It came down to the word *relationship*—elemental glue, gravity, love and hate— intelligent outcomes. I did not understand how they fit, or if *fit* was even the right word. My questions got cut-off, so offered a thought for me to chew on.

"*Relativism*—the idea that wishy-washy labels give evidence for wishy-washy reality—destroys our ability to comprehend the world and our place in it," he said. "Re-ordering *bhur-bhuvah-suvaha* has tragic consequences. For your homework contemplate *proper sequencing*. The basis, its relationships, and their outcomes have unique qualities. For the mind to understand them, it must hold their sequence as sacred. An easy example is the slavery to machines and institutions which exists because of wrong order. A wrong sequence—*man-nature-technology*—has permitted slavery. The basis is human—the energetic field is machine—and that pair must uphold the enfolding purpose which is *nature*. Nature holds the mysterious key to human meaning— technology does not.

"The man-built world could have been a loving dialog inspired by nature to enhance humanity. Instead, technology is an alien god that treads nature under foot. That is its nefarious purpose, to hack into the natural and reconfigure the human. It will spit both out when it is done with them. All because of order."

"*Suvaha*!—the dire situation forces our gaze toward meaning, purpose and perfect resolution—the Gayatri Mantra. This sacred mantra sings the inner coherence of the soul, its nature, and its destiny. Gayatri and Vedanta delineate the threesomes clearly."

We repeated the syllables: *Om, bhur, bhuvah, and suvaha*. Then the lines, *Tat savitur varenyum, Bhargo devasya dhimahi, and Dhiyoyonah prachodayat*. The sage fell silent.

THE INCENSE HAD BURNED to a stub while aromatic plumes threaded their way along imperceptible air currents. Each scene in this room was a snapshot—a stained tea cup, sun rays raking across a scented haze, a couple of worn books, and Vishwamithra—it felt safe, holy, and I didn't really want to go. I gathered my things and left.

The weathered wood door clicked shut behind me. There was a moment to take in the neighborhood panorama from his raised stoop. Morning sun had baked a little chill from the air. Beyond a low courtyard enclosure, the street scene came to life. People tended their daily tasks, uniformed children packed satchels to school, while carts, service trucks and scooters broke the quiet with a surge of engines or the clap of metal. I had thirty minutes before punching the clock in the vast windowless sorting facility that was only a few streets away.

I pedaled my bicycle as slowly as possible without tipping, focusing straight ahead. The snail's pace allowed impressions to stream into me. Tending to the road ahead, looking at the front tire turning, and engaging only enough to remain alert reinforced kinship with the things around me. We were all together, subjects in a realm of change. Despite the introverted mood, my own skin felt intimately connected with a larger world when I left his flat.

The big box came into view—a gray terminus of concrete and metal that occupied the whole field of vision. I breathed.

Om, this, here, now was the totality of life.

Bhur, it appeared as structures, materials, schedules and tasks.

Bhuvah, moods, expectations, and reactions erupted. Trapped by circumstance, free of responsibility, foolish in any case—possibilities brewed endlessly.

Suvaha, sweetness lay beyond the sour rind when fruit ripened. That was my task—to observe the change from bitter pulp into sugar and not eat either one. I locked the bike and went in.

Apocalyptic *by Ashty Hozan*

A vacuum at the old familiar,
Arbitrary points replaced safe-harbor
floating empty in lunar landscapes.

Verses and teachings remained,
material shattered.
Which was real?

Gayatri Mantra
or the Great Work,
Which was stronger?

Clasping at beads—something slipped.
How much of me had ever been,
if history could vanish
so easily?

Part IV/ Practicum

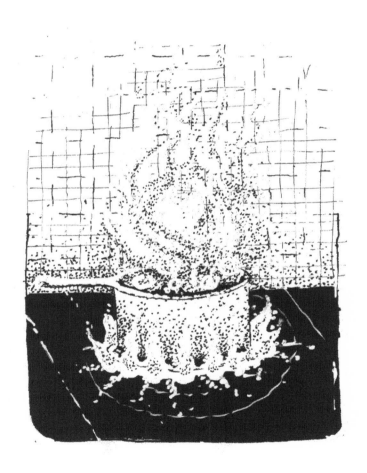

A Useless Word *by Vishwamithra*

To know, you must see through.
Phenomena says nothing essential—
Everything offers relationship.

This word
"grace"
is infinitely far
from its essence.

Hold this Haala Hala and transmute it.
Hear the collective sigh of mute objects
begging for relationship.

GRACE

"Om IS THE ESSENCE of what you are. The vibration of it is like an Avatar that wells-up, filling your intention, employing your body and the voice it finds there. *Ah*, *Oh*, and *Um* are aspects of the avatar, the incarnate God. It begins in silence—its only words are intentions. From unseen depths below the navel, resonance accumulates in the hollows of the chest. The sound births at the mouth, finding its specific personality in you as mouth structures close around it, vibrating and broadcasting into the five elements. Your will is in *Om*, in God, and is not your doing. Receive and interpret—then create. The *True Creator* is cloaked in your unique *Om*.

> "*Master of the Universe, protect us in our study—the movement of Pranava across the body: as geometry, as proportion, as crystal, as flesh, and as voice. May the sound be pleasing, may it bless the world, may all the beings across all the worlds be happy. Om.*"

As the dark morning barely lifted toward sunrise, quiet was dense with character. In the early hours each thing around us expressed lonely integrity. Twisted wood fibers tamed-smooth; floor tile, brittle and defiant, drapes hanging in easy compliance, and the elastic eagerness of my skin each had their precise voice, unheard in non-reactive ether.

"What have you understood about *Gayatri Sadhana*?" he asked in the quiet after the invocation.

"A-U-M implies *threeness* which expands in the introductory words, the *Mahavyahriti*," I told him from memory and continued with my reflections on the core expressions.

"*Ah*, the sound that breaks out from silent intent, points at *bhur*, a word for material, stuff, or a basis.

"*Oh* is an echo of digestion, processing the material presented. *Oh* prefigures *bhuvah* which has energy and electricity. Like relationships, bhuvah focuses on dynamic potentials in the stuff. You called-out *bhur-bhuvah* as particle-wave. They are distinct, yet remain aspects of the same thing.

"*Um* has a counterpart in *suvaha*. We did not cover this completely as you said." I continued, "The logic and progression of the sounds and the ways they anticipate the lines of the Gayatri Mantra are clear enough. It is still unclear how any of it ties-in to my life. They remain only ideas for me. It seems there should be more, that they take on vital relevance somehow." I stated this with little hope that he could connect the mantra directly into my life circumstances.

"Look at your hand—let the fingers move," he said. "How does this happen?"

I said, "The brain sends a command through a nerve network which fires somehow, moving my fingers on a silent suggestion."

"Do you give messages?—for the eyes to look, the ears to listen?" he asked.

"Not in so many words," I said, sensing again that I was on shaky ground. "But a desire for them to act is there, definitely. I cannot pin down the biology or physiology of it."

"We can both agree it is an intelligent act, precise, apparently flawless, can't we?" he said by way of giving a deeper significance. I nodded affirmation and waited.

"It's hard to pin down because you don't know. No one does," he said. "This is unknowable. A different sense is required. Look again. What do you see when you move your hand?"

I spoke and studied the structure of my hand in motion, saying, "Below the skin there is muscle and bone that work together. Words are not necessary because my will connects directly to limbs. Actions happen simultaneous with my desire to move."

"You saw none of that," he said. "Those ideas blind you—concepts serve as the bars of a cage. You are not the fleshy robot you suppose. Let's look again, together." He held up his hand for our inspection.

He clenched hard—I saw anger. The hand opened, palm-up, fingers relaxed—I saw asking, wanting. Then he twisted the hand into a gesture that indicated revelation, demonstrating. He said nothing. Through these gestures of his hand, my mind spontaneously created messages—unambiguous, specific ideas. Where was the interpreter? Who was the speaker?

Then he said, "The bones and muscles are there but they need something between them, ligaments which are neither bone nor muscle. And muscles need something between them, fascia, to keep it from gluing together. Then how does the fascia remain pliant, flexible, yet not binding or ineffective? Between, between—we point at the

180

thing we know and then label it, thus blinding us to the reality that there is no thing to label. We gauge-out our eyes to label the world and accumulate information that we spit out as reality. You cannot find a typical bone, muscle, ligament or anything else. The body itself is more like a flame, consuming fuel, generating heat, radiating light. Ah—but who tends the flame?"

He prodded me even though we both knew I could only ape things he had said. I did not know, and so gave no response.

"Exactly, the true answer is mute. Remember your reply and practice it often. To know the hand you must see through it. Nothing in the phenomenal world contains information—everything offers relationship. Now I give you a word that is far removed from what it tries to express. Its meaning can only be experienced in relationship—the word is 'grace,' the gift of existence. The truer sound of the word is an eternal sigh, a world begging you to go past utility or entertainment. This abode of mute objects is not other than grace—for you, your eyes, hands, mind, for your heart—a silent request is all they have and we miss it. Relate—it is grace. This quiescent place offers communion. Can you hear it? Listen—deafness is tragic. Dull dismissal of the gift results in a golem, hungry, bereft, and homeless. Without communion in the reality of *bhur-bhuvah-suvaha,* the sound of grace might as well be a grunt." The discourse stopped abruptly and he drew into himself.

I studied him as he sat like a stone. I waited—was I supposed to be doing something? Knuckles and veins on my hand caught my lax attention. I stared to see something on the other side, resisting the default into ideas about colors, lumps, cells or veins coursing below the veil of thin skin. At the moment it seemed my eyes could peel back the layers and see something, he began talking again.

"Go slowly. One organ, called 'muscle' has very different tissues from outside toward the center, from connecting point to the meaty middle. As muscle goes toward bone to meet it, to pull and create muscular leverage, it begins to look like bone, then it's called 'ligament.' Bone, again, is a geography of differences—depending on where it meets ligament, bone, nerves and the rest. The labels are arbitrary points for communication. Communication between whom, for what reason—can you see it? Meeting, learning, teaching, expressing—these are the various tissues of grace, *the gift from whence we know not,* that invite relationship. Ashty Hozan, what can I tell you? Every word I could say destroys the subtle fragrance. Draw the aroma of the world into your chest, hold it there, let it become part of you, and expel gratitude slowly. My words are mere toothpicks against

181

machines that manufacture meanings and false gifts that clutter the brain. Let me learn from your efficient reply just a moment ago. *Sita* defended herself from a demon's lust with far less than a toothpick, which offers a more eloquent testimony."

Vishwamithra deferred to another vignette from the Ramayana rather than lecturing on grace, a topic that runs away from words. He leaned toward a potted plant, feeling around the soil, produced a sprig of green and began his explanation.

"WHILE RAMA SIMMERED IN difficulties to cross an ocean, hundreds of miles away his wife blocked the advances of a powerful demon who craved to make her his wife. This was the king of magical beings called *Ravana*, an adept, steeped in spiritual powers, who fell into delusions of egoism. He saw her, wanted her, and took her, assuming that consent and consummation would follow naturally. It did not. Sita was what they called *a chaste woman*, meaning that her only desire was right relationship. She had that with Rama who had yet to rescue her from the dire situation. But was her plight so bad?

"Ravana wanted to make her the crown gem among his many wives. In those days, it was normal for a dominant warlord to take what they wanted from rivals. The spoils included women. A strict realist would see Sita's captivity in the demon's palace as her good luck, an upgrade over her husband who was, at the time, landless, friendless, and sentenced to a shameful exile. Sita found herself among might and opulence that rivaled the gods—meanwhile stranded and powerless across the sea, Rama's options were few. She was aloof and insulting toward her captor, whose resume' far outshined Rama's thinning reputation. We tend to interpret her rejection of Ravana as moxie, virtue, or loyalty. The modern vantage point encourages this. In actual fact, spurning the highly accomplished demon was dangerous, and could be interpreted as a stupid mistake. Cut across conventional interpretations to understand her radical message.

"One day Ravana decided he had indulged her enough. He anointed himself with perfumes, prepared his clothing and crown for maximum effect, hoisted his flashing saber as the manly reminder of his innate superiority over any contender and went to her. She had earlier refused to enter the palace despite the demon's various appeals. Throughout the ordeal she sat Buddha-like against a tree in one of the royal courtyards, enduring the elements, waiting-out this painful chapter of her marriage to Rama. The king strode toward her, trailing an entourage of acolytes and minions. She sensed her time was up, that the full weight of his grandiose personality had finally come to own her or crush her. She trembled and prayed.

"Ravana offered his last, most seductive offer to win her into his bed—she scorned him outright, 'You perverse wretch, you lustful sinner—how dare a common thief such as yourself even hope to claim glorious Rama's woman. I would be damned to even cast a glance at you, you cowardly jackal!' You get the idea. This would not go over well with a narcissist whose sense of fair play had worn thin. Predictably, he exploded and was about to slice her in two with his razor-sharp scimitar when she plucked a blade of grass and held it between them. She challenged such a powerful conqueror of iron will and immense appetite to throw himself against it, and pay the price."

The storyteller raised his own shoot of grass between the two of us and inspected it comically. He passed it to me and I followed his example. After examination I returned it to him. It was grass.

"This did the trick—funny, isn't it?" he said with no trace of humor in his voice or on his face. The single blade lay in his palm, a thin green body that had already begun to wilt. We both stared at it quietly against the lines and calluses on his hand. It was small—honest, straight and dying.

"See grace here," he said. "She did not wag this bit of vegetation at him as a bluff against his earthly might. In this green wisp she held up her very self, naked, and vulnerable—to protect them both—Mother of the Universe who confronted the wayward son. It was Sita's eloquent discourse, truer than any word combination. This is the grace that frustrates labels, formulas, or logic. Ravana realized the truth beyond words and it stopped him cold—the all-accomplishing demon was grass, he would wither and blow with the wind—this was natural law, the same law that created him in a mother's womb. A brute would have forged-on, impaled on that small blade of grass. When the Divine Mother is captive to a devotee, it begs the question, who captured whom?"

I said, "Is the thing called *grace* a game of chance? Does it play in my life? Will the goddess of wealth and beauty ever speak to me?"

He placed the grass in my hand like an heirloom. "She already has. Keep this as a reminder," he told me.

Absent-mindedly I stuffed it in my jacket pocket, out of respect.

Prayer to Sita *by Ashty Hozan*

Behind your stalk of grass you say:
  "Wealth and beauty flow
  toward the open hand and willing eye."

When I grasp elusive treasure,
  the scornful beauty,
  the gloating entitlement,
  the perverted way,
  the aging youth or
  the collapsing support—

When I meet the wall,
  the hollow will,
  the cynical plan,
  the crooked mind,
  the lethal entry to
  the impossible escape—

When I dread the insistent beast,
  the persistent pest,
  the taxman,
  the hangman,
  the angry king and
  the hint of death—

For the sake of grace
  Take my hand and soften it.
In the cause of treasure
  Forge my legs onto the good road.
To bring fullness of life into my eyes,
  always show me your blade of grass.

COOKING

THREE WEEKS WENT BY before we met again. During that time, a friend to whom I loaned money said he wouldn't be able to pay it back in any foreseeable future. I needed the cash and had been counting on getting it back. It was stupid of me, but he seemed trustworthy at the time. Vishwamitra would not likely broach conversations about money so I decided to listen and learn, maybe my dark mood would shift in our lesson.

I entered his apartment. He was not at his usual place by the lamp but in the kitchen tending a large pot.

"Come over here", he instructed stiffly, "The milk is about to boil."

I hurried across the room to peer into a stainless-steel vessel that heated over a blue flame. Steam billowed out, curling against his ceiling, obscuring the liquid as he stirred continuously.

"Milk burns easily. I'm making some cheese, a nice *paneer*. Easy enough, but you have to pay attention. Things move fast once it's near boiling. Watch this; it's a great show. The cheese is bland—the process is something else."

He talked through the steps. The liquid started roiling while he kept the ladle in motion. At some point it nearly burst into foam. He immediately cut the heat and poured-in some lemon juice which had been in a nearby cup. The white liquid abruptly separated into two things, neither of which had been visible in the milk. It was a shock to see white clumps and a clear yellowish liquid where there had been only milk. "It needs something to make it curdle so you can strain off the whey from the milk solids. We'll run it through this cheesecloth."

He poured the concoction into a hammock of mesh fabric slung across the rim of a strainer, washed the curds in cold water, squeezed out excess liquid, tied it off and placed the ball on an absorbent cloth. He brought in a cement block he had been using as a door stop and pressed it flat on the bundle.

"I'll leave it here for twenty minutes until it firms up. Paneer alone is bland, but there is something about it that makes an average dish into a feast. It may be the extraordinary transformation."

I had to agree. The changes in the milk were an alchemical marvel. I said, "There is some anxiety while the liquid heats up and then erupts into froth. Curdling turns it into something I wouldn't suspect in a creamy white material. It's like the acid cuts-through the boiling tension and allows unique characteristics of two very different things."

"It all points back to animal husbandry. They produce continuously and it would be a sin to waste it, so there is yogurt, butter, hard cheese, paneer—all ways to manage the consistent efforts of *the Wish-Granting Cow*." He went to his place by the lamp.

"We'll sample the results later. Let's repeat the mantra."

Om,
Bhur Bhuvah Suvaha
Tat Savitur Varenyum
Bhargo Devesya Dhimahi
Dhiyo Yonah Prachodayat"

The silent space allowed me to review the meanings. Even though I tried to leave my problem at the door, it persisted. So I included it into my contemplative probing until he opened a topic.

"To understand the mantra itself, realize that contemplating *bhur, bhuvah and suvaha* reveals Gayatri. That's where it came from in the first place. The three mantra lines are then able quicken an understanding of reality's structure. Saying the eight-syllable verses while maintaining a sense of their meaning will catalyze meaning in your experiences."

He changed direction unexpectedly and said, "Let's talk about you, because the mantra needs a world to incarnate into. That would be you right now. Describe Ashty's world. Give Ma Gayatri a body to live in."

His invitation was an opportunity for me to vent. "I promised myself to not mention it, but our meditation brought me enough peace to talk without complaining. I loaned money to an acquaintance in good faith and found out it is gone, with no hope of return. It made me angry with him and upset with myself because it's necessary for paying bills. It was stupid. It's one thing to talk about ignorance, and another to become a full participant. Can the mantra help me in this?"

He said, "The Sanskrit word for what we need here is *viveka,* or discriminating intelligence: sorting, accepting, rejecting, storing, reusing and comparing. *Viveka* is like a knife that dissects appearances into clearly discrete parts. What does dissection bring?"

"*Svadhyaya*, self knowledge," I said.

"And what method of inquiry does that imply?"

"Internal heat and self-reflection are part of Kriya Yoga," I recalled from my notes.

He was pleased and took it further. "*Kriyas* are actions that build the fire of discrimination. How can we know what those actions are?" He added, "It's not the thrashing-about most people call personal decision-making. Intention is set through the mantra—Divine Will flows in, cooks us, and brings purpose and effective action. *Pranava* is ever-present in the three realms, with or without our knowledge."

Gesturing toward the kitchen, he continued, "Like the curds suddenly freed from the boiling whey, the heat of kriya separates something edible from what gets poured-off. We will start cooking your situation, the 'milk,' to identify the useful, the useless, and the undecided. Do your yoga and we'll adjust as required. Tell me, where did you go right or wrong in your friendly, financial decisions?"

"I did not have enough information and should not have loaned the money. It was an unnecessary risk," I confessed.

"But you did and the result is here now. The obvious is, *I made a mistake*. Go behind that to the place where it is not a mistake. Add the heat of inquiry, watch the miraculous separation of substances, and enjoy making cheese."

I continued, objectively as possible. "In the future I should get more information and not be so quick to trust."

"Are you learning suspicion here? Is the goal to fatten the bank account? Do you want to be a wise serpent with dove wings? That would be a freak of nature. *Om* has come to you with a gift. Find it. Start with *bhur, bhuvah, suvaha*."

I made step by step efforts to analyze the loan, under his guidance.

"OM tells me all is well and cannot be otherwise," I began. "Nothing can exist outside the creative pulse of *Pranava* which moves in my actions. Difficult as that is to see when I am broke—I will proceed with the assumption that this situation is complete, as it is.

"BHUR is gravity and mass, the material aspect. That would be my dark mood, regret, the hole I see in my bank account, the missing cash. It would be the bitterness I feel at the possible souring of a friendship and the loss of innocence I began with."

Separating the elements of the issue from my reactions took focus. I frequently slipped into confused griping. Vishwamithra shepherded me toward a clearer separation of substance from energy.

He said, "There is a one hundred percent overlap between object analysis and review of subjective reactions. They are two ways of looking at the same thing. Constantly sort one from the other. You said, 'I feel bitterness and a loss of innocence.' *Feeling bitter* is itself an object which is part of *bhur*. Lemons taste sour, like your loan tasted bitter. I used the sourness of the lemon to curdle the milk, in a sense, to ruin it. You now have something bitter, but no use for it, no reason. That is the problem. Bitter is not the problem, lack of reason is.

"You also imply regret at the loss of innocence, as though it were something good to cling to. If milk had a voice it would not want to curdle. This is the point—the milk has no choice in the matter once the process begins. You are in the same pot—the heating has begun. Nursing regrets is just another meaningless ingredient until you cook it. Keep adding these to *bhuh* whenever they arise."

Vishwamithra's discourse comparing cheese-making and thought-culturing went on. He said emphatically, "This process of sorting happens at a higher level of mentality than what you are used to, therefore it seems unnatural. Milk has many delicious transformations, they all involve culturing. Gayatri cultures the mind, which craves this culturing once it sees the astounding separation of *chitta-mindstuff* into meaningful, useful categories."

I doubted my ability to employ the methods he described. They seemed unique to the sage who had experience and insight vastly beyond my own. Going forward, *svadhyaya* generated discomfort and awkwardness that he called *tapas*, or heat.

"*BHUVAH* is a dynamic aspect," I said, "The loan problem stirs me up. Fantasies of stealing it back or getting revenge go round and round in my thoughts. I tell myself, 'You can't trust anybody—might as well get what you can, when you can.' None of these reactions feel good. It happens on its own, regardless of my efforts to stay calm. I understand that some things are beyond my control, but my mind circles back to what I consider a rip-off, whether I like it or not."

Sifting solid, objective issues from their fluid, charged reactions churned in a continuous process through questioning every mental object as it came up. *Was it a feeling or image? What are the objects here? What words would describe them? Are there hooks? How does it snag me—is it like glue, a pincher or a tangle? Is it dull—am I apathetic?* Impressions tumbled over one another while sorting *Bhur* from *Bhuvaha*.

Once the main issues had labels I moved toward the ambiguous next world in the Mahavyahriti, *suvaha*.

"*SUVAHA* is movement toward sweetness, as though pulling from the front," I said, restating what he had already told me. "It guarantees that things have a real purpose. It tells me that difficulties have built-in resolution that may be hidden. Understanding and adjusting for errors in judgment can clear the foundation, *bhuh*. Wrong views send my energy in the wrong direction. Knowing that, I can focus on clarifying the situation. Intentions and actions harmonize in *bhuvah* using Gayatri and clear intentions. *Suvaha* pulls circumstances toward wisdom. A good situation can develop naturally. Really, you began with an idea to make cheese—the combination of milk, heat, and lemon. The starting point was not lemons and milk, it was the intention to have cheese."

The sage took over, "You understand the mahavyahriti well. Make *Om* your intimate companion in this—include that knowledge as part of your very fabric by saying, *Om, om, om, om,om...*"

I joined in. The syllable went far beyond what I could understand. The sound was like a shower and brought relief. Maybe the losses were not as bad as they seemed. Maybe I did have a deeper self, one that guided actions and attitudes better than my so-called logic. It did not have to be a waste. We were quiet briefly. He broke the silence.

"You expected profit and lost your shirt. Your little canoe of give and take capsized. Your bitter reactions are not inherently mean tendencies, as you might judge them to be. Healthy personality traits get distorted in various ways—schooling, cultural neurosis, or simply a lack of guidance allow weeds to grow where you want flowers, or grows flowers when you need food. Problems expose the areas where you are undeveloped. First, realize that financial dangers are abstract— missing a few numbers in an account, or needing more pieces of paper with portraits on them is mostly safe. The mountain climber with a frayed rope has it worse. Be assured the pain you feel is an opportunity to study yourself." Vishwamithra went on to use my concerns to explain the mantra.

"GAYATRI MANTRA PRESENTS THREE strategies to you, one per line. This gives the mind three distinct areas to examine: *the mystery of the manifest world, the insistence of the mental world, and the meaning of both in heaven.* Each line has this structure: *an object in the first word, a quality in the second and a resolute action in the third.*

"Last words in each line—*varenyum, dhimahi, and prachodayat*— prescribe the tasks: to worship, to meditate, and to pray.

"The middle words—*savitur, devasya, and yonah*—are so dense with meaning that they require closer examination and contemplation.

"*Savitur* is the effective, unseen reality behind the sun's rays, and your troubles. It is the source of life and light in all forms and is worthy of worship. Venerate situations that defy your reason.

"*Devasya* suggests the influence of gods, implying it is beyond our grasp of familiar forces. You have no choice but to act and react to money issues, they are so compelling, even blinding.

"*Yonah* is ambiguous and translates as *who*, or *that*—it is *mine*. *Yo*, refers to the first word in the first line, *tat*. Combining absolute reality with an idea of possession should bring linear thought to a shrieking halt. It implies that we have to accept the presentation of things, knowing full well that their true nature is not available to us. There is a wall between what you can perceive and what you can't—you own the impossible task of responding to both. There is a profound gap between what your checkbook says in numbers, what you feel about the amount you see, or how the experience affects the soul. Gayatri suggests strategies for those different levels of experience."

"The first words in each line—*tat, bhargo*, and *dhiyo*—are objective matters: That, Radiance, and my Mind are translations which imply: unimaginable, unworldly and immediate. *Dhiyo* in the last line is your offering, as *Prachodayat*, to *Yonah*. This is the culminating strategy: *I must take responsibility for my mind by offering it to the one who can bring it to the best place—that one is mine, the absolute.* Any translation is obscure."

I felt overwhelmed. Not by what the sage presented—his methods and delivery were familiar enough. Applying what he said seemed impossible. I half-heartedly commented, "Worry about money wastes time and energy—I should contemplate the matrix of meanings. The mantra might shed some light on the problem."

"You don't sound convinced," he said. "*Sadhana* is work—work is not necessarily *sadhana*. They both require effort. The difference between them is *faith*—called folly by the hard-minded realist. Faith is not *assuming something good will happen*. Faith means *your way is coherent and beneficial* because your sources are trustworthy. It assumes the guide is intelligent. You have no will *as such*. Faith is moving forward in trust when it is impossible to know. It recognizes that appearances hide more than they show—the idea of *suchness*, acting *as-though* you knew."

I knew about work—avoiding it multiplied it. Get somebody else to do it. Unfortunately, self-awareness could not be outsourced.

"GAYATRI MANTRA ASSURES US that all is well. Contemplate each word to generate faith in the living source. We experience a coherent world, partitioned down to the atoms. Every piece, from particle to galaxy, works together because they are phantasmal effects of a living wholeness. Imagine it this way. You are in a dark room—that is the stark reality. Tradition says there is a door. It offers instructions to find it. The realist clings to the dark—all the proof is there. The fool feels all over the walls for a way out—lo and behold, the door is there. The fool finds the knob, touches the frames and hinges—still in the dark. There is a moment of truth, to open and leave, or to remain. The door goes into an unknown. The dark, for all its bleakness, is familiar. The fool stays and begins discussions with the realist. The realist assures him the door is not a door, there is still no proof. The fool assures the realist there is a door, if only he had the resolve to open it. If the fool ever does leave, the realist will not notice, because it's dark, and the fool won't return, because he is free. Gayatri practice opens the door.

"*Tat savitur varenyum*—visible light has to have a source. It is not self-effulgent. The sun may be a source of earthly illumination, but what creates that phenomena? The Mantra directs us to revere the cause of illumination, not the sun as such.

"*Bhargo devasya dhimahi*—next, observe that the brilliant effects of the visible world dazzle us and meditation dampens our reactivity.

"*Dhiyo yonah prachodayat*—finally, it suggests a full circle—the unseen gave rise to effects, those effects tend to stimulate reactions, and a true response channels action back toward the unseen origin.

"*Worship, meditation, and prayer* summarize your tasks."

Vishwamithra stood up. "Let's see the cheese."

I had forgotten about his project. We went to the kitchen. He lifted off the block that pressed the curds in their cloth wrap, handed the fat disk to me and told me to untie the knot and pull off the cloth.

Inside the mesh was a round wheel of white paneer. He seemed uncharacteristically enthusiastic, handed me a knife and motioned to cut. The blade sank uniformly into the firm block of curds and made clean-edged squares. He had sweet tamarind sauce waiting in a saucer. Paneer was a sensation I would repeat often with various dishes. One should not be deprived of the experience. He surprised me by packing-up the balance of cheese cubes in wax-paper along with a vial of tamarind sauce. It had been so long since mother made my lunch— I was almost embarrassed at how happy it made me as I rode to work, anticipating the noon break.

Know yourself as the unknowable.
from Vishwamithra

> *You are an offering*
> > *into an eternal flame—*
> > *a miracle of divine origin.*

> *You are flawed flesh and fickle mind*
> > *at the edge of a deep, dark ocean—*
> > *a prayer and a dream*
> > *cast into the unfathomable.*

> *You will come to know the distant unknowable*
> > *as intimate presence,*
> > *nurturing every cell and*
> > *informing every fleeting thought*
> > *—it is your immortal essence.*

Gayatri mantra

Money issues dragged me down. Every random thought, whether it was about work, my family, the groceries—it didn't matter—ended up in a bitter review about my friend and the money. The landlord agreed to give me more time. Payday approached, so rent was doable. Analyzing the issue in the lens of *mahavyahriti* brought temporary relief from the looping spiral, as long as I could stay focused on the process. While *Om, bhur bhuvah suvaha* occupied my thoughts there was more objectivity—but money was money and the loss hurt. My brain glued itself to the problem. The sage listened to my complaints about debts, loans, fair-weather friends, while he surveyed my wayward thoughts.

"The deity rests on an ocean," he said. "The gods churned those same waters to extract the nectar of immortality because fluid-mind is like a borderless sea. Fixed markers of belief or tradition help to navigate open sea. Without guides you blow willy-nilly, lost, confused, and possibly insane. Think about this—on the ocean of consciousness, how is a coherent experience even possible? How can you define an event, whether positive or negative? How is it, in the frothy sea of a nervous system that grabs impressions from everywhere, life is not a confused jumble? The answer is so simple it blinds wayfarers—events and perceptions happen against a still point. The bright spot called *self-awareness* is fixed—to what? A stream flows around a stone in the same way that time flows around the still witness. The rock-witness sees it all—the stream of events knows only compelling currents.

"TAT-SAVITUR-VARENYUM," he said. "This is life! No matter how you suffer under the fat man of obsessive thinking, you have to admit he is impressive and came from whence you know not. Something we call 'Tat.' It is that, simply *that*. Just because you have eyes on the situation, does not mean you created it. Do not rest, until you understand this! Yes, there's poor judgment—yes, there's integrity lacking, laziness, delusion—you name it. That is not the point—notice that life happens to you! You will find no beginning to the loan, the friend and now your disappointment, no matter how far back you trace it. Something stirs the pot. It is not you.

"*Tat* is the sign that says we are beyond the territory of logic or reason—God as *that*. Things that come at us in this world have a source beyond any ability to understand. *Tat* is that which you do not know, you cannot know. Contemplating *Tat* can still the mind and bring *samadhi*, supreme equipoise. Do not bull through! I will say it here once, and it applies to every syllable of this mantra. Each discreet sound or concept within Gayatri Mantra is able to reveal the rest.

"As *Tat* goes past any mental capacity, so *Savitur* defies the physical senses. Pre-dawn light is the essence of radiant illumination, before photons excite, before eyes see. Do not let the sun blind you, that great soul is an effect of *Savitur*. Culture yourself—appreciate a principle of creation that allows us to hail you as *Tat Savitur*. You are an appearance and glow that can be analyzed, but never understood. Your breath alone can reveal that presence, if you meet it properly. Realizing the wonder of *that*, the natural response is *varenyum*, worship. *Varenyum* says, *put conventional thoughts aside and recognize that this is the mystery of living*. Instead of regret, worship—life is woven of mystery and the sacred, however it seems. Notice that worlds of health, friends, and knowledge have superficial relationships to money. They generate their own discreet economies. Your life is woven of mystery and the sacred, however it seems."

"BAHARGO-DEVASYA-DHIMAHI," he said, "is the second line which descends from what is imponderable to what is merely uncontrollable, from the super-phenomenal to the phenomenal.

"*Bhargo* means that it glows—radiance—this financial issue draws your attention. It attracts and blinds you like glare off of water. It seems alive. Sometimes you forget about the loss, distracted. Then it comes back at you, fomenting anger and regret. You want to fix it somehow. The issue and its parts are sticky—you can't leave it alone.

"Who wants to fix it?—the one that gave the money away in the first place?—the one that's afraid of going broke?—the one that hates being a chump? All our so-called motivations are like gods, *devasya*. It means 'of the gods' because if you are honest, you can't find the source of the action. The whole thing might as well be dictated from the beyond. You got volunteered. Why did you meet this person or put trust in him? What made you think it was a good idea and why do you now think it was a bad idea? Do you really have control over those things? There's no proof at all that you control any of it.

"The mantra does not care—it suggests *dhimahi* or meditation. *Dhi* is a Sanskrit root for mind; *mahi* turns the word into 'I meditate.' It says, *Even though you are in a storm of circumstances and reactions that grip your attention, your action should be non-action—meditation—the mind is where the action is.* The mantra directs your one task, simply to observe everything in your field."

As he spoke it occurred to me that analysis was of no use. Combing through the issues had not solved anything and like some song that hijacks the brain, themes of waste and poverty persisted. I did my best to attend to his dissertation on each line, fighting through the obsessive poverty fantasies that had become a default.

"DHIYO-YONAH-PRACHODAYAT is the third line, a strategy of action informed by the spirit of *suvaha*," he said, persistently mashing my woes into the Gayatri mold. "At this point in Gayatri you have appreciated it is over your head. Its origin is beyond your control or understanding and you make yourself an alert observer. Put reactivity to rest or at least include all your reactive emotions and thoughts as more stuff to observe. You have drawn a circle around the issue, large enough to contain all of it.

"*Dhiyo* translates as, *mind content as such*. *As-such* means it is not possible to do full mental accounting. Sanskrit achieves precision by making context an essential part of understanding the vocabulary. The lost money, the acquaintance, the poor judgment, and all the other aspects of your current concern are *superficially* yours because you can only be responsible for what you survey. *Yonah* offers ambiguous references to the *Savitur*, saying *That (which is) mine*. If the meditator can't be fully aware of mind content, claiming some possession of godhead is even more unlikely.

"*Do not stop there*—below the surface, the field of mind works in ways that are beyond you. You are in a double bind. It is not your fault and there is nothing you can do about it—yet, it is all your responsibility and you have to act. What can be done? *Prachodayat* delivers you from fate and gives you full responsibility. The most skilled action is to offer it back to the entity that cooked it up in the first place, the one who holds any real power over events, people, bank accounts, et cetera. *Prachodayat*, means *give it forward to the effective One— pray*. And who is the effective one? There is only one," he asked.

"*Om*, Pranava," I said.

"And who is that?"

"It is my essential Self, the one that knows how to create life circumstances and digest food." He nodded affirmation.

"Is the bad loan a price worth paying to help you meet the still point, the essence, the Self? You could not have known this aspect in any other way."

"I know what you are saying, but no matter how it spins, it was a bad decision. Surely there are cheaper ways to meet *the Self*."

"None of that matters as long as you pour your situation into this mantra as a continual offering of worship, meditation, and prayer. It is connecting you to the arranger of these things. This power deserves a chance to do right by you. It will complete its work. In other words, 'Do this practice, appreciate, digest, and assimilate the bitter food of a bad deal.' Tell me how it turns out. Be honest with yourself. This is Gayatri, the savior of the world in this era of manipulation.

"It is a profound process of enlightenment through learning and insight, the gift of the Creator-Shakti known as *Saraswati*. She is the Goddess of Wisdom who inspires all study, instills the urge to know, and builds true culture. If you intend to heal and grow, she is there to help you pick up culturing tools and use them. It is about culture, what is essentially valuable, finding the tools to truly create and critiquing the mechanisms for making things. Having more or less money could be either a blessing or a curse. There is no way to know without discrimination, and Saraswati is your wisdom guide, eager to help you sort out those differences." Using the mantra-structure to analyze my situation had merit, but seemed too esoteric for me to employ the technique myself.

He wrapped-up our meeting with, "There are alternatives to Gayatri that you can seek out. Devise your own solutions with the tools you have available or you can find other disciplines through a vast array of religions and teachers. Those options are somewhere else; Gayatri is right here. Small choices ripple out in their effects. Know that even whimsical decisions collect mass and importance as they grow, going-out from you, shaping your life and those around you."

For the time being, I was stuck with habituated worry and whatever relief I could manage by doing analysis by the lines.

EKALAVIA

THE LESSONS HAD BECOME difficult. The problem was not the teacher or my ability to grasp what he was presenting—the material was taking on a certain life of its own and that made me nervous. Earlier enthusiasm gave way to practical concerns. The sessions took time and they siphoned attention from trying to make more money.

Yes, the morning appointments were pleasant and informative. Yes, Vishwamithra was uniquely capable and effective. No, it did not create critical strains on my time or pocketbook. Yet, occasionally, I wished for at least one good reason to quit. I could not make such a decision myself—it would be shortsighted, like cutting off a finger for an insurance settlement.

Who could put a price on a finger? An insurance company?—economics in those terms were macabre. How on earth would I choose to leave the sessions with the sage? Another question naturally arose. "Why discuss it if it's positive and does not burden other aspects of your life?" Here's why.

Leaving the farm was not easy and did create some hardships for loved ones. Their emotional support was guaranteed only in a certain context. The emigration away from the life I had ever known was intended to bring improvements to the ones back there. I would succeed, send cash and upgrade my contribution from simple rote chores to assistance with their needs for capital.

These lessons with the sage could be part of that unwritten contract on the condition that they put me *back in the saddle*, which would be improving my station so I could uplift theirs. Instead, I was developing repugnance for the saddle, horse, bridle and the entire dusty pointless trail over the horizon. My developing attitude seemed like a betrayal of my family and our agreements.

"If thine eye offends thee, pluck it out," was a piece of advice that never completely made sense. In any case, some cherished limb or other would have to go. These ideas simmered on the back burner of my

mind while we went chanted the mantra and he invoked Ma-Gayatri.

Wasting no time he introduced another story, saying, "I want to tell you something strange and sublime, a reminder that logic or reason cannot fully comprehend meaning and purpose."

"IN AN ANCIENT KINGDOM just before the greatest war, there was a teacher of martial arts named Drona. He was charged to prepare a royal brood of adolescents with formidable fighting skills. Out of the mixed collection of brothers and cousins, his special pupil was Arjuna, the half-human, half-divine son of Indra, god of thunder. The academy of warriors was deeply involved in practical lessons when a village boy interrupted. The innocent intruder's name was Ekalavia, which means *One Thumb*. He sought instruction from Drona, whose unrivaled reputation as an archer was universal. The great teacher refused because the kid was a common villager and lacked qualifications. The boy bowed and left."

The sage shifted his posture and tone to make a side comment.

"There seems to be some class prejudice here unless you understand why Drona deflected the well-intentioned request—the boy was not of the warrior class. The *full* reason that the guru sent the boy away was much more intriguing—Drona *himself* was not of the warrior class—he was a priest, practicing in willful violation of that religious trust! This is one of the many conundrums that can only be solved in the lonely corridors of self-study. Judge no one. Instead, discover the profound truth for the cleric to adopt the garb of the soldier, defying accepted conventions!"

Resuming a storyteller's inflections he said, "Some years later, Arjuna found a dog wandering around with its mouth laced shut. On closer look he saw that someone artfully wove seven arrows into a tight contraption around the snout to keep it from barking. Arjuna was shocked—*he* was supposed to be the great archer.

"Drona's star pupil ran to complain about what he found. 'You said you would teach me the most advanced techniques and skills,' he complained. 'And here is this miraculous demonstration of archery thrown away on a mutt!' Arjuna's sense of entitlement came back to burn him with tongues of shame."

The sage explained, "The teacher understood the student's accusation—that he held back the most advanced teachings and that Arjuna was in fact *not* the best. Someone out there was a lot better. Led by Drona, the brothers searched the area to find the one whose talents outshone their lesser lights."

Vishwamithra interrupted his story to say, "Think about it. They found a flea-ridden dog who was shooed into silence with the skills of an angel—what a waste! In those days they didn't run around advertising their egos. They were still of a mind to respect physical abilities as divine privileges and use them with appropriate humility. Think of the speed and accuracy! What arrow bending magic would allow an archer to tangle a box around a yapping dog—when hurling a rock would have done the job?"

In the dramatic pause it was possible to imagine the uncanny movements he described. He continued into the heart of the story.

"The search party found a youth practicing marksmanship in a clearing. From a hidden vantage point they watched phenomenal feats of archery. He followed each session with devotional offerings to a life-sized clay statue which he worshipped with garlands of flowers, fruit, incense and all the trappings of bow and arrow. This was obviously some prodigy, an advanced pupil with a transcendent source of instruction. Drona, who was as miffed as the others, strode out for a confrontation, saying, 'Skilled archer, what is your name, and what is your lineage? Who is your esteemed teacher?'

"The young warrior's face beamed with joy and his manner was calm. He placed his hands in prayer, bowed low and disclosed the source of his skill. 'Drona is my master,' he said, 'my teacher and guru.' His mirth at the meeting was yet another mystery. What did jt mean?"

"Drona barked back, 'I do not know you.' and with a sweep of his arm toward Arjjuna and the others he added, 'These are my students.'

'Ah, this is a test! You definitely know me. My name is Ekalavia,' he said and cast his gaze at Drona's feet, continuing to describe the means of his mastery.

"The adept related to them his indirect communion with the guru. After being rejected for master teachings by Drona, his commitment redoubled. He erected an image of Drona and wholly devoted himself to it. The clay likeness of the supreme archer and guru instructed Ekalavia heart to heart. The boy's devotion grew, as did his skill. The teachings proceeded from rude beginnings through every nuance of mind over matter. In that way his access and application of Drona's wisdom was limitless.

"'You are my holy mentor,' he said. 'There is no other. I owe you my life.' Ekalavia waited, silent and empty.

"Drona issued his gruff reply, 'As your guru, I request *Dakshina*, the traditional gift of student to teacher.'

"'Anything you ask,' the youth said. 'Let my offering please you.'

"Drona told him that he wanted his right thumb. The skilled student-archer in one motion drew a razor sharp blade, severed the digit, wrapped it in linen, bound it in a tassel of silk, and offered it to Drona. Again, he bowed low before the teacher, the stump on his right hand tied-off with gauze."

"Unmindful of the wound he said, 'It is so small a request. Would anything else please you?'

"Drona replied, 'All is complete. I bless you.'

"The meeting ended thus. The brothers followed their teacher back to their usual place and took up lessons where they had left-off. Nothing else was said about it. The exchange confused Arjuna who learned later, through pain and blood—*the battle for heaven always requires the most precious thing*."

But Vishwamitra withheld his conclusions. The bizarre request, the meaning of such a gruesome payment—the request by a teacher who should have been wiser—would remain a puzzle for me as well.

I said, "Drona's demand seems out of character, even cruel. Surely the point of it does not end with such hurtful protocols. Please shed some light on these things that strike me as irrational."

The live guru before me deliberated. Slowly he said, "Legends like these are flowers, with roots that reach down into the ancient truths of this world. They can only survive for thousands of years because of those life-giving tendrils, surely not the sense they make to a senseless generation who would just as soon forget or rewrite them. The flower itself is incomprehensible, a thing of beauty to be appreciated."

Vishwamithra continued, "You can know the meaning of the story yourself by following the bloom—the plot, the characters, their victories, defeats, and foibles. Trace them down the stem and leaves through the emotional challenges presented. Don't stop there— continue down into your resonant feelings, attend to them closely. That is the loamy soil. Those feelings are an admixture of *Ah, Oh,* and *Um,* your primal expressions. The Holy *Om* activates the stuff of what you are, uniquely. At that point, you are the story. It tells itself in you and there is no 'making sense,' any more than you are a thing to be analyzed and understood."

He smiled and kept talking, "But this thorny rose has a particular beauty and my ideas about it are bound to strike your ears. First let me ask you, where will Ekalavia's genius take him?"

He touched the sore spot. I blurted, "Far, if only he had a thumb to continue his advancements! Drona has mercilessly disabled him. Here the student's virtues outshine the teacher. He sacrificed his art...*his* art, the one *he* developed...to the rank whims of the supposed guru."

"Remember your outrage," he replied to me "It is not other than a hint of the vast fortress of ignorance your generation has inherited. The human creature must dismantle it as happily as the youth severed his own thumb for *dakshina*. Here is the reason."

Vishwamithra flexed his hand in front of me. His slender, strong, calloused digits moved in an orchestrated dance, stretching, and twisting. "Notice the thumb," he said. "The opposing thumb activates and empowers them all. The thumb is the embodiment of doing. A hand without a thumb becomes a mitt and the bereft fingers spontaneously seek a replacement. The thumb is their servant, the humble *Quasimodo*, comical in a way, misshapen, funny looking compared to the stately fingers—which are straight, long, and move in graceful agreement. Yet, without the thumb, the royal court of four remaining princes can do very little. When the thumb is gone you will realize the fleshy appendage is only an outgrowth of mind—to pinch or clasp, to hold and draw in—these are concepts. The *urge to grasp* is the nearly imperceptible razor-edge that this story balances on."

"Tell me more," I said. "The bizarre details of the myth leave an odd stench. It festers like an open wound."

"Let's focus on the odd, anxious state this story breeds," he began. "The question is *where would Ekalavia's skill have taken him*? I say the flower of his art fell and came to fruit—all at once—on meeting his guru only the second time for those brief moments. What efficiency— Ekalavia the sage was born from the perpetual student with so few words and only two meetings in the flesh.

"The exchange between student and guru was so rarified that the brothers missed it completely—most people can't understand what happened between them. The thick-headed princes would have to witness untold miseries before they gained Ekalavia's wisdom."

He went on. "The boy's talents had taken him to the edge of physical application. His prodigy was so over-full that he wasted it on a yapping dog, without noticing the misuse. Advanced skills degrade into levers for power if they are not dedicated to the highest good. Drona recognized that the student, lacking a material teacher, proceeded in a physical vacuum. In such a medium the student had become as subtle as his mentor who was a spiritual essence. And he was not a warrior by cast, so the bowman's arts were at risk of becoming embellishments, festoons with no practical, moral use."

Vishwamithra went on. "He slowed Ekalavia down, removed the flashing edge of his talent so that spiritual fruit would have room to unfold. If strange turns in the fable cause discomfort, hold it close. When you speak its language you will hear about the limits of personal willfulness."

I said, "Once before, you issued warnings about learning *how* things are done. Are you saying that enforcing limits may require violence, when skills are greater than the wisdom to use them?"

Vishwamithra responded, "If Drona had chopped the thumb himself, it would be violent. He did not. There was no violence at all, to the hand, the ability, or to the boy's psyche. Pruning a tree is not violence. It is husbandry which involves an exercise of skilled power.

"The teller of the tale leaves you to continue the story in your own way. If bitterness or any kind of bad feeling emerges from the hearing, that is the hearer's work, not the bard's fault. A good story will 'ring your bell.' Self-study is listening to the resonant tone and responding with disciplined action."

Vishwamithra turned sideways so I could not see what he was doing with his hands and then came back to face me. His left was palm down, the right palm pressed against it, right forefinger covering the left thumb joint.

Holding that curious pose he said, "Dakshina must be given, but regardless of the disciple's perceived loss, remember, it's more like this." And he gave a convincing demonstration of pulling the top joint of his left thumb off and sliding it along the flat hand. He repeated the illusion several times, clicking each time it "detached."

"See, not so much blood," he said and opened his fingers flat to expose the trick.

It was funny, more for the way he abandoned a sense of decorum than for the corny parlor-stunt. Whatever his intention, the gimmick amplified my queasy feeling about Ekalavia's situation—it brought the cost of discipline that much closer to reality.

THE ASH PIT

SOMETIMES IT SEEMED THIS practice could actually bring me some relief, that losing the money was a surface play. The heart of the matter was just what the sage suggested, *svadhyaya* through *tapasya*—finding out who I am by enduring the hot-seat in an intelligent way.

Inevitably, self-accusations came up. Disaster fantasies fed each other when I dwelled-on how stupid I had been—images of policemen at the door, forced penniless into the street, vagrant, or thrown in debtor's prison—if there even was such a thing. My mind could generate whatever it took to make me feel impotent, small, and vulnerable. Forget philosophy. After all, most of the world did not have the luxury to crow about self-knowledge or whine over a few lost dollars. Ironically, I felt entitled to pursue higher, spiritual aims, even though I had trouble enough with basic finances. My tiny, all-consuming problems bared their teeth again and again.

Those futile thoughts were depressing—maybe I should chunk so-called self-improvement altogether. Making money might be a better way to make myself useful. The work ethic was there—but greed didn't pair well with altruism and couldn't motivate me to try that hard in any case. In spite of such confusion, I applied the Gayatri method as possible and repeated the mantra in a rote manner.

On our appointed day I arrived at his front doorstep with an irritable, disorganized mind. My ill-wind targeted the sage. What did he know? He was in a sort of fairy land of spiritual peaks and was no more familiar with the real agonies of the masses than I was. Was this throwing good hours after bad in the same way the money went down the drain? In this cynical condition I took a seat and waited for him to open our session.

He did not. He swept ashes from a hearth in the corner. The ever-present flame had been extinguished. He gathered bits of half burned wood and gray dust into a metal pan and transferred it into a brown bag. I cleared my throat—it seemed he was unaware of my presence.

He glanced at me over a shoulder while he continued. Energetically scurrying here and there he busied himself with taking the bag to a half a dozen potted plants inside and on the balcony, carefully placing ash around each one. After a look around, he cleaned-up whatever bits he had missed.

It seemed we were about to begin—I was wrong. Now the sage poured water onto the tiles and made a clean sweep of dust. He returned with some fresh wood in a hopper and a stack of newspapers which he placed at the ready for his next fire. Eventually he settled and began with three Om's and Gayatri repetitions. However, any chance I might get centered had been shattered by his activities.

My attention was riddled with a barrage of thoughts and reactions. *That was rude. He did not respect my time. If he could not honor those established boundaries maybe he was not as he claimed. He might be a fake, just another "priest" bucking for donations. I had to work for a living, what did he do? I didn't know. It looked like he hung around his place avoiding as much entanglement with real life as possible. He was striking up a good time for himself—I was conned again, an idiot, stumbling through without a clue, always looking to someone else to deliver me, bail me out. Now this Gayatri thing; it was always something else. When would I learn?* Such was the script of my "silent meditation" as we sat together. He still had not spoken and the stultified silence persisted long after I felt any minor benefit from sitting there that morning.

My skin crawled. I felt like running out screaming. How long had we been here? It must have been close to an hour. I was in disbelief. It had been a long time since feeling so disregarded. Finally he opened his eyes. I had been staring at him for not less than ten minutes. He smiled and talked.

"I thought you might like a change of pace and some more quiet time. I hope you enjoyed it." He stood up, stretched, and moved across the room, showing me to the door. I mechanically followed his lead and left in a stupor. The metal latch clicked shut behind me.

On the walk to work, I alternately wanted to curse or cry. Faltering strings of maledictions fell out, strained and empty. Tears seemed justified, but those were theatrical at best. Stuck in the experience, there was really no good reason to feel victimized. Work and its rote series of mindless motions would offer welcome relief—this was the real thing, the more of it the better. The day ended. Instead of going directly home I went to the tea stand to lick my wounds.

Freckled, funny Azeeza was not there, nor her father. A relative tended the operation while they were apparently out of town. He was efficient and aloof. I missed the familiar faces.

To treat myself, I ordered a latte instead of the usual cup of black tea. I carried the beverage and a package of sweet biscuits to a table and opened the spiral bound notebook where our sessions got dutifully recorded week to week. The drink was bland and tepid. I took my problem back to the counter to swap for coffee. "Sure," I thought, "*keep the customer satisfied*—he has to."

The improvement was short-lived. A quick sip burned my tongue and now I could barely taste anything. The dry cookies hurt the scorched tissue in my mouth. My sit bones dug uncomfortably into the thin, unstable, metal chair. My pants grabbed at the crotch. I chewed anyway. Tears welled up. The open notebook was blurry.

"I am pitiful," I thought, mashing the cookie and coffee together into a sweet, bitter paste, "an entitled baby surrounded by petty cruelties." The pen hovered over the paper, unmotivated. I slurped with pained restraint, swallowed the objectionable snacks and closed the pad, all the while observing these reactions that embarrassed me. Water fell out-of my eyes onto the table. My mind was blank and I breathed. A breeze kicked-up and swept away some loose papers. Erratic gusts cut through my jacket. I battled fickle wind and dust by fixing things in place with the elbow that still supported my heavy head. A wounded ego held ground against the conspiring elements. I continued awkward sips and chews in this forced posture, wobbling stupidly with every draw of liquid and motion of my jawbone.

A memory from the fourth grade floated in—the student next to me placed his chin on a clenched fist which in turn rested solidly on the desk. A picture of boredom, he popped his mouth open and closed. His distended jaw, sloped forehead and reduced cranium size presented a profile similar to Cro-Magnon man in our science text. And as a bonus, the irritating poem he composed on the playground began a relentless loop in my mind:

> *...See, black isn't blue and blue isn't black,*
> *Your damaged brain makes you want to attack,*
> *If it makes you see red 'cause your mind has cracked...(see black isn't...)*

Abandoned by dignity, I laughed caustically and chewed. "Why now?" I wondered. These trials were apparently not worthy of respect, even to my own subconscious. I wished it would stop, and yet something in me did not care what I wanted.

Guru, *by Ashty Hozan*

I want to tell you something.

People in relationship are not like debris in a river
Appearing and disappearing, vanishing in currents,
Flowing under bridges, bumping against banks and each other
On their way to God only knows.

They are not like random verses in a song sung by life
With tunes that loiter and caress the mind in idle moments,
Catching us off-guard, depositing lilting phrases
Then losing themselves in the noise of the mind

Relationships are meteors that crash into the planet Narcissus,
Survivors of varied size and composition that leave pits,
Craters and deep space fragments, lodged in permeable flesh.
They defy all defensive atmospheres.

Dredge the radioactive remnant for fuel.
Donate chunks to the Museum of Self-Regard.
Display them all in life-like dioramas.
Delegate an official task-force to fence-in the smoking hole.

The wound is a birth canal,
The fetus crashes in and crowns down—
Born in reverse, it craves a womb and
Creates coitus to explain its existence.

You are now that permanent resident, fuming in my tissues.

POWER

My mind was in a more balanced state than before. Our opening verses were a welcome touchstone. We sat in comfortable cross-legged postures on floor cushions. I usually watched him for cues, while he closed his eyelids about halfway. He began: *Aum, aum, aum. Om bhur bhuvah suvaha. Tat savitur vareyum. Bhargo devasya dhimahi. Dhiyo yonah prachodayat.* After nine repetitions, he added, *May she protect us. May our study be brilliant. May we not antagonize one another. May she reveal our life as our study. May she lead us from falsehood to truth, from lethargy to bright spirit, from morbidity to God's eternal optimism. Om.*

"How did your week go?" he asked.

"Better than it started," I replied.

"Did you arrive at any insights during your mantra practice?"

I said, "What is an insight? What's the use? When it comes down to it, I'm a victim of whatever I think my circumstance is. The immediate situation makes its demands and doesn't ask if I'm ready. It's all mine to manage, regardless. There might be some small victory in sadhana and then—*wham!* a lot worse than a money issue erases the petty progress. It could be disease, a drunk driver, a tree limb on my head, winning the lottery. It doesn't matter does it? In the end, every person runs a random gauntlet, no matter their good intentions."

He studied me and said, "*Tat savitur varenyum,* that's what we're talking about today. Do you know what a *gayatri* mantra is?"

I had to suppose this was his reply to my observations. "There are a lot of them, three lines, eight syllables each, but the one from the Upanishads is *The Gayatri Mantra,*" I answered.

"Do you find anything strange about *Tat savitur varenyum?*"

I did not know what he was talking about.

"Count it out. There are only seven syllables in the first line. A problem for an eight syllable line, don't you think?"

It was obvious. To get eight out of it, you had to do something to three-beat *varenyum* to give it four beats—va ray-*ay* nyum or va ren *nee-*yum, either way it was unnatural. "Is that a mistake, like some kind of scriptural typo? It does not make sense that the *Gayatri of gayatris* would be flawed," I said.

"Take a minute to understand the problem," he replied. "First of all, is it really a problem or can we just ignore it?"

"What would be the point of critiquing a mantra with such a venerable reputation?" I asked.

He came back with another question, "If you were the author of record for the unique glitch in this mantra, specifically called it *gayatri* and were well-aware that the label specified exactly eight syllables per line—tell me, *what exactly what would be your intention?*"

I said, "Laziness or lack of poetic talent has to be excluded because the mantra is precise in every other way. Of course it was no oversight. There is only one reasonable explanation—the author intended it."

Vishwamithra smirked. "A no-brainer, as they say. We are not talking about a kit with a missing piece—this is the *Mother of the Vedas*. Adding the missing syllable ignites the mantra. Let's learn why."

He led me again in three slow repetitions of the mantra. The teacher gathered himself and began a discourse about the genius of omitting a syllable. "We already discussed the meaning of three," he began. "You assign solid meaning to numbers because you and the concept of *number* are intimate partners, born out of one womb, the One Mind that exists before any concepts."

Months ago he had discussed how each number had its own qualities that spoke directly to the mind. *Two* was duality; this against that. *Three*, stabile triangular relationships, were tangible aspects of abstract unity. *Four* described material solidity, four directions, four seasons and the rest. *Eight* related to four somehow. The sage elaborated on the way *number* made Gayatri effective.

"The discoverer of this Mantra saw its deep creative purpose," he said. "Line one has *seven* beats. The chanter transforms it into a thing of *eight*. It is important at a subtle level, so it earns the label *metaphysics*. The difference between seven and eight is profound at several levels: physical, mental-emotional, and spiritual-archetypal. Participation by actually 'plugging-in' is the essence of Gayatri practice. Listen."

I braced for something that might well fly over my head and turned to a blank page in my notebook. He said, "The number *seven* represents human progress through cumulative steps. It involves time, advancement and patience. There are seven chakras, seven sacraments, seven heavens, seven yogic disciplines. Sevens imply that a goal can be achieved through effort in a staged-sequence. Standing alone, *Tat savitur varenyum* implies such a process with its seven syllables."

"Taken just as it is, with no meter added, Gayatri does not have full efficacy. The burden is on the chanter to take the necessary steps. It is conceptually and spiritually perfect, but it is not yet truly a gayatri. A great moment confronts the one who enters the mantra actively, adding the required syllable. This is your creative portion of *savitur*. Chanting it this way turns the key and ignites the mantra into an engine of effective action."

Praises and claims heaped onto the Gayatri from every commentator. It seemed unlikely that Vishwamithra could clarify the faith-based accolades. I was wrong. He said, "The glyph for eight, in most languages, shows a simple change of direction, as though the essential character of that number is 'change.' With the extra syllable, *seven* becomes *eight* through your active intent. Step by step progress turns into effective transformation by adding the syllable. So far this is only an idea. How would it work?"

I wondered how the *meter* in Gayatri had anything to do with the mantra as *relationship*. He intentionally asked *how*; a word he had emphasized in the context of discipline. I asked, "Isn't there a danger in turning the mantra into a tool rather than a spiritual practice?"

"Oh my!—what is a tool anyway?" he nearly shouted. "If your practices are not tools what are they?—festoons?—artifacts? Beyond the obvious need for spiritual tools, the mantra invites the chanter into relationship." He continued, "It's not that the chanter seeks to use the mantra to gain advantages. The living Mantra gives her treasures to one she recognizes as suitable. If you do not participate by inserting the extra syllable, the two of you stand apart, separate and therefore, inert. When you change *varenyum* into *varen-eeyum* and embrace relationship with her, a different entity emerges. She first asks, *what is your intention?* The divine mother charges the chanter with her effective powers, the same powers that illuminate the sun and infuse reality with all its dynamic qualities. The lines of the mantra prescribe beneficial changes to reality. It is not magic or manipulative. It is a quickening of *meanings* into *effects* by actively pulsing eight syllables, three times, anchored within *Om*—her grace." The thought dangled while he dug for more. *Do not throw pearls before swine* meant don't waste wisdom on those who wallowed in entrenched viewpoints. My ability to receive his pearls was still under scrutiny.

"Develop relationship—this woman is the five-faced goddess," he said. "She waits until you come to her in the manner she prescribes. It is courtship," he said in an unfamiliar tone. "First become the *Om-transmitter* to catch her interest. She's not sure. She watches and waits. Show your intentions by contemplating *bhur-bhuvah-suvaha*. She is *suvaha,* sweet resolution that pulls you. The mantra proper is like an inert formula with latent power—in that way it is *bhur*. You are *bhuvah*, the romancer. The syllables come out of you as the sound of *Om, Pranava*—now She recognizes you. The mood is set. You and She are together. W*orship* dresses you in the essence of Gayatri—her power is in the act of surrender. The mystery of this power tantalizes, and you fall into *meditation*—this is intimacy. You want nothing, so she gives all. The responsible suitor does not take advantage of her willingness. Return the gift of awareness back to her—she cannot resist this *prayer* and quickens your worthiness.

"Dwell with her in this proper relationship and you can't be disappointed. You become *kin*. It is the spiritual equivalent of a blood bond between mother and child. It can develop into a marriage and ultimately, a new life. This is the way the mantra works, based on symbol, effect, spirit, and the nature of matter. It is a miracle." Then he emphasized, "Every relationship has challenges. The remedy that calms the storm is in the relationship itself. Working through them is part of *tapas-svadhyaya-ishvara pranidana,* in other words, growing-up."

He picked-up my notebook to sketch cursory diagrams.

"This circle is you," he said. "It is your stabile, comfortable world, the one you expect when you wake up in the morning. In the middle you have a command post; it's like a forest ranger tower. You monitor every possible vista from this seat." He placed a central dot. Sketching in a thing like an asteroid or meteor with streaming tail, he said, "Something comes at you from the outside, an impact. Little events don't do much—they might cause a ripple at the edge—but big ones, relative to what you are used to, will create big dents, bends, or even holes in that boundary." He drew impact lines as the object crashed into the self-circle. "The event might run its course and allow you to heal. Some impacts leave permanent wounds. You may have to move the command post to recover at a safe center."

"Spiritual practice should strengthen your nervous system and provide a more fluid, flexible circle. With practice and awareness your comfortable territory can tolerate huge deformities that float back into place more and more quickly." By now the page had various amoeba shapes with differing issues. There were dull impressions, sharp points, cuts, and multiple hits, all of them pushing the edge and jostling the center. He continued, "Events will have a less catastrophic effect. Like physical exercise, *sadhana* needs intelligence in practice. Concentration and focus accompany aware repetition to bring the desired results."

He added more arrows, lines and circles within circles, becoming eyeballs, with pupils and irises and said, "The eye is a real-life diagram of the sort I described. It registers the health of your body through changes in shape, pattern and color. On the surface, an iris surrounds the pupil. That muscle-ring controls the amount of light allowed to enter. The hole enlarges in excitement and contracts in concentration, responding immediately to every subtle mood. There are other structures: nerve ring and various fibers and spots. All of these map the reactions we already talked about by reacting, zone by zone to events in the body. Some people have a tame, controlled, nerve-ring nested in silky smooth muscle—they feel strongly, but don't react. Other people have a lot of fibers, spots, eccentricity in the nerve ring—they make noises and blurt statements without control. They display their highs and lows, shaking with fear and demonstrating reactions when electric energy spikes within the body and mind.

"The body is an analogy, a metaphor of sacred realities. Observing the body and its reactions is spiritual practice. *Sadhana* has to bring physical, emotional, and meaningful benefits or it is not *sadhana*." He returned to his diagram. "Look in the mirror to see what there is to work with. Examine the story in your iris. Notice how the eye-map and the reactive-self mirror one another."

I commented, "Eye structures are interesting enough, but how does it tie in with mantra study." I was still looking for something to soothe my growing fatalism. Mantra might be more icing on a stale cake.

"This reality is responsive and intelligent in every aspect," he said. "Worship the facts, meditate the effects, and offer your prayer into the one who gave it. The three-stranded body of discovery, knowing, and integration is your immensely powerful vehicle. Learn to ride it. Love the journey. This mantra will tune the world and your experience in it. You have to see it—wake up—here is this fabulous graphic map of body and mind, rippling with every touch of experience. Here you are to witness. Ah!—discover it. Oh!—Examine it. Umm—Enjoy it. What is the mantra?—It is a metal file smuggled into your prison cell. If filing the bars is too hard, it is a treasure map of coded instructions. If you don't like following directions, it's a girl, waiting for you to get up the courage to introduce yourself. And if all those present too much of a challenge, look in a mirror and ask *who are you?*

The Baby and the Bath

notes from Vishwamithra

Don't suppress negativity.
Negative thoughts and emotions
are powerful, vital forces
that have their life in your deepest desires.

Squelching dark fantasies,
anger, or negative looping
may fix the immediate mood
but it does that by
strangling the life urges behind it.

Observe them, identify their trends,
and while they are full of force,
follow them back to their source.

Their ultimate Origin has to be
intelligent and full of creative power.

Have the courage to discriminate
what is from what is not.

RESISTANCE

"Every relationship exists because of pure joy and is restless to return there," he said, lighting three candles after we settled in our places. "We have described *bhur and buvaha* as terms for something solid and something that moves—their endgame is always joy—joy is their reason to exist in the first place. You can call it bliss, or in Sanskrit, *Ananda*—the gayatri calls it *suvaha*. The world of static things and its parallel universe of bumping, grinding motions want resolution. They strive for peace and when they have it they say, 'Job well done!' and retire. But there is no rest for creation, it is as infinite as Gayatri Mata. She loves the endless game."

Without warning he said, "Invoke your god. I have performed as master of ceremonies all these months—bring your *ishta devata* to us. Ishta Devata is your deity, your god—the one with sway in your life."

Despite working with the practices he had suggested all along, I had never thought of having a deity. This put me on the spot, because of course, the over-arching Power had to be there—but this was Vishwamithra's realm, whether it was *Gayatri*, *Vishnu*, or anyone else. I winced and accepted his order, searching my mind and feelings for God. There was none. No face, name, or form came forward. I was godless. The realization washed me and I felt lost, precariously hung on a cliff face, going one hand-hold to the next, praying to no-one for sure footing. And yet footing was there. "*God,*" I began, "*You are my God of the godless. You have protected me when I was too stupid to know I was in danger. You have guided me when I was blind to my circumstances. You brought me here...*" I cried. This was unexpected. "*Bend my mind to your will for me. Tame my delusion of control. I am sorry that I do not know you. Come, be with us here. Thank You.*" Slightly embarrassed I was quiet. He had seen worse.

Eyes closed tightly, Vishwamithra was again someplace else. "*Om Namah Shivaya. Jaya jaya shambho,*" he repeated to himself. He opened his eyes and smiled, saying, "This is Shiva, God of the godless, *anatha - natha*. Among the forms of deity, this one asks nothing. They say he is

Shambo, a font of blessings, because he only requires one thing—your sincere request. So he is here, of course. Meanwhile, *Om*, which seems faceless, is the eternal beginning and ending point of all. It is complete, containing the whole affair no matter how you label it. Back to my opening statement—any relationship forms out of *ananda* and has to resolve in contented satisfaction. Does that make sense to you?"

At the moment, nothing made sense to me. A chord running through my body still jangled from doing our opening invocation. Why tears? Why not joy? According to him, trying to relate to God should make me happy. "Honestly," I told him, "when I seem most sincere, it leads to melancholy, not happiness. Many things are painful though the truth of the teaching as bliss is sublime. How can anyone understand that all things are born in bliss and resolve in bliss when there is so much misery in so many wretched ways all around us as we speak? Why would the invocation bring me tears?"

He said, "When you address *That*, reaching past your conventional ideas, tears cleanse the eyes so that the soul can see. Other tears are *Haala-Hala*, the poison Shiva transforms into nectar. So, all tears have God's attention, one way or another. If you probe your tears from a moment ago, you will see they spring from a fountain of bliss. Tears that prepare the eyes for divine sight invite pure *ananda*. Other tears prove that the mourner resists reality."

He explained how, in this universe made of joy, misery dominated our perception. "Evils occupy our awareness for a simple reason—the blissful ground, the working substance for everything you see, touch, taste, and experience, is perfectly constructed and so becomes background, the white noise of reality. If we celebrated every time DNA, gravity, or biology did what it was supposed to, nothing would get done, so we mostly pay attention to the problems. Give me an example of pain you have experienced." The sage would surely issue his critique of my thorny situations.

I told him, "My money woes persist, so, once again, I'm again not able to pay the rent. But my discomforts are superficial—I recently visited a friend who has been paralyzed for years. He fell out of a tree and broke his neck. His body is wasting and he can barely feed himself. He considers his financial burdens as the least of his problems. Unfortunately, I'm so preoccupied with my petty issues I don't feel much sympathy for him. That seems wrong. What right does anyone have to expect happiness?"

He said, "Suffering alone causes sober introspection, *svadhyaya*. Don't wish it away. When bliss takes on a body, it apparently needs regular doses of misery to stay attentive. It is a profound conundrum. For example, financial issues only bother you when they bring pain, otherwise you don't notice. Freedom is natural—constriction makes you resist. If you had lots of cash, that issue would not arise, so you are right, lack of money causes a problem. Knowing that *it's always something* does not help either. Of course, you'd rather have the rich man's problems. That's right too. Poverty strikes at survival, wealth brings on the problems of the gods: mortality, cynicism, stagnation. Pain of any kind has nothing to do with *Sat, Chit, or Ananda*—but in this realm of contrasts, pain is essential for knowing the Truth. Our craving for comfort is the shadow of bliss. It drags us toward the real.

"Our lot in life is to grab floating debris, lash it into rafts, and stay out of the storm as often as possible. *Building boats* means using what you have, flawed as it might be, to course toward the truth. It is Yoga. Humans bridge the gap between the absolute and the relative with every breath, every thought. Local, petty, painful situations are your opportunity to build a bridge to heaven. Forgetting or ignoring that fact *is* suffering, regardless of cash on hand or good legs. The human drama, the struggle away from pain is not sad. Building connections back to *Ishta-Devata* is the center piece of our condition—it is not the failure of it. Squirrels collect nuts and stash them for the winter—we forage in consciousness for the truth of it all. Our brothers and sisters fling themselves into harm's way because of ignorance. The casualties will be there as long as there is an ocean of consciousness to navigate."

Directing his attention to my situation, he said, "You must have noticed that your relationship with money—a negative, painful one at that—has not changed much. It comes up again and again. Again and again you want it to go away. Your money woes are as persistent as your friend's paralysis or the abuses heaped on innocents. These need miraculous cures. Gambling on miracles has no place in Sadhana."

"Notice that your pain increases with the outward gaze. The more you examine the rent, the paralytic, or the scorched earth, the more suffering increases. Your first reaction is to ruminate on how dreadful it is, even though no solution exists there. Now, go back to your problems and tell me what you find, beyond a depressed reaction."

I thought of my lame friend, once young and full of ambitions, his limbs wasting from a simple fall. Poverty-stricken masses lacked basics like clean water, washing, excreting and drinking at the same source. Elite controllers only used their plight to squeeze more money out of them. I got weary of going from high to low. With a little money I would forget my cares. Suddenly, the economy sagged and guaranteed sleepless nights, anxious about the future. I deflated there in the privileged atmosphere of our spiritual discussions. I said, "What do I find?—problem on intractable problem with not a hint of *ananda*."

He said, "Negative feelings indicate that you are pouring your attention away from the basis of all this, *God, Tat Savitur*. It goes, not toward your friendship, which is joyful, but to the body's unsolvable wound. Reverse the flow of attention back to *Tat savitur*. Feel the flow of it away from you, stop it—and send it in the opposite direction. They say that when you are buried in an avalanche you spit to find out which way is down—then dig the opposite direction to get out. That is the essence of awareness and Gayatri. Feel how you attend to anything *out there*. Catch it and bring it back to its source in you. Try it."

While ruminating on my problems, I recognized that they accumulated, reinforcing each other in a negative spiral. I said, "Do I reverse the flow of negative thoughts by suppressing them? Using mantra? Meditating? It seems useless. Nothing changes."

He said, "Don't suppress negativity. Negative thoughts and emotions have power—you feel it. They feed on vital forces that have their life in your deepest desires. Squelching dark fantasies, anger, or negative loops fixes the immediate mood by strangling the life urges behind it. Affirmations miss the opportunity to become aware of what bubbles out of your core. Don't wish-away afflictive emotions as though they weren't there. Admit that those ideas seem to have a life of their own. Observe the nature of their power, not their content as such. While they are full of force, follow them back to their source. The source will always be intelligent and full of creative power. Think of the fantastic imagery in cinemas—it is often blatantly perverse, intended to drag your emotions into the deepest hole the arts can create. But the talent, the skill, the sophistication!—these are from the gods! Find the sublime source of the negative scenarios you produce."

He encouraged me to try it. I allowed the concerns to fill my attention. They whirled in no particular order; money woes morphed into self-pity that led to guilt and false altruism for a friend that led right back to my checkbook. Jumbled feelings played like a random juke-box; familiar, unwanted tunes that resisted my preferences. His only instruction was, *reverse the flow of thought*. I imagined the objects of my attention thinking back toward me and got lost in fantasies about what I could do about them. The flow was not reversed, just relabeled.

Changing tactics, I pushed against my attention, like someone swimming against the current of a river. The inner dialog about global disasters, my friend's misfortune and poverty continued. They rested on a conveyor belt, consciousness that went out, dragging me with it. With effort it was possible to note the direction and push against it, using focus and persistence. It caused a subtle sense working around each negative package toward the place where the movement started. The boxes rolled past me like white noise, even while they persisted. I was neutral in that place, moving over and around, away from them.

I imagined the rolling conveyor at an airport baggage claim. I ambled toward the door flaps and the room hidden beyond them. I popped through a thin wall between *out there* and *in here*. On the other side I could stop the machine, put it in reverse, or send out other luggage. It was an awkward flipping back and forth, going from the visual metaphor of clambering against a flow of obstacles and then back to examining the content of the moving parcels which were in fact my complaints, packaged, boxed and rolling outward. The new options were unfamiliar. Habitual tendencies pulled at me with force. I resisted the process which tired me. I told him what happened.

"That is analytic meditation," he said. "Notice there are two things, *bhur* or packages, and *bhuvah*, which is direction of flow. Until these are clear you are a spectator, waiting for what comes at you. Here is another way. Tell me about your money concerns while maintaining an effort to reverse the flow of thought. It may 'cramp your style' and create inner friction, even frustration; that's good. The difficulty is also called *tapas*, a concept which should be familiar by now."

I took a breath and began the strange effort of speaking words out to Vishwamithra, and at the same time drawing my attention in—all the while reviewing the current status of my lease.

Me: "I am two months late in payment."
Vis: "Do you feel pain?"
Me: "The landlord does. I am afraid."
Vis: "Do you feel his pain?"
Me: "No. He will evict me."
Vis: "What does the landlord feel?"
Me: "I don't know. I feel fear."
Vis: "Give fear a name."
Me: "Poverty."
Vis: "Speak for Poverty."
Me: "No one likes me. I'm alone."
Vis: "What should he do about rent?" (Ambiguous, who is he?)
Me: "Never pay." (Me is he.)
Vis: "But they will evict him."
Me: "He deserves it for the stupid loan."

Vis: "This is a closed loop. How can you open it?"

Me: "Talk to the landlord."

Vis: "Solve your problem now."

Me: "I can stay with my brother if it comes to that."

Vis: "You can stay with your brother if it comes to that. My back veranda is also there until you gather your resources."

The stilted conversation came to a natural end. The words I spoke were effects of the effort to maintain an inward flow of attention. They were not important. And I said them whether they made sense to me or not. The exercise strengthened something and wearied me at the same time. It was like pedaling into the wind.

He led me in repeating the mantra, "*Om. Om. Om, bhur bhuvah suvaha Tat savitur varenyum. Bhargo devasya dhimahi. Dhiyo yonah prachodayat.*"

My body felt shaken. From the opening prayer to my efforts at raw honesty during the exercises these were muscles I did not know existed. I asked the sage, "Am I cursed to be haunted by unresolved issues—the money, leaving home, letting people down? I don't expect a magic wand to fix everything, but these persistent anxieties make a universe of *ananda* seem delusional."

The teacher replied, "Today is your day. *Nothing can cling to the blue, blue sky. Clouds slip off no matter how they try.* You tell me—are you cursed with your concerns? Will you always be broke? Is your friend a hopeless case? *Look up higher, past overcast and gray. Tell both of us what the oracles say.*" This was no multiple-choice question and I could only fall-back on what my imagination served as an answer.

Blue—there was one day, back then, when the intense transparent blue of the sky had luster—when time was more forgiving and every moment held possibility. I was with a cousin on my mother's side. They actually lived not far from where the sage and I sat during these meetings, which only just occurred to me. It might be why I moved to this area after leaving my family. On a summer visit to relatives, when mothers and fathers talked, and children were *better seen and not heard*, this boy and I trekked out to a hiding place he knew of. We followed a creek bed and arrived at a cluster of hardwood trees, gnarled survivors of agricultural development which leveled all else between there and the edge of housing. Train tracks ran from town to the flat horizon. They were gleaming metal bands separating the grove from a stream bed where rippling water spread-out, glistening over natural pea gravel. We waded-in up to our shins, exploring. I was in paradise. My heart rose into my throat with the thrill of minnows darting past fat pollywogs that awkwardly scurried under stones to escape our interest.

Bullfrogs watched us from their safe distance, while we upturned rocks or teased schools of fish. The shiny green amphibians were the length of a forearm, streaking a meter or two through the air if we got too close. The visions of nature were rapturous. My cousin yelled for me. I looked. He held-up a stick that dangled a clamping crayfish. The beast spread-out the size of a dinner plate, like a star, flexed to attack. He tossed it, stick and all, far onto the bank. We sloshed-over to trap it, to examine this wondrous monster, absolutely armed and armored to fight us to the death. My pulse raced as it reared-up tall; thumb-sized pincers poised to sever us. We cornered it this way and that, all the while it clicked on deft legs, sideways and backwards, weapons ready. The crusty thing worked us toward tree roots where he scooted through, hit the water and shot into the center of the creek, lost under the silvery, broken surface. Meeting God would not be more dramatic.

What did the oracle say when I looked into clear blue skies? Beauty and potential lay around my mind like treasured heirlooms in a dusty attic. They would never abandon me, although I might ignore them.

"No curses," I said. "Fate has always been far kinder than what I imagine for myself. If there is any curse at all, it is that I will be okay." With that, I left to go to work, longing for the tenacious grip I lacked, the muster to grapple with my mind and its contents.

Recognize *notes by Ashty Hozan*

There is something absolutely beyond you.

Tat savitur is a distance that can never be bridged
   because *to become aware* is the only valuable part
   of the quest *to know* anything.

Human meaning speaks vividly at the *sandhya**.
   The essence of your creature hood
   is forever *sandhya.*

Stand at the place where darkness meets light.

Actions that are not worship are a waste.

Sandhya:
honoring, offering + of the mind;
Junction, union, holding together.
The three transitions—dawn, noon, and dusk.

LIGHT AND DARK

"LEAD US from falsehood to truth, from darkness to light, from death to immortality. Allow us to meet in your presence so that these studies are radiant, bear fruit and go out from us into the world. Keep us from argument, from anxiety, and protect us in the three worlds, physical, mental, and meaningful, that we might realize Om."

"WHAT ARE WE DOING HERE each week?" he asked after our verses.

"You are the teacher and I want my life to mean something," I replied, "to recover a sense of purpose, to develop peace, tolerance, and love for my fellow man. So I am here to learn."

"To learn," he repeated under his breath. "This world is full of wonder. Birds migrate unerringly with no map or compass. Tides move in geometric precision—who plans the ebb and flow? Structures in a leaf, tree, and vast root systems, interconnected with populations of insects and fungus, so much like a human nervous system. You, I and everyone we know or ever knew are in a constant chorus of *Om* in so many forms. The flux of hopes and dreams is a song of longing sung by every molecule in the panorama of *Om* unveiling itself. Beauty is everywhere. It *is* every thing if we have the eyes to see. And every eye craves that vision. We could get lost in so many subjects—animal patterns, plant chemistry, millions and millions of worthy subjects. Open your eyes to the whole wide world that is your extended self.

"Yet, blinders on the horse and a crack of the whip will keep the buggy out of the ditch and on the road. The living spectacle drags at attention—such a dilemma. When you are thrown from the boat, all that matters is swimming—Sanskrit and eye science are useless at that point. The human race is in a stormy sea with no sight of land. The boat is breaking into bits—it's time to swim vigorously!"

"What storm do you mean—what are you talking about?" I asked. A shadow lingered behind the teachings, slipping-in uninvited—he never failed to introduce disturbing specters that rattled my cage.

"Religious techniques and our conversations both exist for a basic primordial purpose—to resist a process of forced mutation. Natural law applies to our reality of three dimensions. There are entities that coax, seduce, cajole, and chop the richness of height, width, and depth into a flat plane. Management is their function, so simplification is their objective. The goal is a planned world—one that runs as they see fit. Find the tendencies in yourself—valuing plans over feelings, nurturing things more than people. See electronic screens all around you, telling you what you are—and notice how you comply. However it gets expressed, the natural way can only survive through applying human discipline toward self and other. Freedom in consciousness requires a self-imposed process of discernment. We, as creatures, were born for this battle. Some call it the quest for enlightenment."

I said, "Sage, I still can't take this kind of science-fiction agenda seriously. Yet you insist, and so I want to understand in plain terms."

He said, "Call it *sin* if you like. The trouble with terms like *sin* and *God* is they were mashed into conventional attitudes long ago. *Oh, sin—that's just people behaving badly, blah, blah*, you would say. They are small words that do not bring light to the topic. As I have said before, humans stand apart from nature. Animals and plants do not have sin or gods because they don't have concepts. Human reality is a *conceptual* realm. We live inside of it as though it is natural. It is only natural to humans—and the unseen hand we call *evolution*. What is evolution? Has anyone seen it? Is the proof in better screen resolution? There are dramatic choices before us all as to *what is human nature*. The five-faced goddess Gayatri exists to lead through—*through what?*

Vishwamithra elaborated on his mention of *sin and God*, saying, "Entities have gained control of human culture. They show themselves blatantly in education that does not educate, politics that does not serve people, business that is a parasite, money that has no value, banks that have no money, children that think they are adults, adults that think they are children, churches that seek popularity, and a population that has no guidance, tradition, family, friendship, or security. None of it happens like leaves, blown in the wind. The deviations are planned. Confusion is intentional. Do I need to go further? No, there is no need to complete the long litany of evil developments we accept as normal. The human person is under attack—human consciousness itself is the ambrosia which these parasites gorge upon." He stopped, gazing slowly around the quiet room as though examining the air itself.

"You know the situation," he began again. "The blind can't see roaches crawling all around them; dust piles-up thick on a high-shelf, out-of reach, the deaf are oblivious to an oncoming car. The usual senses have their limits. They need other means of detection. Roaches have a sound and smell, the dust has to be assumed, the traffic vibrates. Let's rush headlong into Gayatri. Let her be our uncommon sense to guide us beyond parasitic forces. Understand the intentional challenge posed by the faulty first line—say it and count!"

Reacting to his urgency I blurted, "*Tat savitur*," and counted on my fingers, inserting the additional syllable, "*varenee-yum*," to make up the prescribed eight counts.

He exclaimed, "Wonderful!—we are saved for today. You have brought yourself into the mantra."

I felt like a player in a scheme beyond my grasp. His approval had nothing to stick to—I did nothing to earn it.

Then he announced quietly, "I see you shining, accepting the mantle of a spiritual warrior, one who has picked up the sword and buckler of Sovereign Mind. It is our task, everyone's task to raise the polished blade of discrimination and cleave away two-dimensional demons that pollute human goodness—toxic music, imagery, foods, and ideas that assault the nervous system and offend genuine culture." His tone shifted into a rant. He raised open palms in front of us, with fingers stretched, separated and straining. He seemed to catch water from above, only to let it roll off and away.

"For it to be genuine, it has to culture a human being. Culturing, culturing...what does it mean? It stimulates change toward the good. What is the good? Relationship—with another being, with the Self, with the mind—discipline!" And he quickly clasped, holding tight.

"Be sober. Look! Hackneyed scientists butcher the blueprints of life. Bankers garnish every type of true wealth, distributing shreds of paper in return. Native peoples everywhere have been plowed into the dust, along with their ways, their forests and streams. Love itself staggers from door to door, bereft of a home in a human heart, held hostage by twisted entertainments and crooked institutions. Don't be deceived. We're not engaged in idle pastimes, you and me. Anchor your soul's intent in the fray—take refuge in the mantra!"

I had never seen him in such a state—though seated in front of me, it was like he stood on a high peak. He shone with an inner fire, brandishing his mantra at swarms of shadowy jackals. Vishwamithra banished them all and we returned again to quiet.

My mind played the verses involuntarily: *Om, bhur bhuvah suvaha, Tat savitur varenyum, Bhargo devasya dhimahi, Dhiyo yonah prachodayat,* forming a

223

rhythmic soundscape during his scathing critique.

He said, "How can I tell you the wonder of it? I can't. You will find it. The mantra reveals itself. We are privileged to insert ourselves, to create worlds by adding an eighth syllable to the first line of seven. The perfect teaching is incomplete until you add yourself. You become the mantra, it becomes you—when you add the missing meter.

"*Tat,* simply translates as 'that.' It makes no attempt to guide our opinion or perception of this world. *That* is the truest name for God.

"*Surya,* the Sun-god pulls the solar chariot across the sky. *Savitur* is the effulgence of dawn light. It is *before*-light, *proto*-light. It coaxes you to follow visible proofs as evidence that phenomena are shells protecting truths. You see light, it speaks of radiance, but what is the intelligence in Radiance? You think a thought. It speaks of conscious-ness, but what is the inner *bright* of awareness? This practice is most available at the *sandhya,* the transition between day and night." He went on to describe the sublime qualities of time as moments slipped one into the other, changing their essential nature as they moved.

"THERE ARE TWO GATE-KEEPERS—the dark *behind* the dark holds the night and faces into it, never receiving one photon. *Savitur* faces the day, holds it in open arms while blackness falls on his back. They press together and yet never mix; absolute lightless meeting absolute darkless. *Viveka,* separates them. Discriminative intelligence splits the visible 'this' from the invisible 'that' with a razor so fine it fits between those denizens of the dawn without touching either."

He asked me, "How does one act in the presence of *Tat Savitur,* that unworldly source of every illumination?"

"*Varenyum,* I worship."

"And what is worship?"

"Reverence, bowing, ritual action, constant remembering," I said.

"But what is the *Savitur* of worship, the invisible radiance behind any reverent feeling?" he asked, pleading.

He would offer a richer answer. I waited. This was one of those moments between us when the teacher, the teaching, and the taught blurred together and we were no longer two. My ear and his voice belonged to one transcendent conductor.

"I stand before the absolute and prostrate," he said. "Listen closely. It is a symbolic action that celebrates the fixed distance between me and the unknowable. This ritual tells me I must recognize what is forever beyond me. Why is *tat savitur* a distance that can never be bridged?—because *becoming* aware is more important than *being* aware.

224

It is the boundary between *known* and *unknowable*. The meaning of what it is to be human speaks at the *sandhya*. The essence of your creature hood is forever *sandhya*—standing at the place where darkness meets light. Actions that are not worship are a waste."

I interrupted, "Please, let me be sure I grasp what you are saying. Awareness is like the pre-dawn potential for light. And *the desire to understand* is like the light itself. That seems backwards. Doesn't a person crave knowledge and then grow into awareness, in stages?"

"You heard me well," he said. "Awareness precedes the desire to comprehend, despite the seeming conundrum. You think, 'What would bring you to the City of Wisdom if not the road of knowledge?' It is not that way. You have to wake-up before you can learn anything.

"A mirror was inserted in the many-faceted mind. It allows self-awareness. We can either go mad, following the infinite reflections, or we can be aware of the phenomena—our minds are a mixture of illusions and truth. All of it is a flattened version of the Real. Knowledge, information, or even perceptions have nothing to do with Wisdom, which is above and beyond any of them.

"*Om* is the first step even before cracking a book. The ten-thousand things are only an excuse for a local-self to realize it is a thing of consciousness, a child of *Om*. The reflective nature of the human mind shouts-down animal instinct until panic breaks-in, then behold the beast! It is your responsibility to notice you are consciousness pasted onto an instinctive creature—an edge of divine light in your dark."

I asked, "Is it enough to meditate on the mantra at the break of dawn and the *sandhya* at evening? You said it teaches us from within, that it is alive. Am I missing your point?"

He replied, "Meditation and mantra practice is not a peaceful feeling or a conceptual high. It is settling into the Om-fire regardless of any smoke and fumes you have to endure. Flame may consume cleanly and efficiently, it may smolder, but the fire is the same and always burns away dross. Meditation without tapas-friction is a car without wheels—a smooth ride that goes nowhere. Imagine what gold might think as it experiences the refiner's fire, or rough wood—how the grain resists the craftsman's ministrations, how the material suffers. Fine millwork and a gleaming chalice are elegant testaments to partnerships in matter and diligence.

"Wake up, attend to the moment. That makes any time of day your *sandhya*. No matter what I have said, no matter what you have understood—relationship with Truth, Consciousness and Bliss is immediate, fresh, and alive. If I seem to have given you formulas for success, destroy them all! Be aware. Be awake. If Gayatri becomes a rusted tool, abandon it. She instructs in the ways of relationship and like a woman, she wilts if you neglect her living presence."

I felt particularly calm sitting with Vishwamitra in the aftermath of his pointed discourse. The silence tucked around me like a blanket.

Outside the window, children laughed and played in the street. Mental pictures of their games formed spontaneously. Was that a ball bouncing? Were their scuffles a race or game in the open street? What did I hear in their playful voices—jokes, challenges, or was it simply their joyful chirping at a new day?

The ambient noises were no different than the dance of words issued by the teacher. His sounds merged with theirs, an aural palette that comingled and yet conjured distinct snapshots of the moment. Pondering Gayatri was a nest—meanings wove a reassuring mat below while abstract concepts fanned-out as sheltering branches above. The single flame of awareness diffracted toward me in a dappled play of light and shadow, enticing me into spontaneous meditative attention.

Part V: Polestar

Smoke *by Vishwamithra*

Fear is smoke that obscures the fire of love,
Clinging is water thrown on your fuel.
The burn will be slow, painful and dirty.
Wet wood smolders and fumes.
You fight the billows to stoke the flame.
Noxious clouds bring on tears.
Vision stings and the smell ruins everything.

The fire is there somewhere
So be happy in spite of fear and worry—
They can only exist on love's account.

Moods change in the coming and the going.
Pain measures how tight we grip.
Hanker for the sun at noon
and morning will be anxious waiting.
Cling to that high point
and afternoon will bring on sad laments.
What would you say to a grief-stricken soul,
Waist deep in a stream,
Forlorn because the water flows by?

REVELATIONS

WHEN HE WAS IN THE ROLE of teacher, occupied with preparations like setting up the tea service, lighting incense or paging through some text or other, his lips moved with the bare hint of saying mantra to himself. His attention seemed to be elsewhere, so one might assume the session had not started. In fact, if I was there, we were engaged whether I understood the nature of it or not. He was sharply aware of everything around him, especially my state of mind while waiting. It was necessary to 'pinch myself' mentally and avoid 'spacing-out.' His lips moved now. Half of him was in shadow; half was illuminated by filtered rays from the early sun. He sat on a patch of thin carpet. One foot rested on a thigh, leg bent. The other stretched in front of him. Without stirring, he began the invocation. I followed where I could.

> "*Aum. Bhur bhuvah suvaha. Tat savitur varenyum.*
> *Bhargo devasya dhimahi. Dhiyo yonah prachodayat.*
> *May our bodies be protected. May our minds be protected. May our hearts and homes be protected. May She be present. May we dwell in Pranava. May we not quibble with each other. May our lessons be brilliant. May we save the world. May the rains fall and nurture the fields. May the gods smile upon creation. May all beings be happy and blessesd. Om*"

The room glowed soft and warm. Bird sounds and the neighbors' activities came in, carried on the cool morning breeze. During these moments before our lessons I had the opportunity to examine the surroundings, running a finger along the smooth stone floor or reading the spines of a few books he kept nearby. He cleared his voice in the manner that usually signaled a story.

"I want to tell you some things about mastery, desire, and layers of the phantasm we call, 'Life.' The middle of the story is Gayatri. Let's begin there and work forward and back. No one invented this mantra. It has no author. It is the pulse that interjoins all the various levels of the great creative dream into mutual responsiveness. This illusion-world that we move around in, talk into, and expect responses from is rich, organic and purposeful beyond any remote ability for a mind to grasp. Yet, grasp it will. You remember the situation with the two-dimensional beings we've discussed—those who dominate others, do so by truncating the truth that is inherent in matter, flattening the object of their desire. *Om* determines the interplay of things and sets right order between them. Consciousness is that *Om* as it meets creation. Altering or stifling the relationship of *Pranava* and any creature is vandalism."

He went on, "A self-conscious being, intoxicated by the illusion of free and independent action, disfigures absolute freedom by grasping at it. The spirit of one who grips is likewise distorted when they clutch at their sense of *I do this*. The gods, saturated with feelings of influence over what they consider lesser mortals, play this delusional power game and bring pain to everyone involved.

"The gods—it's good to know something about them. They mean no harm, but they are the source of almost all of it. And where do they live?—up there? And where is that? Where is *Mithra* of the dawn and friend of the well-placed, or *Varuna* who controls oceans and metes out justice? *Brihashpati, Yama, Aryaman,* and *Vayu,* or all the other ten thousand luminaries who take care of wind, rain, the days, the moon, the nights, an elbow joint, your hair follicles? Where do they live? What do they do? You can only guess. They control, but do not mix with the commoners, in a social spirit, anyway.

"You can be sure they determine every nuance of your second by second experience, including sleep, dreams, digestion, evacuation, and flatulence. They leave nothing unattended. Each and every one guards his realm and executes his duties with impassioned, territorial fervor. They fight. They step on each others' toes. They rob Peter to pay Paul. They bribe. They hire goons. They create a furor to keep the status quo running smoothly so their vast eons of time are spent giving the cosmic clock a little twist every now and then. They don't work that hard and when they are forced to, they all consider it a major catastrophe. You could not live without them and yet a heaven full of them is not worth a thimble of your consciousness. That is their world—their earthly footstool is the electric flux that runs you from tiny toe nail to facial fuzz.

"A proper priest is a tool of the gods as well as a pawn in the game of dynastic control—kings extend the gods' agenda onto the Earth. My soul-nature was a hybrid of the two. The priest in me took on kingly aspirations while the regal part of me had a yogi's temperament. You might think it would lead to internal conflicts to be a King by succession and a priest by disposition. In my case, royal bearing and ritual asceticism was an engine for accomplishing material conquest in spiritual worlds. I remain thirsty to husband the ethereal realms so they supply the infrastructure for human dharmic activity."

Vishwamithra looked toward the ceiling, raked all ten fingers across his scalp and clasped both hands there momentarily. "I can tell you, I once lived these things and will, once again. In fact, it is alive in me now," he said, releasing his grip to converse eye to eye. "My autonomy threatened Indra and his divine sycophants. They are skittish, having so much to lose. Being a god means being in control and likewise, controllers assume god-like airs. They are at the top of the food chain. They employ or deploy kings or priests as desired. Heaven-drenched autocrats avoid discomfort, which is the price of evolution, by casting a shroud of ignorance over everything under them—they call it *Indra's net*. That is how they answer to none but their own appetites.

"You might have heard that the so-called net is woven by CEO of gods, *Indra*, and those intricate geometries of intersecting chords with a fabulous diadem at each intersection adorn his palace on Mount Meru. The diamond vertices reflect one another infinitely in all directions, so the story goes, a dazzling structure of jewel nodes and lines that mirror one another endlessly—don't fall for it! They want you to give it to *Indra*, the universe, metaphor and the rest. I'll tell you what it is, flat-out—it is a mirror facing another mirror in your own head. *Indra's net*, the intricate cosmology of the universe, is your gray matter. *That* is the confounding web of godly origin. Let me walk you through it. All life is *sentient*—it feels—it is constructed of insentient elements, which are organized and animated. It was accomplished with a mirror, or gem, that transmits consciousness into matter like a diamond reflects light into the eye. It's DNA. To create a *self-conscious* realm, insert another mirror into the mind. The result is an infinite regress of images as the light bounces back and forth between the mirrors. The cumulative power of infinite reflections becomes a *sense of self*. Self-*awareness* recognizes the game. Humans are trapped inside the game of infinite reflection, unawareness, by design. If human beings could ignore the webbing, or at least identify one coherent strand and follow it out, ignoring the reflections, they could storm the gods. They would be hungry souls claiming their share of heaven—flesh and blood penitents confessing ignorance, staking claims on Godhead and conscripting righteous teachers. That is the last war, the holy war, the end of this meat market and the birth of meaning; the revelation of truth in radiant mind.

"I ruled Earth for eons, performed intense tapas for ten-thousand years. I built towers of spiritual pride so high than none could touch me—and sank in cold, dark hells below mortal reach. I was a wise cynic, thoroughly enlightened, with brilliant insight that only bittered from disuse. There is no *happy ending* in God's plan for men—it is nuclear fire, burning the center away until love falls into truth's arms. Their coitus is *Shiva's Tandava Dance*, the beginning and ending, the only noise worth hearing.

"I saw Him dance. His swirling matted locks are galaxies sweeping space near light speed. His ankle bells are super novas. His smile is the mouth of a baby, searching out a woman's breast, sucking empty space until it latches-on and is satisfied. Mahadeva locks eyes with a mere girl, the Earth-maiden and they fuse, creating in her the Cosmic Mother. Not even Indra, the celestial monarch, knows the beauty of this heavenly place called 'Earth.' God wants to be known. *Knowing* is the human way—by contrast, gods are *know-it-alls*.

"Despite my innate superiority, Indra and his clique would not have me in their club. Instead they sent damsels to seduce me—I am a man after all. They didn't bother with physical torture which would be useless since my diamond body had been long tempered through austerity. The lofty milestones I accomplished were turned into millstones through their intrigues. They dragged me subtly by stages into the mediocrity of pleasure and success.

"Emperors create false religions to ensnare the mystical temperament. They want to control the priestly core of creative power. I would have none of it—neither priestly hypocrisy nor the falderal of the palace. And it was revolting to see where iron will and holy perfection finally delivered me. Purity of intent, the holy *Om*—not rebellion—caused me to create my own universe, replete with a better leadership than Indra's neurotic pantheon. Living beings need options and I was well on my way to building a dharmic kingdom. The battle really starts with this—the gods are entrenched bureaucrats—and bureaucracy is bad for consciousness."

Vishwamithra's face was open, eyes intense, focusing on images beyond the ceiling and walls. One might wonder about his sanity, railing about esoteric scenes, so ethereal and fantastic. I did not. I had accepted his world as more real than the absurd arrangement of boxes and habits I inhabited. My story was one accident after another, his complied with demonstrable truth. I cherished these causal journeys.

He returned to insider hints about the brood in heaven, matter-of-factly saying, "The sum of their good deeds is a prison of red tape to consciousness. It actually blocks the power of *being*, which is your simple-awareness. I stared squarely into Indra's net, the trap of striving for control or holiness, and saw only a corpse. Pretensions in godhood are dead ends that I resolved to bury. You hold the wrist or neck to discover if blood is still moving in the patient, to see if it's a lost cause. The doctor's interest is proof of the pulse, the presence or absence of animating spirit. That was how I heard *Ma Gayatri*—cicadas at dusk, wind in a canyon, distant surf—*bhur, bhuvah, suvaha.*

"She is the refreshing antidote to the gods' control-grid debacle. My *righteous universe in the making* rests on a cosmic back-burner by mutual agreement. Though they can be difficult, the gods are immortal, so relative reality is stuck with them. The human race is not prepared for radical honesty—it would drive them mad. Until such time that I take up the task of world creation once again, *Gayatri Mantra* is the cosmic gate to a Godly Universe built solely of Truth and Love rather than the patently unfunny divine comedy you inherited by default."

HIS PLACID DEMEANOR RETURNED, as though nothing were said. He traced the edge of a paver with his finger, mirroring earlier motions I performed in reverie. The work he implied troubled me. I did not have the Mahayogi's intensity or his strength. Writing in my journal, taking in a cool morning and watching people in their routines buoyed me when I might have sunk. He described a struggle between life and death. "Burning out the center, so love and truth could unite," was a metaphysical drama way over my head. I didn't want to even think about it and yet the sage confronted me here. I stared out the window, avoiding his gaze. A mature cottonwood grew in the small dirt courtyard that protected his house from street activity. A concrete wall taller than a man wrapped the intimate enclosure and buffered us from the hubbub which could blare into chaos at certain times. The tree trunk rose straight up, branching-out beyond walls and over rooftops. Crows perched there and heckled each other. They used it as a base to raid the carts of fruit vendors or passersby in the busy lane. Cawing, wing flaps, the play of light on surfaces, smells in the air, an intimate conversation, the strength of a wall to shelter and yet allow the city to enter, an ink pen in hand, drawing a line, writing a word—realizing the vulnerability of these pleasures made me sad.

"Sage, isn't life—the beauty around us enough? Do we have to turn up the heat? Don't ever to go—these days should never end! Let me

233

hold onto these simple pleasures at least. Can I say the mantra and avoid drama, tragedy, bullies, and my own mistakes? Surely, there are allowances for good intention. You have the heroic fiber—in practice I'm mediocre, half-baked and afraid of being steam rolled by the kind of purifications you allude to."

"Here's a cheap trick—you need a talisman," he said, raising an eyebrow toward me. He felt inside one pocket, then the other and clasped something in his fist. "A fakir living in a cave outside of Katmandu used these in his practices." He offered me a strand of seeds that had been threaded by hand—a simply-crafted, well-worn japa mala.

He continued, "The man's wife had died. He was so distraught, I sent him into the mountains to meditate. A villager charged with his mundane needs looked in on him one day and saw a very small being, about the size of a loaf of bread, sitting in meditative posture on a pallet in the fakir's hut. Startled, the well-wisher ran away. Later that week a rainbow appeared over the hermitage. The villager brought me this rosary which he found on the cot next to a sack cloth the penitent had worn. No one ever saw him again. They say it was his spiritual attainment. Keep this. Use it. Be prepared to give it back to the old guy if he ever returns. I doubt that he will. Hold those beads—they won't let you down."

He went on, "'How is that?' you might wonder. They are a metaphor for an innate power that can never fail you. Perceptions become feelings which stimulate thoughts that lead to actions in the circle of life," he said. "Neither sleep nor death can end that cycle if you remember the connecting thread—consciousness. It does not belong to you. On the contrary, you belong to it. It chose you. It is not fickle, so it will never let you go."

I could listen to him indefinitely. "Your fear is like smoke that rises off a fire. The fire is love," he said. "Accept the telltale sign that it has ignited and let it burn cleaner. Wet fuel causes smoldering, fumes and is obnoxious to everyone. Even if smoke obliterates everything else, you know the flame is there somewhere. With that knowledge you can be happy in spite of fear and worry. We both know that things come and go, even the mood outside changes from moment to moment. The wetness in the fuel is sentimentality and emotionality, which are other words for clinging and attachment. The intensity of the pain caused by change depends on how tightly we hold on. If, for example, you grasp at the noonday sun, clearly, the morning will be all anxious expectation and afternoon will be regretful lamentation. What would you say to someone waist deep in a stream, lamenting because they could not hold onto the flowing water?" He waited for my reply to the absurd scenario.

I said, "My first thought would be that they had gone mad. If I had to counsel such a wretch I would say, 'What you want is impossible. If you had a bucket the size of a lake you could not stop the water from flowing or possess the stream. Flowing water cleanses the land and nurtures every life form.' I'd sit by them, talk, and appreciate the river together. We could throw twigs and watch them drift downstream."

"Grasping at the impossible doesn't have to be a neurosis," he added. "It can be a ritual practice that ultimately makes neurosis useful. Spend the time before high noon in happy anticipation. Use the falling sun to reflect on cycles of time. And what is swimming but the stylized ownership of water? Think of those lunatics that dedicate their life to crossing ocean channels, climbing frozen peaks or shooting for the stars. Those are nothing but religious rituals infected with an ego that says, 'Look what I did!' instead of saying in honest humility, 'I bow to you and offer myself. You are the greater.' Such is life—worship, meditate, and pray! I understand not wanting to lose something you have grown to appreciate. Platitudes don't help when the things we love are pulled away. Arid neutrality is no solution—it becomes a form of necromancy, an embrace of endings, missing the beauty of the gift. You want practical reassurance. I will give it."

He held his own strand in his palm. Like a jeweler displaying a gem, he delicately suspended the first bead between the index and middle finger as he spoke. "Repeat the formula, ponder the meanings, and become the mantra." He stroked the reddish globes one at a time, demonstrating how his active forefinger caused individual beads to flow away from him or toward him over the stationary digit. "Let it replace as many vagrant thoughts as possible," he said. "Let your daily routines be a vigilant pruning of useless mind-stuff. Return to the polestar again and again—

Om
Bhur bhuvah suvaha,
Tat savitur varenyum,
Bhargo devasya dhimahi,
Dhiyoyonah prachodayat

—that is the pulse of life. It cuts through smoke and moodiness," he told me. "It exposes the fire, your own inner heat. The smoke can and

235

will overwhelm. Even so, say the mantra."

He squinted and continued the advice, "Say it in panic—hold to it like you are grasping the mane of a wild horse. It might be like the lifeless body of your own child—stare into the precious face of Gayatri even when you are at once gored by pain and gripped by love. Let the broken tethers of your mind flap uselessly while you make empty repetitions, spinning blind in confusion. Ride, and let *it* keep you, if you can believe it. This is sadhana," he said.

The discourse continued in a torrent.

"Practice is the only way.

"*Familiarize yourself with the exits*, they warn on the plane. Why wait for a bomb threat to learn your way around the building? It reduces the experience to random chance.

"Vigilance for repeating the mantra and knowing its meanings will turn random chance into divine intervention. Practice increases the likelihood of a lucky break, avoiding the tragedy, transforming chaos into something useful. Luck is on the fringe of skillful means— increasing your skill will expand the likelihood of good fortune."

He sat forward, stared in a dramatic pause and suggested, "The Gayatri Mantra, said with attention, charges and organizes subtle material, the thought space around you—I will go even further."

With pursed lips and focus narrowed toward me, he continued slowly, "While you broadcast your three lines of eight syllables into the ethers, you affect the future in your present. The plane engine will *not* fail—problems *will* be caught in advance—or the whole thing could be a delayed and you'd miss it entirely. Attaching to the mantra is clinging to the *Savitur*. Your Karma has to happen, no doubt. Even so, cause and effect can operate more cleanly and burn completely. That is the way to avoid pain, the smoke that outgases from soggy fuel in the form of fantastic, useless, or untrue thoughts. Is it magic? Yes. But it is the natural magic allowed for the ones who have agreed to save the Earth." That was how our meeting ended. I would appreciate his prescience later on.

UNHOOKED

For some weeks I had been waking near the dawn transition, *sandhya*, to repeat the mantra. When the alarm sounded, my hand felt for the japa mala he gave me, the threaded *Rudraksha* seeds that had become my companion. Lying on my back in the still dark, I held them in a fist over my heart and repeated *Aum*. That syllable alone could have been enough. The primal expressions *ah, oh, um*, the feel of the beads rubbing against one another and yet firmly bound by a thread was a harbinger of blessing, a comfort embossed on my mind.

It was common for me to wake-up with negative thought—*Om* reassured me that life was new, it was there for me, and its essence was good. Then I did three repetitions—five lines, thirteen words, and three strategies—sometimes contemplating the meanings, sometimes not. Analytic methods helped me peel-apart the contents of my mind. Taking extra time to lay-out the objects, energies and ultimate directions of my thinking in the light of Gayatri prescriptions didn't impose on my schedule. I spent less time wandering aimlessly, which seemed to create time.

I opened my computer as usual to check mail. The plan was to take care of miscellaneous errands that had pile up. I logged-in but could get no further. A system message over-rode efforts to get past. White letters on a black screen might be an irritating sign of a virus or hard-drive issue. This was worse.

> "Your area is under a level orange security advisory. Enter your Personal Binary Code for specific area instructions. You will then proceed to one of the locations listed below. An orange alert is issued when there is a high probability of threats to life safety from one or more points of origin. Local and national law enforcement requests your cooperation by following public service instructions carefully. Thank you."

A cursor pulsed inside an orange rectangle waiting for my citizen identification number. Below it, three locations were listed as check points. There was a long description of available services and supplies that the shelter would have on hand. The time-span was vague but emphasized that authorities were clearing possible sources of threat as quickly as possible. There would be full internet and cell connectivity at the refuge nodes, something that they managed to block, in my neighborhood anyway. I had never seen anything like it. I paced the room for maybe half an hour, frequently rechecking the screen between orbits. It still might be a virus. I could check the radio.

Sitting in a corner of the kitchen, away from windows, spinning the dial, I was not relieved to hear mostly the test signal. The high-pitched, honking oscillation associated with nuclear war or violent storms played across most of the dial. A human voice broke-in when I found the local station. An emotionless public service announcement interrupted banter about the weather and regional trivia. The message offered more or less the same reasonless, terse instructions as my lame computer's "black screen of death," but the sound of a human voice calmed me. The reassuring sound told me I was not alone—when a quick glance out the window indicated I was.

Since meeting Vishwamithra Gayatri Mantra had become a lens through which events had coherence, beyond superficial narratives offered by media as fact. Something stank. Why? The tacit order to file into a local shelter for an uncertain amount of time did not connect to any prior information. It did not make sense. Persistent crime, violence, war, economic insecurity and the disaster *du jour* angered and frustrated me before using *bhur-bhuvah-suvaha*, and the three strategies of the mantra. The assumption that society's best hope was in full-access to mediated cues for sighing and crying had unraveled. Gayatri revealed a joyful core inside tears, and that truth squeezed through the edited facts. Strategic mantra analysis suggested skillful actions in place of collective hand-wringing. My confidence in a social-political machine that would tend any particular need was gone. Faith in humanity itself had increased tenfold—human persons had beauty, depth and a holy potential to see every molecule through God's eyes. Mechanisms of wealth and control were not human. This was the rub—I loved being human.

The naked instructions imposed on my computer came from no "hand." At best it was an innocuous public bulletin. At worst it was a contrivance. I wanted more information before committing myself, mindlessly. There were risks if I did not reply to the pulsing rectangle. Beads rolled between my fingers while I paced the room. *Don't be paranoid. It's what's on the plate,* I said to myself. I typed my numbers into the space provided on the emergency screen display. My finger hovered over "send." A subtle tap would send word I was up and running. This brand of anxiety was unfamiliar. Clenching the beads I said mantra under my breath, hesitating. On second thought, the feeling was like a time in grade school I was sent to the office. My ten year old self struggled to keep from urinating at the mere thought of a scolding by the head prefect. The visit was brief—they asked me a few questions and sent me back to class. There were no punishments. It was only years later I learned it was because of unusual scores on an intelligence test. Maybe this current situation was set up to check my Intuition Quotient.

I closed the computer and put on the japa mala as a protective necklace. By now there was movement outside that complied with the screen request I resisted. There was a general exodus toward the school, mostly on foot. People carried children and overnight bags in a grim parade. My decision to ride this one out, created peace—*Om, Om, Om.* Was this a drill? Maybe it was some real thing. It didn't seem like a real thing. Then again, kinks in the chain of expectations created anxiety, or panic. What about me? I was afraid. That was no reason to act. The ominous screen gave only the vaguest explanation. Were reasons necessary? Did I trust the liquid crystal display to give me good advice? The Yoga Sutras said there were three ways to get good information: *direct perception with clear faculties, inference using reliable precedent, and reliance on scripture or a sage.* Did the screen qualify as one of these true sources?

Why didn't I trust it? If it was an elaborate security drill, I would rather not be a lab rat. If it was real, what did that mean?—bomb threat?—terror attack? Why not say? Governments were not altruistic, regardless of what press releases implied. Ancient sages didn't mention *political apparatus* as a source of wise advice—and I was too shaken to believe my own eyes. That left Vishwamithra. He lived a couple of miles away. Could I get there without looking suspicious?

I couldn't imagine him checking in at the local grammar school and filing into the basement with a crowd of others, each one clutching their little care package. What would he do? It seemed like he would avoid the whole situation. Most people do what they are told, especially if "safety" is involved. The patient cursor waited for the only answer it understood. Would I be safer there in the basement of a building I had never been in, with people I didn't know, under circumstances I didn't understand? Should I assume that would be wise advice? At this point, the grammar school was less desirable than taking my chances. Was this an authority problem? After all, what was the sage?—he was an authority. Was it a mistake to trust my own shaky judgment rather than paid authorities? They neither decided things nor judged the situation. They only passed instructions from one desk to another. I would go to Vishwamithra.

The task was to stay out of the dragnet of police and guardsmen. There weren't that many. I abandoned the laptop which was reduced to a one-answer box, stuffed a jacket, nuts, raisins, and a bottle of water in the pack and headed-out on my bike. Breathing deep at the back gate of my apartment complex, the plan was to cut across some alleys to the levee. It had an overgrown path that kids for walking to school which ran alongside wetlands. If somebody stopped me I'd say my dog was loose. This would take me near the back of his dwelling.

There was a gravel parking lot between me and my immediate goal. A pair of policemen talked between two taller buildings. The armed, black-clad law-enforcers went door to door, clearing out stragglers with gentle, insistent reminders. My anus twitched; maybe I was in over my head. Authority problem or not, getting arrested would not be good. Somebody told me *people leave you alone if know what you are doing, so act like it.* I found that to be true and summoned some control. *After all, it's a free country.* Uniforms went out of sight. I gave them some time to go the opposite direction from mine, swung the gate enough to clear the handlebars, eased into the open, and talked under my breath, "Hmmm, where did they say that safe-zone was, anyway?" Peddling like a "man on a mission," I passed through the clearing, into the rutted lane. Minus trash cans, busted window frames, and a couple of rusted cars, it was a scenic byway that led to Vishwamithra's.

I stopped at a three way intersection where the alley met the road. A low hill blocked my view beyond the street. Past the berm, the weedy grade fell-off toward a thin waterway and rambling path that ran through scrub trees, the last leg of my trip. Yellow warning tape marked the neighborhood blocks as "off-limits." This section looked abandoned. I walked the bike forward.

"Sir!" a sharp voice shocked me from behind. "This area is secure. Where are you headed?"

The contents of my body pushed for an exit. I felt faint, end of game. Touching beads that draped over my chest, I turned with deliberation, casually as possible, given the sudden load on my sphincter muscle and looked at him. Maybe half a head shorter than me, sunglasses, bulletproof vest, he had a black pipe-shaped firearm with arched clip and shoulder brace at the ready. His boots were shiny, with black metal toes. He stood with feet angled at ninety degrees to each other, *like a ballerina,* I thought—curious, considering my predicament. A leather baton dangled from his belt and an electronic clipboard attached at his hip.

"I made it all the way to Sector D Middle School and forgot my laptop. I'm in the right direction aren't I? Right there, down the street?" appealing to the helpful public defender in him.

He responded, "Yes sir. What's your name?" I told him. He checked his board. "We've already sealed your unit. It's a federal offense to go back home. Are you aware of that?"

"I saw that. Will we be Ok? I mean, how serious is the danger?"

"All I know is what I'm doing." he replied. "They'll take your name and clear you when you get to collection point D."

I mounted my bike and rode down the street toward the shelter. The back of my head buzzed as he stared. Luckily there was a turn that took me out of his view. I found an alcove and breathed again. Now I was officially dodging the law. "Nothing wrong with checking on an old man in these troubled times," I invented my alibi, and rerouted toward the creek bed, eager to get passed the pavement. Bike in hand; I gladly ducked down the hill toward scrubby woods.

"This must be how animals feel," I muttered. "*Get me away from these people!* We destroyed all their hiding places, and then don't want them around." Talking to myself, relieved tension. "Things that want privacy are out of luck these days," I complained to no one while keeping an eye-out for passable shelter among the shrubs. The bicycle bumped along the rutted footpath, hidden in vegetation and below site lines from inhabited areas. Gayatri, I had been chanting in a distracted way since leaving my place. It was a good chance to recover my wits and savor the lines before finding the whereabouts of my teacher.

"*Om,* all is well, all is well, all is completely well—*Bhur,* the stuff going on, the people, the places—*Bhuvah,* my reactions, my stormy emotions, my fears—*Suvaha,* everything resolves into the original intended order," I counseled myself under breath.

"*Tat Savitur Varenyum,*" I continued. "This danger, imposition, or manipulation, is worthy of worship. It's got unseen roots that go beyond the obvious."

My mind raced, but the sense of panic had burned off.

I said the second line, "*Bhargo devasya dhimahi,* fear blocks the ability to understanding anything. It results in quick decisions just to avoid stress. *Meditate,* I will comb through every part of this situation."

"*Dhiyo yonah prachodayat*," repeated quietly, and brought peace that I could feel. "It's all beyond me, let it go, notice the nuances and send it to the source that brought these events into my experience in the first place. What do I know?—nothing. Hide like the scared creature you are and wait, then find Vishwamithra." The brush was good enough for taking stock and avoiding another encounter with the law. There was a hollow in the vegetation that looked like it had some tradition— cigarette butts, beer cans, a few gin bottles. Flat, knotted blankets stuck to the ground. I crawled in on all fours and got comfortable. A squirrel watched with some interest. "Who is the new neighbor?" it seemed to say.

"I'm not here for long," I answered his implied question. "Then again, you may feel the same way about it." He flicked his tail and shot up the tree, continuing to monitor my activities.

No police in sight and distance from dangerous announcements comforted me. The surroundings were grungy at first. They improved steadily with passing moments. I decided to stay until the sun was low. That would be in a couple of hours.

CONCUSSION

THE ABANDONED SHEET AND thick blanket had been rained on a few times. Stiff and dirty, but not mildewed, they formed a solid block of wrinkles. I had to pry them apart, mash-out molded, twisted folds and give it a few hard shakes, careful to stay contained in case of nearby officials. The bed-spread had an angular pattern on one side and brown stain rings on the lining that had been in contact with bare soil. The neutral face made an acceptable gray-cream mat. The lime colored sheet got folded and placed to the side.

Cross-legged, in stocking feet, I ate and surveyed my new venue. Twisting back a couple of saplings gave enough head room to sit up straight. I pulled the beads from around my neck. The talisman in my hand was a gateway, a potential. Each rudraksha seed contained a mantra, offering more than any laptop or safety advisory.

It was a line to Vishwamitra, my teacher, now... somewhere. I doubted that he was still in his apartment. I tried to imagine him "going along" with drills, real or not—it wouldn't happen. Thinking of him brought Gayatri back into focus. That's what he would have me do, establish a thought strand to the wisdom source that gave the mantra its potency, the *Om, Pranava,* me, somehow.

"*Bhur, bhuvah, suvaha*"—laying back was easier, dead leaves and ground cover provided a natural cushion, the leggy shrub formed a canopy, and above that was another, created by leafy tree limbs.

"*Tat savitur varenyum*"—I could be grateful for these unnerving events—in a real way, they wove this sanctuary around me. There was some food, water, quiet. This shelter could be *Adi Sesha,* the Primordial Snake that formed a hood over Vishnu, the Hindu god, at rest on his Ocean of Consciousness. Resting deeper, the texture of the beads played against my fingertips.

"*Bhargo devasya dhimahi*"—I analyzed the circumstances that led to an unlikely resting place. The police did their jobs, I did mine. They might need to kick or shoot someone in the name of protection. That should be avoided—can it?

"*Dhiyo yonah, prachodayat*"—If I had faith, it had to be in a world of purposeful resolution. I saw no meaning in the school basement or gymnasium, whatever scene was happening over there, not far from here.

Dhiyo—this was mind-stuff, delivered into my life by mysterious processes.

Yonah—it was mine all mine, to move toward the One who could deal with mystery in an effective way.

Prachodayat—nestled among the undergrowth I stared up through a filigree of tiny limbs brushing softly against one another, responding to the late afternoon breeze. I sought out that One, transfixed by the bare rhythmic motion of light shafts feeling their way through layers of green to rest on my eyes. Half-formed ideas tumbled over one another and I dozed.

I DREAMED THAT A gang of hooligans stood around my bicycle. I wanted to ride it but was afraid. There was no option, I walked toward them, braced myself for trouble, but there was none. They stepped back, seemed younger. Then they were like children. I told them about the bike, described the gears and brakes. They touched it and wandered away, distracted. The scene shifted.

On a beach, a steel gray sky and glassy, crystalline ocean; waves broke the surface more like facets than liquid. I was mesmerized. A woman approached from the side. She asked, "What do you see?" I saw that this was the skin of an immense creature, the undulating surface was reptilian; it started to stand. Its movement stopped and then blew apart.

An explosion caused me to bolt upright, breathing hard. I did not know where I was and pawed at leggy shoots that raked across my face. The air was thick and dark with a metallic cast. I just managed to orient myself and recall the events of the day before.

Another concussion reverberated through the dense pall. It was a deep blast of physical pressure, pushing at ear drums like balloons inflating into my brain and convulsing my chest cavity. The sensation had barely registered and the sky flashed white, a full second of silence, followed by a wave of sound and force deafening enough to register as

244

yellow sparks in my brain.

I felt thrown, but had not moved. Time-sense and physical space seemed upended—like stuff in a box, shaken hard against the sides and things came to rest in piles. Trees bent, leaves roared in an artificial wind. In no words I thought, *the end, they have done it,* and felt the calm of prey, dragged down from behind, prepared, void, dry.

I kept my eyes closed. I did not want to see what might have happened to my body, the damage. Thinking rattled, certain this was hell, delivered by those soulless creatures in the shadows, I went still, as though any slight motion would sever my tenuous contact with reality. My head throbbed. Inching a forefinger toward my ear to feel for blood, they were chiming, hissing, and dry.

I worked the encrusted blanket around me into a cocoon, lay on my side in a ball, pushed hands into jacket pockets and absently felt the bits of stuff that had accumulated there. There was a loose thread. No—a memory—it was a twisted blade of grass, wilted, shriveled, still green—Sita's defense given to me by Vishwamithra.

Lying there, I pressed the grass and beads together, moistened by my sweaty palm. Face buried in the comforting, stale smell of the blanket, I cried. Wracking started behind the ribs, breaking up the armored muscles that tensed against the assault. Forced repetitions of the mantra rafted my anxiety past waves of confusion while I waited.

There were no more explosions. The sobs were choked back; they rattled my frame while stifling any noise that might disturb the beast. Comforted in a fetal position, I abandoned myself to the gods, to superstition, called on Om, on any god, asked Sesha to protect me and begged them to guard me, the ones I loved—a world of people who would not ever know why bombs dropped on them or why their bodies, lives, or children were crushed for no reason. The dark woods were a shroud and petitions carried me to sleep.

It was pitch black when I woke. My body seemed whole. The cool air smelled burnt. Tenuous movements met no obstruction and registered no pain. I crawled out, uncurled to stand, stretched and pressed the grass and beads back into my pocket. It was hard to see my hand moving just inches from my face. The first man on Earth, I walked gingerly toward the path.

The stars looked like they were about to fall out of the sky—as though the explosions blew away every shred of haze along with the electrical grid, allowing stars, planets, and constellations a rare cameo appearance. Trees and building parapets were lightless cut-outs against shimmering nebula. The cool silence was amplified by distant, indiscernible voices.

My fear was gone. I mounted the hillock to a row of buildings that had become featureless blocks against the stellar glow. I navigated toward the sage's dwelling, ambling toward the huge cottonwood in his courtyard—its familiar canopy silhouetted against the Milky Way.

The wooden gate would only open a few inches. Mounded debris made objection as I pushed into the walled enclosure. Virtually silent, I maneuvered over broken tile and glass at a glacial pace. Going forward as though testing thin ice my mood soared: to be at the place where we sat, anticipating the single flame of an oil lamp and holding the sacred books if they were still there. This was his temple, my sanitarium.

Vigilance was essential, some uniform or other would have to fulfill the obligation of the uniform. I made myself invisible, weightless, small, and lowered my upper body through blown-out windows, both hands finding the floor. My bulk pressed into fleshy palms on shards and broken mullions. Knees and then feet cleared the sill until I finally stepped down without disturbing anything but dust. No one could see in. Walking to the other end of the unit, I stood unprotected in front of the window and faced the garden off the street. There was no movement in this section of town. Satisfied that this zone was cordoned off, that I was alone, I felt along the wall to his altar.

Touch revealed a sheaf of prayers, butter lamps, Ganesh, and a box of matches. The sulfur-tipped stick flared with one strike, the cotton wick lit easily and there was vision. It was as we had left it. A drape pulled carefully across the fractured window would obscure my presence to anyone who might see. I wove a path through the damage to where we had spent hours in discourse, and sat in my place.

Bhargo devasya dhimahi—how many times had he warned me against the urge to jump up and do something, to solve problems, to give in to restlessness or fears? That was never a reason to act. I stifled the impulse to flee the spot before being seen. Action—what was it? I didn't decide to breathe, eat, or drop a hot match. There was a world of accomplishment without forced motion or blind reflexes.

The sage lived in that realm. He acted all the time and it was never in reaction. He was free. I wanted that freedom. Withdrawn into those thoughts, hidden inside the cubic inches of space my body occupied, stillness descended. No one would find me. There was nothing to find. In that state I returned to the ghosts of the guru's lessons. They lingered, saturating the walls. Even if his building had been obliterated, the truth structure he built would remain, unaffected.

The scattered remnants of a chaotic force lay around me, a thin veil that failed to obscure Vishwamithra's presence from me. My spirit rose as calm joy, at the opportunities presented here. There was gratitude for the teacher, the teaching, and the tradition. I said the mantra like savoring a delicacy. Each word was a morsel held on my tongue, releasing its unique bouquet of flavors.

Tat savitur varenyum—There was every reason to worship. The *Savitur* radiated even behind jack boots and weapons, behind explosions, ignorance, and the rest of the coarse, dull skin that held life's nectar. Attacking or dreading the covering of a fruit made no sense. If you wanted to eat, peel off the husk and throw it away.

Tat—the word was nectar. *Tat, tat, tat*, so simple. It was a syllable that told me, "I do not *have* a meaning—I am meaning itself." *That* summarized the full, proper name for God.

Human lips could not form a better word than *That* to describe God, the original conscious impulse. Personalize it, give it clothes, a location, a time, or a task and always, *He, She, or It* came back to *That*. The malleable, miserable, or magnificent world was in the end, mute. Truth began where words, descriptions and plans left off.

Bhargo devasya—Events lit my neurons like a fire. Their glowing coals shimmered in the aftermath. *Dhimahi*—I watched them without stirring the flames or quenching their heat.

Dhiyo yonah prachodayat was my prayer—

Let me receive consciousness; clear and clean, rushing around and over the world's jagged rocks. Let my practice be a flood that wears the world's evils smooth. Allow every scheming mind to froth and burst like a bubble into your rush of bright awakeness.

Ganga the goddess-presider of rivers gave the lesson—master the tests and trials of the world by flowing, flowing, flowing, bringing life to dry plains, and constantly returning to the Source.

> *Om*
> *Bhur bhuvah suvaha*
> *Tat Savitur Varenyum*
> *Bhargo devasya dhimahi*
> *Dhiyo yonah prachodayat*
> *Om shanti shanti shantihi.*

The World is Full, *by Vishwamithra*

The world of wonder is full.
Birds migrate unerringly,
Tides ebb and flow perfectly.
Plans, maps and compass,
There are none—
Who plans the perfect movement?

You and I and everyone we know or ever knew
  are a constant chorus of Om in so many forms.
The wild flux of hopes and dreams is longing,
  sung by every molecule.
The panorama of Om unveils itself as beauty everywhere
If we have the eyes to see—
And every eye craves the vision.

SEEKING

BLACKNESS LIFTED, MAKING WAY for the radiant dark. There was still time to move without being visible. Holding to a contemplative mood, I packed the brass vessels, his hand-bound book of Sanskrit verses, and whatever food he left behind: dried biscuits, fruit, and candy he called *sweetmeats*. At the rear window I faced into his apartment, pressed palms together, bowed, and left the way I came, maybe for the last time.

Curious to find out what happened in my neighborhood, I backtracked along the overgrown trail, scrambled to the T-junction and took a long look down what had been my street. Nothing was there. It was hard to tell how much was gone because any possible anchors were also flattened without a trace—no three story flats, no time-worn tenement structures, only the sobering sight of a smoldering plain. My refuge in the wooded scrub was now *home*.

A neighborhood and the memory that hung there was a vacuum. What had been my residence was an arbitrary point, floating in a now-empty lunar landscape. Dream overlapped fact and I was left with his teaching and those verses. They remained. Material shattered. Which was real? Between Gayatri and the social hive, which was stronger? I clasped the beads through my shirt and felt something slip. I could not tell how much of me had ever been alive if history was so easily erased.

A faint glow on the horizon silhouetted tree trunks and pierced through foliage. Pedaling minimal rotations, my story rolled forward on no axle, uprooted, light, and cored out. The footpath was a depression between weedy clumps to either side. I meandered to the sapling fortress, my vegetable bungalow. The squirrel came halfway down the trunk in greeting. Upon seeing him, a rush of intimate feeling startled me out of a fugue.

"I have to go," I said. Its tail twitched and nose felt the air. "He who hesitates is lost. Strike while the iron is hot. God watches out for fools and drunks—the rest of us are on our own." I whispered while the attentive rodent listened. "I might be back, but this is a little too close to the action," I said under my breath. He understood better than me what to do when the nest gets plowed over. The daypack had plenty of space for my stuff and the few things from Vishwamithra's.

"Bye, I'll check on you soon," and blew a kiss. At that moment the furry acquaintance was my comrade. I rode further on the path in breaking light, checking intently over both shoulders until the way was clear and beyond any residences.

I remembered the undeveloped buffer between the town and perimeter fields, the place where my cousin and I ventured on rare summer afternoons. My only alternative was such a sentimental refuge. In twelve years, anything could have happened to it—ironic that my best bet for safety was a wisp of momentary feeling by a kid who existed in my head, a child that did not age. I didn't know what to do but dig backwards for safety, while forging ahead. Dirt paths eventually turned into grasses pressed flat until there was no clear trail. If you walked-on toward an oak hammock, there was a creek that opened into shallow water and gravel expanses. It would provide sheltered vistas down railroad tracks toward a distant two lane highway and more importantly, an objective view of the place I just left.

My recollection was accurate. It was an oasis, a grove, a sanctuary past human traffic. There was a tended-quality, lacking overgrown wildness and random litter. I leaned my bike against a sturdy tree trunk. Stout branches twisted out and up from just above head height, splaying to form an organic symmetry of foliage. Acorns lay all around. I used my shoes as an *asan*, a seat to avoid sitting on rocks and sticks.

This was an upgrade from the bush-hut by the levee. A cool snap in the morning breeze was refreshing. Real clouds amidst remnants of smoke made me happy. I felt clean. There was enough food for three lean days and the nearby stream was adequate for washing. It would afford time for assessing my circumstances. For now it worked. I leaned my back against the trunk and intoned *Aum*.

When in doubt say *Om*, long and loud. It curled around my battered eardrums with fingers that caressed the insides of my head. Last night's explosion obliterated thought. It felt like rape, brute force that screamed me down to a cowering ball.

The sound of *Om* was the opposite. It invited my smallness into largeness. Thought ceased in *Om*, but was not crushed. It matured— flowering and fruiting into quiet. I would need more than the *Pranava* or even Gayatri to get by...but maybe not. How could I know if I didn't do the experiment? When would be a better time? I bargained for this when I dumped my computer and ignored the public service announcements. I commenced saying the mantra in a conversational voice, singing it on some repetitions. Then quiet again, except for some robins blustering about their nest and the ocean-like sounds of leaves as they brushed one another during warm gusts. The ground heated in the rising sun. *I'll make tea,* I said to no one. *That is civilizing.*

Having arranged four sticks in a square, I placed a small pyramid of tinder inside. The inner structure would ignite easily, spread, and burn the bigger branches in a sequence from tiny to large. The bicycle and pack arranged as effective windbreaks. One paper match and one strike began the wood pile burning. I set out my cup with a tea bag from the stash of goods in my pack.

Where are you? I thought as I imagined meeting him again, discussing the *Savitur,* hidden in all things.

Bubbles covered the bottom of the pan as water was about to boil. I hesitated before pouring and set out another place. His tannin-stained, porcelain cup was among the things from his apartment. The familiar memento connected me to him and conjured his subtle ways, how he sipped or rested it on a thigh. I poured tea for us both.

Steeping spices wafted into the air with aromas of cardamom and cinnamon. My chest hurt for something solid, as old insecurities met the familiar perfumed scent. My mind's eye saw him preparing for our lesson, and I spoke-out loudly, "Swami Vishwamithraji, where are you?" Woven into the sound of rustling grasses and the hum in my brain I heard, "I'm here, let me finish my prayers"—words scattered among chirping birds and the voice of wind in the trees.

The hallucination was welcome and comforted me. Shocking jolts from last evening were grim reality. I closed my eyes, tracing back to memories of our conversations held in dimly lit mornings. Every perception was only a symbol of an ultimate design, gifts offered by the brain to a self, hungry for experience.

Illusions all around overpowered my mind and senses—convincing me they were real. He did not fall for it. He was acutely aware of the things around him and they had no power to distract him from their inner reality. Tree bark dug pleasantly into the skin of my back through a thin cotton shirt. I looked in the direction of the town while imaginings swirled about what actually happened and the things set in motion. Leaning into the sharp woody texture gave me gratitude for sensation, perception and waking dreams.

From above I heard, "Watch out, I'm on my way." A thick knotted rope let down the trunk and bumped my shoulder. Torn between astonishment and alarm, a sickening possibility crossed my mind—I might have been hurt worse than I thought. Maybe it was brain-damage. Maybe I had actually died.

Sandaled feet scuffled against the trunk, careful to avoid me. The sage stood there, brushing at leaves and dust that clung to his clothes, magically transported down his hemp stair from above. I looked at him blankly with no basis to understand what this was—metaphysical symptom, or crossed wires in an addled brain. I wobbled to my feet.

He said, "This is a surprise. You have taken the time and trouble to make tea. Why come out here of all places?"

The Tibetans had a term *bardo*, which described the intermediate state between births. He might be an aspect of *the clear light of consciousness*, ushering me through a death sequence. I looked for cues. There was no sure way to tell fantasy from projected memory. My own subjective sense was all that might tell hallucinations from fact.

He gathered handfuls of long dry grass to create a loose pillow. In a smooth motion he sat down, reached for the steeping cup, and gestured that I do the same. I sat opposite, unsure of the nature of this experience. Earlier, when the concussion burst in my ear...it had also been dreamlike, an absence of other people...I might indeed be dead. The thought was disturbing and peaceful. The worst would be behind me. All my dramas would be over. He had the same mannerisms and smile. It was him, no doubt. Had he died also? I hoped it was him. Morbid as that might seem, it would be the best luck.

"What good are ants without a picnic?" he sang in a spirited mood while settling-in. "Refresh my memory—where did we leave off."

"Yes, here we are...What are you asking? What do you mean?"

"I left you with an idea that needs more clarity—order does not come from chaos. Order reveals the nothingness of chaos. It is not accurate to say, 'Order is more powerful than chaos,' because chaos has no power at all," his matter-of-fact line of reason continued.

"Chaos, disorder, pain, trouble—the form of evil does not matter, they are utterly powerless. Each exists as a discourse on Discipline and Order. You might wonder how that would work. Use a favorite form of difficulty—pain for instance."

I was glad to let this discourse run, still doubtful about its fabric.

He said, "A person in pain will not argue for its virtues. Pain sucks you in and proves your unworthiness. The god of pain demands worship—and gets it. One cannot ignore the least discomfort. Is it even a good idea to try and overlook pain? Pain is nothing but a demand for painlessness. Agony is a black mass for a false god, a 'nothing' that has been enshrined on an altar of fear. Bow, genuflect, offer food, make incantations, form institutions around it—pray. The false god cannot hear or respond to rivers of tears, much less, a half-baked appeal because there is nothing there. Instead, attend to all the sensations of pain and suffering—become aware—and you will detect something in the void of meaning. Echoes of something real resonate in that hollow—it is a call to discipline and order. Inquiry is the first doctor to arrive. Meaning is a salve that heals pointlessness. Medicine in any form is 'Ishwara,' your personal God. *Ishwara pranidhana...*"

"...is the essence of *Kriya Yoga*," I interrupted. Being captured in the stream of teaching was bliss itself. My head and body ached. I let the words come at me as balm. I cherished this form of superstition and did not care about the science of it.

"I apologize. Please go on," I said.

He smiled at my eagerness to complete the thought. "Like shooting fish in a barrel, isn't it?" he said. "The Yoga of Pain—indeed! What *kriya*, what action comprises this practice?" I quickly shrugged to avoid entering too much dialog. The sound of his voice was enough.

"Discipline requires these key questions:

"*What is the voice, the nature of this particular pain?*

"*Who expresses it?*

"*When and where does it happen?*

"*Are the causes internal or external?*

"The goal of these inquiries is to find out *who* is having the complaint and *why* it is there." He stopped for a moment. Some birds chattered over a distant sound of sirens. We listened. He talked again, more quietly than before.

"So many sounds," he said. "How can a kriya-yogi know which ones to attend to, or which ones will benefit from the *puja* of analysis?" He stopped again and intoned "*Om.*"

I joined in. My voice cracked. All channels had been either shut down or overused and *Om* was restorative. My voice and sinuses opened. It amplified some head pain, but added an intelligent order to the throbbing sensation. My body aligned naturally along the vibrating syllable. *Om* and sirens, they fit each other. And the birds, the rustling of the leaves—they were clearly *Pranava* itself. Moments passed and he picked up a twig to etch on the dusty ground.

On an edge between joy and doubt, I watched him draw a circle.

Waking *by Vitthal Mishra*

!
had I
been asleep
?
bolt upright in
bedroom disarray
pointing purposeless
to weeds in an unkempt
mind.
blasted morning sun showing
stuff all over the place.
it had always
been you
!
the window
light-beam stairway
to above and beyond my precious coma.

INQUIRY

"HAVE YOU HEARD OF PARIKSHEET?" he asked. I had not. "Only such a sage-king can bring discipline and order into the empty dramas you contend with every day.

"There was an era when titanic beings we call *gods* married themselves into terrestrial affairs. A race took shape from divine boons, cosmic gifts and impossible acts of stoic devotion. The story holds that they incarnated by acts of will, coming and going as they pleased. Later they became increasingly enamored of mundane life and became trapped in their cages of flesh. Through this they learned, first hand, the tragic price of decadence."

He described an ancient time when humanity decoupled from heaven, felt itself falling. High-bred beings began the earthly project with divine powers and virtues. Yet, the flow of time worked like an acid that ate away the nobility in their fiber—honesty, humility, and compassion slipped toward delusion, grandiosity, and cynicism.

He continued, "Words had always been a God-given power. Words spilled directly from the mouth of Truth and the impact of these syllables was good and binding, a force of creation. Words then did not *represent* something—they weren't symbols that one could master in order to express ideas. They were agents of God's hand in the world—they were the sounds of incarnate divinity."

"Human minds began to harden," he said. "Personal whims like, *what benefits me* or *our good is important* became what we would call *discursive thought*—sacred syllables decayed from godly impulses down to gross tools for leverage and personal gain. In a sense, men kidnapped words from Heaven and sold them into forced labor on earth. Words got rounded up, reinterpreted, gathered into groups like chain-gangs to forge human happiness out of sensual whims."

Vishwamithra spelled-out these *slave-camps* as vocabulary, grammar, reason, sentence structure and rhetoric—our accepted rules for language usage.

He explained, "Truth slipped-away from human thought even as societies became more sophisticated. The ancient heroes in this story felt the dimming. The more they struggled to understand and save the absolute truth, the more they tangled themselves in ideas, false oaths, cynical pacts, and useless plans. The situation ripened into the war between two groups of cousins we have talked about several times. History records this as a fight between good and evil, but even now it is clear—humans lost their way and became unable to recognize the truth. They compulsively hacked God's Reality into dual concepts which forever pitted one idea against another in mortal combat."

As long as he kept speaking, the real world and its frighteningly pushy plans for me remained over there, physically close, but comfortably far-off—as long as he kept talking. And he did.

"These highborn men and women were trapped in the middle of two tragedies; the truth was falling from its zenith while the *way of the lie* enjoyed its nadir in unstoppable ascent. Nowadays we can easily look straight up and see falsehoods glint and sparkle as false gods.

"The *Mother of All Wars* was their last-ditch effort to purge evil out of good and save truth for coming generations. They succeeded, heroically. Despite the apparent reign of untruths today, we could not have these discourses without their prescient actions tens of thousands of years ago." His analysis went on and I waited to hear about Pariksheet, for whom all this was a mere stage set.

He said, "Their war was Armageddon. The task was like removing oil from paper which has to ruin both materials. They ripped entitled self-interest away from social dharmas—this wrecked the so-called *inheritance of noble blood*. It also pitted idealism against skill, a struggle of austere romance against sensual realism. The Great War exposed cowardice in heroes—it elevated timid souls to courageous heights. The bloodbath mutilated bodies, tormented minds and crushed spirits—it was total annihilation, except for one..."

Holding up his forefinger he announced clearly, "*Pariksheet.*"

He described the scene at length: battlefields were carnal nightmares, wails gasped out of the few survivors, gardens turned into putrid wastes and worst of all, nothing at all had been gained, only loss upon loss because of a bitter rivalry among kinsmen.

"It was the end of the war," he said, "Fields of death shined red in the flickering glow of torches through smoky, fetid air. Last moans wheezed from the dying while mourning cries issued from every corner. Drona's son, *Ashvatama*, became battle-crazed. War's tragic waste dealt a fatal blow to his nobility of spirit. He was mad, rushing from one innocent to the next, exterminating the kin he saw as enemy. His blade shined crimson with kindred blood. He rejoiced to find Arjuna's unborn grandson, growing *in utero*. He aimed a missile directly at the mother, one of ten-thousand grieving widows. This would be last of the line, the final hope of the half-divine warriors. He considered it his morbid privilege to obliterate that seed."

The sage stopped, sipped, and looked toward the town where plumes of black smoke went skyward in thin wisps. The light in late afternoon brought a glow to his untroubled profile. We examined the fumes, rising off the city—my mood lifted unexpectedly. It might have been an auspicious sign, incense from the ashen remains—new life.

He began again, "The child there-in was Pariksheet, Indra's grandson, three generations removed from the throne of the gods. An era of truth had died and this was the last hope for human dignity. Krishna's subtle form is what stepped into her womb to shield mother and child from an assassin. The embryo saw both the missile and the deliverer who absorbed the blow. The growing child formed around the question, *Who?*"

Vishwamithra continued emphatically, "Here was the saving grace, a simple question. We might call Pariksheet the 'giver of inquiry.' His mind was branded by the quest for *who*. He became a force for discovery—rediscovery in fact. See it and be thrilled. A prodigious race of heroes and demi-gods missed absolute extermination by the width of an infant's hair. Out of the bloody pile of ignorance, passion, and greed, a wonderment emerged—*who*? The curious king discharged his duties admirably, in spite of his restless soul. He would have no peace until he knew the prenatal protector. His question is DNA, transmitted to generations eking a life in the Dark Age, the invincible flame to know the nature of *the one who saves*."

He dropped the story-teller voice and adopted a hollow tone, saying, "Stories recall the king as a hero. Supermen do two things, they inspire great deeds and they cause laziness. It depends on how you understand yourself. If Pariksheet was the last member of a luminous clan, shining through myths and legends, he is worthless to us. If we let him inform us by giving him life in our actions, then the tale does more than instruct—it saves us." He traced an arrow in the dirt, coming toward the center of the circle. He abruptly erased the diagram with the back of his hand and began again.

"Pariksheet was aware, even in the womb. The enemy sought him out, driven by the insane wish to snuff out goodness in the world. God himself took the blow. The salvaged king used the balance of his life to find the one who gave him that life. The name *Pariksheet* means, 'continuous inquiry.' His parents were 'Persistence' and 'Strength.' This sage-king was the first person born into the Dark Age called *Kali-yuga*."

"Did he ever find that savior?" I asked. "After all, what would it look like to an unborn baby to see or recognize anything? It seems to me such an ambiguous quest was doomed from the start. How could Pariksheet know what he was hankering for, or recognize it when he found it?" When I thought about it, Pariksheet's efforts would be worse than finding a needle in a haystack. All his energy would be poured into clutching at prenatal moods and feelings. How could he ever find satisfaction?

"Put yourself in his place," he said slowly. "Think like an embryo, which is peace incarnate. You would perceive a threat in your fresh cells and brain. But that idea would have no meaning yet—there is no sense of other, much less a danger coming from the outside. It would form in the mind as an all-pervading feeling of doom. There would be no direction or source, only a full-bodied awareness of 'ending.' Even the idea of 'unfamiliar' is unfamiliar, so you would also feel confused, trying to live in an aura of pure harmony and yet process complex global threats."

The tale's action from the outside was all about means and ends, weapons and targets. However, in a fresh, embryonic mind, the threats, the things threatened, the fears, and the reactions would be jumbled into one experience, prematurely struggling to sort itself out. I understood what he told me and struggled through my distracted musings on immediate circumstances, juggling two disjoint thoughts. As a fetus, how could Pariksheet possibly resolve the threat of extinction? And more so, how was any of this happening at all, this surreal conversation out here on the edge of life and death?

Vishwamithra continued, "The need to understand restoration, redemption and saving grace branded his brain. The future king would search forever—until he was back at the precise place where inquiry began. That *ground zero* had to include threats to idyllic harmony, mysterious external forces, just like in the womb. He had to anchor his adult experience in dreaded endings so that he could *wonder at the intervention* that restored wholeness, as before. These tales are profoundly wise. The story tellers used *curses and boons* to give spiritual truth in a way we can recognize as cause and effect. Pariksheet re-entered the existential threat through such means. An angry sage cursed him to die young, adding the condition of enlightenment before death. Pariksheet would experience the form of *Krishna-Pranava* He would feel awe in the discovery, awareness in the knowledge, and integral satisfaction in relationship to the one that saved his life before it began. Most importantly, his perennial question would have its answer, in truth. The legacy of the king was inquiry."

I hoped that the story could go on indefinitely. It would not.

He concluded, saying, "Witness the beauty of *suvaha*, poetically told as an epilog to a blood-stained debacle. The seeker eventually mounted his death-bed so he could have his epiphany. The gallows was his platform for *samadhi*, supreme equipoise.

"This story is told in *The Srimad Bhagavatham*, Song of the Krishna-avatar. A wandering minstrel transmitted the keys to awakening, moments before an untimely death. Receive the same epiphany—*we are the no-thing that passes. God is immortal essence.* Knowing that presence is true consciousness, the rest is sleep walking, death on your feet."

The person in front of me was like a spectral bard, filling my mind before an end I could barely sense was hurling in my direction. "It is darker now," he said. "This living king is your opportunity to ask questions, to find meaning. This is the last light, a light that will not be extinguished."

Discriminating Cheese *by Vitthal Mishra*

Milk takes forever to boil.
When it finally happens, it's too fast.
Cut the heat—throw in the lemon.

It goes crazy!
—like it was alive
—like it wanted to bolt
—like it finally had its way.

Then the harvest—
Dump liquid that wasn't there before and
Keep solids that appeared from no where.

Press it into a new thing,
Smooth and perfect.
It says, "I am here. Taste me."

Part VI: Upadesh

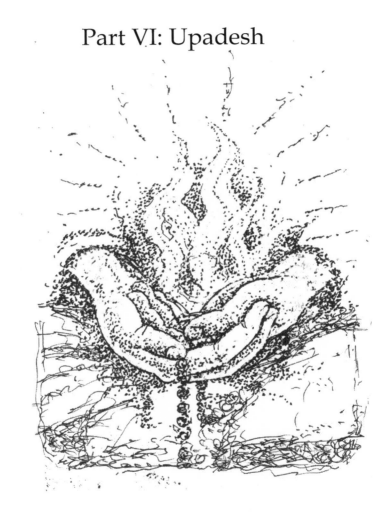

Roots and Flowers *notes from Vishwamithra*

Life in the spirit has its opposing way
—mere existence in flesh.

Expansion in consciousness is an outward movement
—the flower of relationship.

Contraction as flesh is an inward cycle.
—rooting down and away to survive.

The two modes exist at once.
—opposite poles of a single axis.

Their extremes negate humanness
—and define it.

KARMA

VISHWAMITHRA PRESSED *QUESTIONING* AS the lifeblood of the mind. "Throw away the need to find solutions. Embrace questions and become Pariksheet," he said. "Relationship builds on questions and intent. Even if pain mangles your ability to be lucid, listen, find its coherent voice. If your agony resists any effort to find meaning, then it could be an alien affliction. The frame of pain can be larger than you.

"Collective karmas are economies of flesh and blood that require humility to accept. Blame, if any, is scattered cross time. Racial debts go generation to generation until someone gives them an audience. Blame ignorance, but pay—making peace with them heals the past and the future, beyond your framework. It's sticky business, an act of love.

"It could be an unknowable source in the present. Things you can't see, hear or feel directly can excite the nervous system to excruciating extremes. The pain continues until you get away from the source. This type of suffering forces weak, indecisive people to act, if only to find an escape. Use Gayatri analysis to avoid leaping from one fire into another—it prevents random, stop-gap solutions that lead to serial suffering, often extending the pain, dragging others into the soup.

"A third type is like a phantom limb—a ghost of sensation whose causes are no longer there. Build discipline by asking, *where is the pain?* Find the edges. Does it spread or have a firm boundary? *What kind of sensation is it?*—sharp or dull, steady or pulsing. *Does it change or is it the same, no matter what?* This way you relate to the sensation. It can go from a vague, unwanted burden, to a single point or localized spot. You may find it is not so much painful, as unwanted."

He continued, "I knew someone who became a great yogi by means of his paralyzed body. They told this tapas-surfer that feelings could not return below the heart vertebrae of his broken back. The so-called paralytic did *samyama* on the silent tissues and found subtle movement there in the dark. Paralysis has a silent, internal voice, meditative. The yogi discovered *Tat Savitur*, the effulgent ground of sensation that abides in living tissue whether it has feeling or not."

"And in the fourth cause of unwanted pain," he said, "the sufferer maintains a belief in animal sacrifice." He waited for my reaction.

The stream of ideas about pain had to gurgle around my rocky concerns—that a war was in progress, that my life anchors had been destroyed, or worse, that I was dead. I engaged him to keep the apparition intact. Besides those distractions, his fourth condition for persistent pain made no sense at all.

"I understand generational healing." I told him. "There are racial aspects or inherited traits that link to trauma and they can't be ignored. The second one you mentioned, 'sources of pain outside of us that have to be physically abandoned,' is clear enough. That could include toxic materials, regions wrecked by famine, war, environmental disaster and the rest, epidemic risks, destructive electro-magnetic sources, or certain people and social situations. I have also heard of phantom limbs; pain that some people feel in an arm or leg that is no longer there. I suppose psychological versions of the phantom pain syndrome exist as well; when certain circumstances are no longer an issue, but the reactions to the old affliction persist as fears or dreads with no present cause. I understand these."

This last one about animal sacrifice seemed completely exotic. I asked him, "Only backward and ignorant people slaughter animals for religious purposes—how does this figure, even in an exotic sense?"

He said, "There's an ancient, pervasive belief about the body. It is the foundation of slavery, leads to dark magical rituals and sprouts from laziness. Mastering thought and the senses requires disciplined effort, time, and humility. An ancient experiment mixed animal nature with a programmable consciousness. It causes misinterpretations of reality. Resisting hard work is a mistaken form of conserving energy that leads to class differences with all the inherent problems.

"The mind has powerful tools; some are more effective than others. *Projection* is such a tool. It is the ability to throw one's own personal qualities onto another. There are benefits to projecting your positive or negative traits on another person if you are aware of what you are doing, It can be easier to work *out there* and then incorporate those efforts *in here*. *Projection* provides a way to remain objective when subjective feelings might block progress. There are risks.

"Judging, laying personal faults on others, is a negative form of projection that buries one's mistakes and shortcomings in the body of someone else. Far extremes of that distortion lead to murder or worse. Conveniently, goats and chickens become mute victims of such ritual purification. More common versions are kicking the cat, self-criticism or pushing past healthy limits to prove a point. It happens a thousand times a day.

"It could also be the abuse of a child, whose innocence and lack of voice is kin to that of an animal. All these are projections where a perceived problem gets laid onto another being. Slavery starts with the simple desire to get someone else to carry your load. Whole groups devise ways to use people like tools, against their will, wittingly or unwittingly. Every abuse is a shadow of relationship. They are all ways for one individual to avoid relating to another, in discipline."

But I saw a need to push through, toughen up, force others to act, identify weak links in the chains of relationship. I said, "Circumstances can dictate relationships that may look abusive, coercive or dishonest. *Eat or be eaten*—sometimes that's an intimate, all too sincere, and unavoidable meeting that has to be considered."

"None of this can be determined without *Pariksheet*," he replied, "the restless search for *relationship as the one who saves*. Can you see that harming another human being is a macabre parody of relationship? If you find yourself in a situation that requires you to kill a man, slaughter a goat, or drive toward perfection, first ask the questions—*who, what when and where* to enter relationship. One has to approach the object and inquire. *Samyama*—holding them in mind, hearing the sounds they make, watching the things they do, dwelling on their outer form, exploring their chosen environments—these bring you into full immersion and they reveal themselves in *samyama*. Without this kind of questioning, mixing dissimilar people ends in violence."

He stopped and puzzled over something. Momentarily pressing his eyes shut he said, "Animal sacrifice leads to human sacrifice and eventually, cannibalism. It comes back to the basic problem I started with so long ago—alien influences and the flattening of consciousness into two dimensions. Efficiency leads to over-simplification. Monsters breed in clever minds that reject true discipline."

While he spoke it was clear—our paths had crossed again, somehow. This was no apparition. I would have to ask him about the nature of our meeting...at some point. More pauses and he plowed forward, telling me about the fourth kind of pain that resisted samyama and Gayatri. This fourth category, apparently, was so different from natural paths that it required more. He proceeded.

"Life moves. It will either evolve on natural paths or involve in incestuous ways. Living in Spirit requires dedication to finer sensibilities. It moves life toward more and deeper layers of subtlety. It leads to an appreciation of three dimensional constructs as a perfect platform for the Spirit to know and observe itself. Because of duality there is a way that opposes the natural path of expansion. Some choose to *use* spirit, to trap and enslave it, to lock onto material reality, forever. That would be *damnation*."

I asked him what it had to do with the fourth type of unsolvable pain he had been discussing. He lavished attention on the subject of "animal sacrifice," but his point eluded me.

"By mysterious design, life in the spirit has its opposing way—mere existence in the flesh. Expansion in consciousness is an outward movement. It happens as *relationship*. Contraction *as flesh* is an inward cycle. It is non-relatedness that *sinks into itself as an answer*. These two modes exist at opposite ends of one scale we'll call 'incarnation: formless spirit adopting bodily form.' Extreme forms at either end negate the way of becoming a full human. Pure asceticism and vile decadence exist as inhuman dead-ends, yet they have to exist for the *middle way*, which is human.

"Animal sacrifice and even darker expressions of cannibalism and incest will manifest as long as there is duality. Every form of non-relationship: involution, parasitism, vampirism, slavery, incest, cannibalism and so many unimaginable horror stories continue as perversions...all due to the inherent freedom of consciousness. In that way, to answer your original question, animal sacrifice is the ever present shadow of consciousness. Be aware and avoid."

I spoke tenuously, "May I ask you a question?"

"Certainly," he nodded, sipped, and waited.

"Are we...dead?"

SPEECH

His face turned somber. The cup rested on his thigh. His chest rose and then fell slowly, letting out a long, barely-audible breath.

"We are dead," he said. "For all the swirling complexity of creation, only the light of conscious awareness, the flame, *Jyothi*, is alive."

He did not understand what I meant so I repeated my question.

"But were we killed? Did a bomb land on us and end our lives?"

"It's a simple question. I'll give an answer in kind." It was understood—my current confusion was not much different than the larger ignorance I had always tolerated.

"No, we are sitting under a tree on the edge of town. You are visiting me for reasons I can only guess. I am here because I like this place, distant and near to my flat. I come here often. You do not. Is that clearer?" I was only partly reassured by his clarification. The idea of death settled in with me as a good way to avoid the problems of living, back there anyway.

I said, "I have lost track of time; it seems so long ago. Something is going on, serious. Maybe it was a bomb. A huge explosion completely destroyed several blocks. I got a message on my computer and ignored it, hid out because the police were corralling people into various shelters, and then the explosion. I feel beaten. I'm worried. Is it a war? You're out here. Would I be safer in the middle school basement?"

My questions were rhetorical. He would not answer them directly because all of it was surface effect. Vishwamithra heard them as a probe toward the center. My panic felt staged—even I did not believe it. While waiting for a response, I tried to reformulate my question. What did I really want to know? He spoke while I puzzled.

"Distraction, invisible strings, and the thrill people feel at being fooled," he said, smiling, "are essential tools for magicians. Don't let noises, images, or reactions take your attention away from *Om*. Reason can get warped by unexpected changes in an environment. Use these times to expand the perimeter of your practice. Make the ability to stay on a fixed point more durable. During confused moments, simulations of truth can be slipped in by those who would take advantage of disorder."

Specter or real, Vishwamithra taught me as though nothing had happened. Under a tree, away from the city, he seemed a little lighter than what I recalled, like he was on a small holiday.

"The question might come up," he said, "Why is there evil, chaos, death, and destruction? Listen closely—there is no answer and the reason is simple. Inquiry into evil becomes part of evil. Evil seeks attention, a flow of energy toward it, involution. You have to *think* like the devil to understand him. To know God you have to *be* God. *The good* is an outgoing creative flux. Yet, if we don't probe into evil, we betray discriminative intelligence. Goodness in a dual world requires inquiry, insight, and discipline. There is not so much danger when you cross a busy street—just don't try it with your eyes closed."

He went on, "If we don't continuously identify the problem, self-absorbed narcissism can creep in and substitute for the journey to the Self. Our perennial task is life, let's say it together."

> Om.
> Bhur Bhuvah Suvaha.
> Tat Savitur Varenyum.
> Bhargo Devasya Dhimahi.
> Dhiyo Yonah Prachodayat.

The sage seemed immune to events.

He said, "This little grove is a handy hermitage, my private campground away from the hum and buzz of electricity and traffic. Out here the body-electric operates without distortion caused by devices and machines. I came here after our last meeting. The explosions last night were loud. The last one sent up a huge billow lit by flashes from below, very dramatic! I didn't worry about you. It seemed I would find out soon enough what the situation was and here you are, enlightening me."

"I avoided the official procedure so there's no telling," I said. "Everyone was forced to evacuate. It seems like my neighborhood was the target. I did manage to get a couple of things, the rest is now a crater. Your apartment had minor damage, except all the windows blew out. If it stays open to the weather it will be a mess. I collected these when I went by." I opened the pack and showed him the prayer book, lamp, and food.

"Good, keep them. Old Town was the most affected, wasn't it?" he asked.

"Yes, the historical zone," I told him, "the only district with any character. Maybe it was the racial tension that's been building up. It could also be religious. They've brought in the immigrants, a certain percentage of them are extremists. And you know, the traditional inhabitants go back over a hundred years, so there are the vigilantes who resent the policy. My mother's side came here six generations ago—even she thinks it's a terrible idea. I hope it wasn't a transcontinental missile. It seemed big enough to be an attack from over there. There are so many reasons, all speculation. A brain can concoct any explanation. I guess it's lucky they cleared out the area. They acted quickly for a change." I knew it was chatter.

"I'm glad to see you here," he said. "Your intuition must be up and running. Let's spend a minute with these current events; maybe we can understand something about how the mind works."

The unhinged sensation lifted. The sound of his voice was a base for me to recompose. The teachings had become more important to me than usual comforts like meals on schedule, coffee breaks, or even the familiar surroundings of my own apartment. This, right here, was real and not replaceable. I listened while he talked.

"We are confused about objects by overlapping the word for it, the meaning, and our ideas about it," he said. "If we can discriminate one from the other, the inner language of anything reveals itself. You must have learned that Patanjali's sutras offer practical truths. Examine mind stuff through the lens of the *mahavyahriti* and the yogi-sage's terse lines prove-out."

He added, "Before you ask any more questions or tell yourself more stories about last night, let's grasp the inner language of that particular 'boom.' It went *boom*. That's all we really know, so let's not call it an act of war, hatred, a bomb, or anything—*boom*, a big noise, lots of damage. Apply *bhur, bhuvah, and suvaha* to analyze last night's events. Then move on to the three lines."

I was used to this by now and relished the rare comfort of treating meanings or perceptions like blocks of wood, cutting, shaping, or connecting them with mind tools—especially in his company.

I turned my attention to the fire in front of us. The burnt wood had become a bed of hot coals. I stategically placed more material to keep it alive and dropped on a bigger branch that would burn longer. It was all like the flame of consciousness—a metaphor for analysis.

The tinder, twigs, and sticks were like the topics to consider.

Analysis acted like the fire that consumed whatever was placed there—the cleaner the fuel, the better the burn. Last night's trauma, the concussion, the events leading up to it, the news in the weeks preceding, the actions of authorities, my own actions and reactions would be placed one by one on the fire of awareness. Some ideas went to blaze immediately, others more slowly. I started talking to the sage when it seemed the issues were "well ignited" in my thought process. Meditative analysis burned away the most obvious ideas to reveal subtle, cleaner issues that glowed more brightly.

"The neighborhood had sentimental value to the town. A research institute broke ground on adjacent vacant land which drove real estate values upward. While the price of the land skyrocketed, controversy over how to deal with long-time residents became intense. Those in favor of development wanted to mow down the old and rebuild, others wanted to preserve the historic core. Immigrant minorities had established insulated communities in the old buildings over decades. Their isolation alienated local residents, created bad feelings and made matters even more complicated. Beyond that, the city seemed to intentionally let beautiful old properties go down. The whole area became run-down, even dangerous on some streets. It didn't make sense to me while it was happening—renovation became almost impossible. At the same time, a national endowment was available for new art and culture ventures that could support the boom of research and development. It seemed unlikely that our town would be picked because of the tension between resident factions."

Connecting the dots was obvious.

"They blew it up. It was a demolition," I said.

The sage replied, "Keep that thought and tell me the inner language of *boom*. Words and meanings are not political. Politicians only use them to achieve their ends."

I continued to contemplate the violent concussion of sound. "It offends. It is one way. It carves, hacks a hole. It is not interested in discourse," I said.

I settled below those observations and thought about the source of my words. Depending on intentions, words could end a conversation, begin one, or explore ideas. One explosion, "talking" to another explosion was war—the clash of single-sided statements, one aimed at overpowering the other. It would end when one side went silent. When an unarmed community took the blow, it was genocide, terminating beings, making people into statistics. It worked.

Who would say "boom" in our region—only a well-resourced force from the outside that wanted to dominate—or eradicate. It had to come from beyond local political structures.

I continued my analysis, "A huge creature, an alien, has arrived. Anyone living here will have to listen from now on. There will be no discourse. It is too big. We are too small."

Vishwamithra said, "And the soft-spoken community invited the bellowing beast. They lost affection for their own discourse and bought the sales pitch for huge aggressive voices. The bomb is only a last word on a certain kind of noise that has built over time."

He continued, "More powerful blasts are on their way. These will be laws, anti-cultural fences that will continue to cut across human discourse. Organic conversation has to stop to make way for plans and programs—the fingerprints of the two-dimensional beings we've talked about. Continue with the Gayatri Mantra. Use the three lines to suggest how to proceed."

I began, "*Tat savitur varenyum* tells us to worship. But what thing is worthy to be worshipped?—the *savitur*, wisdom guide hidden in every particle and action. All phenomena are also *Tat*. Truth disarms my understanding, so I fall prostrate. It is humbling."

I went on to the second line, *bhargo devasya dhimahi*, saying, "When understanding stalls, meditation is spontaneous. The violent event stirs-up reactive fear. Bombs, displaced people, lives upturned, and narratives about attacks are in the end *phenomena*. The only action to take is toward whatever center I can find inside—Ma Gayatri resides in my center as the vitality of the mantra, not the mantra as words or phrases. Looking anywhere else is to look away from the true solution to my anxious state, blinded by the glare of appearances."

I depended on this man in front of me—my great good fortune, dreamlike, to prepare for an uncertain future that bore down on me. It would end. Everything ends.

"*Dhiyo yonah prachodayat,*" the third line completed what *Savitri*, the wisdom mother, would have me do. Whatever came to me here would be my guiding hand. I said, "All this is an apparent world I have the privilege to discuss in this quiet moment. This is a blessing. May that blessing go on...in your form—the appearance I have come to value..." With raw nerve endings and naked exposure to the fates I wanted to cling to the only solid object in mt world, Vishwamithra.

Returning to the mantra I continued, "*Prachodayat*—I pray. I offer the content of meditation to one that can receive it, despite worry or distortion. Once these are placed with there, I proceed with that One, my choice, my guide. Faith is the way forward."

"Uncertainty is her way," he said. "It is wise to grapple with uncertainty through understanding and faith—the mantra prescribes worship, meditation, and prayer. Meditative analysis with Gayatri leads spontaneously through the yoga of action—*tapas-svadhyaya-ishvara pranidhana*. But you know these things."

Practical knowledge was a world apart from spiritual awareness. I had to pinch myself hard and wake up to all this—time marched, events swirled. Uncertainty continued to be uncomfortable.

I asked him, "The explosions, the wrecked village, future implications, surely there is something I should be doing. This thing called faith seems insubstantial. Are there no guarantees of any kind? What needs to happen next?"

"Relationship," he said. "And there is only one of those, really, You want to act. That's natural. Faith is not a goal—it's a way of action, all its own. You can also think of faith as *the process of yoga*."

He leaned forward, reaching for my shoulder. He gave it a hard squeeze and sat back again. The gesture was new.

He spoke to my concerns, saying, "Your mother, father and sister were relationships. They are there now. You only have to go a little way into your memory to find them. With effort they are fully present. And we here, you and me; this relationship is happening now. And yet, there is intimacy hidden in this that you can only find in my absence. It could be longing. It could be recalling old sentiments. The colors of relationship are infinite. That is because there is only the one relationship, the *Aum* resonant in your own fiber. I'll always be here. Worry if you want, but better yet, offer that worry to Her. She's the real friend; the rest is chit-chat. But there's that raging beast back there whether we want to talk to it or not! What to do?"

The magic of it dawned on me for just an instant—a faint smell of metallic smoke, this secret place, a twisting trunk of oak, the spent dregs in a cup, my rattled frame. Silent space separated one thing from another, one word from another, one event from another. Gratitude for nothing rose up, washed me from below, the sweet presence of nothing—*thank-you for nothing*. Ashty Hozan was an empty frame that saw the image of Vishwamithra sitting there. The image filled the empty frame. There were no tombs, only empty space.

LANGUAGE

HE POURED MORE WATER over the spent tea bag in his cup and swirled it. "There is nothing to discuss when a bear enters. The beast's presence dictates all future thoughts until you get away from it. Let the two of us create some distance from that immense, insistent creature."

I sensed an ending. He was wrapping-up. It startled me and I said, "I would rather not! Tell me I won't lose the aura of your presence. You are the bear that sharpens my senses. When I'm around you, my mind quickens and my soul finds depth. I will be all the worse if you leave. Teach me a method, your instruction, in a way that won't fade, one that stays fresh. Grant me *upadesha*. Is any of that possible, or do I have to resign myself to the mortality of even our time together?"

"The rate of change does not increase, only the quality of your perception varies. When you examine a flower you don't perceive change, even though at first you are looking at the stem, then the petals. The image of the flower is held inside your concept of the whole flower, so you don't say it's changing. With a little bit of effort, your concept of that same flower can enlarge. It can include the life of the flower from sprout to bud to blossom. Try it."

He found a dandelion, wriggled his fingers around the root while speaking under his breath, and handed me the plant.

"Open your mind enough to include the living aspect of the simple thing of sprout and root. A dead dandelion is not a dandelion—life is essential to the living! That's obvious. While holding the living plant, examine it in time, going backward and forward."

In the small, vibrant, yellow blossom, the long delicate stem, the deep green base with jagged leaves, and the finely branching root, I sensed a real compliance by the plant. It encouraged this experiment as though the plant spoke to me in no words. From the interaction I knew the sage promised to put it back and water it.

I received more information about one wild weed than I ever thought possible. It was as though the sequence of growth from the puff-seed to its full blossom, maturity, and will to propagate was there at once. I only needed to choose a place to look in time. It was an ideation of all its developing forms that lived in the dandelion. They came from far beyond the plant.

The yellow in the plant was "Sun" there in my palm. That tremendous incinerator, so far in space whispered to me in the dandelion. It had secrets completely available for the asking—secrets about beginnings in a Living Pulse—beyond even the black voids in space. The voice murmured in an intimate calmness, patience. It was indefatigable, insistent. Its words revealed flowers within flowers within flowers, on and on that could not be quenched. I could stay with the flower forever, but the dandelion was finished and wanted to go back.

I handed it to Vishwamithra. As expected, he gently replaced the root. He watered it with the cooled remains in the pan I used for tea.

I said, "The dandelion conveyed intelligent information to me no different than when you and I talk—profound and sacred. The language was not speech or even image. It was a thought-form, like seeing a movie from the projection booth, removed from the outer visual aspect and immersed in the dynamic internal aspect."

"Contrary to the words of the anthem, the times are not *'a-changin'*—any more or less than they ever did. To notice the way social forms shift over time requires adept seeing. They can't be held in the hand, so their essence can't speak as easily to you as the dandelion. However, their message is available. If you develop the talent to hold the living reality of the town in all its complexity you can know the seeds that sprouted these events decades ago, as well as their maturity and death in a distant future. Remember, time and space are different ways of describing the same thing. It is not about flux. It is an object of varying dimensions, a thought form revealing itself."

"Are you also telling me our time together has to end?"

Even as the words came out I knew what his answer would be. "Find out for yourself," he would say and then going further, "Contemplate our sessions from start to completion..."

Giving me no reply, he raised an eyebrow and waited for my results. It was obvious, clearer than the life of a flower.

"It won't end. There's no stopping these sessions that I've enjoyed. They will chan..." I refrained from completing the word and said, "It is complex, all a part of a continuous fabric, the teacher, the teaching, and the student. There will be a full range of perceptions from all angles. But you, the timeless sage and I, the learner are aspects of the unchanging truth. It has always been this way."

"Well said—you are catching on. *Sat Chit and Ananda* is in eternal relationship with itself. It does not need us because we are only aspects of it. However, we are 'boots on the ground' here and now, completely precious, unique and not expendable. *Satchitananda* does not 'love' anything since it *is* all things and is love itself. The ocean can't be thirsty, yet all water is destined to be embraced there somehow or another."

I said, "When I am with you all of life seems orderly and meaningful. I could not imagine you being killed, but I did experience gut-wrenching separation when I saw the damage to your flat and that you were not there. What can be done about that? My world can shrink very small and far away from *Satchitananda*. Even *Om* can seem abstract, despite the balm it offers when I practice it."

Vishwamithra gazed intently. He examined me from top to bottom. It seemed he would have kicked my tires if I had been a car. "Gayatri also means 'she who protects.' I want to give you something. First, look at me hard. Scrutinize me with all the depth you can muster. I give permission."

I stared. He was a man. His eyes had a greenish light as though illuminated from the inside. It contrasted against olive skin. His forehead was broad, open, with a slight sheen. Latent lines that might deepen into furrows ran horizontally and vertically. His hair was salt and pepper, a tight carpet at the sides, thinning to speckles on top and around his face. The jaw, cheeks, and mouth were delineated by distinct folds that animated his expressions. When he smiled, laughed, or spoke they distinguished the curving surfaces of cheek from jaw, jaw from chin. His neck was lean and sinewy. White-gray tufts of chest hair disappeared behind a melon colored, long-sleeved shirt open at the collar, revealing a wiry-powerful build. Razor-creased, gray-green cotton pants were cuffed and complemented his brown, bare feet. His toe-nails, like his finger nails, were wide, well formed, trimmed. When he scrambled down from the tree his body moved gracefully, deliberately, with surprising spring and strength. Below the surface of his attractive, not conspicuous presence, was something inscrutable.

The more I examined and opened to what I saw, the more his body became empty, a conduit. Vastness flowed under his skin like a river under ice sheets; the two were separate from each other, agreeable, and detached. I did not tire of looking at him.

"Have you finished?" he asked. I nodded. "Only now I will give you a way to stay in the presence of the one who protects. She is your mother. She wants you to know her—you already do, so this is easy.

275

Invoke her with the mantra. I will stay quiet.

"*Om, Bhur, Bhuvah, Suvaha. Tat, Savitur, Varenyum. Bhargo, Devasya, Dhimahi. Dhiyo Yonah, Prachodayat.*" I made audible repetitions.

His eyes trained toward the remnant of fire that sprang sporadically among charred sticks. Smoke rose straight up in lilting trails, losing itself in the hazy air that hung below the tree canopy.

He said, almost too quiet to hear, "Repeat and repeat, generate feeling and see her. Embrace the whole mantra. It is the body of your mother. Inside that body is your own flesh, protected, safe and clear like from the beginning. She holds it for you in trust, waiting for you. You will arrive. Generate feeling. Feel the whole mantra, much as you held the living flower a moment ago."

I did as he suggested. The words came softer to me, inner-awareness balanced outer-sound. The Sanskrit syllables formed non-specific images in my mind. Idea impressions developed contrasts, became folds, like a linen dress—simple, light, an unbleached cloth that comforted and veiled. It gave way to contours evoking skin, arms, legs, belly, and breasts. I repeated the mantra more evenly, like a shadow following the breath. The intimacy startled me.

The Sage said, more quietly than before, in words that barely structured the air they rested on, "There is nothing to be afraid of. Take her hand. Allow yourself to be her son. Go back."

I settled and trusted. Now, I was in the veil, sheltered behind a gauze screen, a smell of rose. The cotton took on flesh. Firm, pliant, soft, and supporting, it held me, wrapped me in embrace. From head to feet, a pulsing womb surrounded me, safe from the world beyond. She was also that world. She was both. She held us together and separate.

I felt a rush of cool air beginning above, flowing in progressive waves. A crisp breeze washed my head, then ears, neck and shoulders. It extended down my back, spreading wide across lateral muscles. Refreshing, bracing, not cold, it moved down into my lungs, abdomen, and pelvis. It continued, refreshing my legs and feet. It faded. The tangible vision of Gayatri was done. I drank the sensations of it.

He again whispered into my reverie, "Discipline, hold to your discipline. Collect the Mother's presence, hold it and see."

I checked my impatience, the urge to leave the abstracted state and become normal. I woke myself out of dreaminess and held to the vision at the same time, returning to mantra.

"*Om. Bhur, bhuvah, suvaha. Tat savitur, varenyum. Bhargo, devsya, dhimahi. Dhiyo yonah, prachodayat,*" I repeated. A vision of a girl appeared, as

276

though over my right shoulder, a surprise.

Silently, I asked, "Who are you?"

She laughed, shy. She said, "Mata." She held out a pink iris with a red orange burst and vanished abruptly. Like a wave seeping into the sand, all of it was gone.

Neither Vishwamithra nor I said anything. Awareness of our bonds and destinies diffused into the landscape, grasses and a breeze. Our physical weight pressed down like every shape in our field—wood of tree, a silver snake of water moving goalless in a depression—all held to earth's bosom. Insects, birds, a town in flux, he and I—we shared the dense material ball, the planet that gave support while we pushed down. The balance was perfect, for a leaf, for a boulder, or for a tangled web of steel. The edge of my body was arbitrary.

The teacher reached into my mood and parted the seamless garment we shared.

"What was your experience?" he asked.

I described it in detail. Words were empty and yet necessary. I concluded, telling about the apparition. "A young girl appeared briefly. She seemed very real, an average villager. She was attractive. I was caught off-guard."

"Repeat this practice when you can, best at night. It will provide protection and a sense of calm. It is the goddess herself. Like any relationship you must attend to it. She waits and is more steadfast than you can comprehend."

He reached under his shirt and produced a pouch. He searched through its contents while he spoke. "Gayatri is alive. She is not a personality in the way that we are. Yet, as much as you allow her, she will be more personal than anyone you know. More real than those who walk and talk. We could and may well maintain these discussions for an eon. It's a shower of grace that God gives. Imagine a world where it is this and only this: neither living to eat nor eating to live, all of it poured into conscious discourse, romancing the mystery. Do you need rockets to the moon?"

He found what he was looking for, a photo, held it face down on his thigh, and waited for my reply.

I said, "Technology has been the vanguard of our development. I hope someday that rockets to the moon, computers, medicines and all the works of the human race will be used for good." Wars and violence posed a depressing puzzle. Thinking back just a few hours ago reminded me of how far away we were from my idea that technology could serve the highest aims.

He went quiet and scrutinized me. It seemed he searched for words that I would be able to understand and weighed them before speaking.

"You are young and want to sign-on to the *great work*, to realize a luminous vision of a sleek, trouble-free world that extends to the stars. This is karma and nothing I say would convince you away from the trap. All karmas spend themselves and generate new ones—Gayatri will protect you while this one also consumes itself." I noted that his fingers pressed the photo, felt the edges.

"Machines and fantasies are addictive drugs, *their* substitutes for grace," he said. "I told you, months back, about a flattened consciousness that is hungry to re-experience the juice of three dimensions they forfeited, the feelings, love and pain they sacrificed to a fantasy of progress. We find these dynamos and gizmos appealing because they clearly make life easier. Without exception they enable the lowest expression of a man. There is not one trick performed by one techno-magician that does not block the light of consciousness."

He continued, "All this, every tear, every sigh, every breath and laugh is our own *human-ology* of flesh and spirit. The technology of human reality is complete in itself. 'In-ventions' are just as the word implies—alien arrivals. They come to stay, to disrupt the organic technology which we have as 'man' or 'woman.' The true magic that takes us to the highest peak of humanity is complete in us, our inheritance. The machine agenda will—behold the truth—enslave and kill. It will endlessly provide comforts that end in crushed hopes and dashed dreams." I spontaneously checked the presence of the beads and felt for them against my chest, reassured when I detected the threaded strand.

He said again, "*Ah, Oh, Um*, these are at your hand, now and forever—why?—because they are inherent in your consciousness."

There was something different about him. He was trying to make a point. I did not remember him *trying* in anything before. This was a confidence and he seemed vulnerable, human, and intimate—less the formality of teaching and more the warmth of friendship.

Without pause he said, "I'll answer my own question about rockets to the moon. You do not need them—or any of the other things you mentioned—*they* do. This is an alien agenda. I have a different question. Who are you? Are you a machine, walking the earth, executing commands from your maker? Or, are you consciousness, free and independent?"

"I'm both, aren't I?" I said. "Hormones and cravings command me, seemingly from outside. All at once, I love the freedom to choose."

"Yes, you are both. You chose neither and are responsible for both. You and I inhabit these fabulous things called bodies—sophisticated hybrids, designed to ensnare consciousness and harness *Chit* in a net. The trajectory of the body is toward utter enslavement, every mechanical choice you make takes us all there. Then there is the other, a luminous awake-ness, the thing that is being harnessed—it is *Sat Chit Ananda*, Truth, Consciousness and Bliss. You contain these two roads—one leads into slavery with no end—the other is totally open and free. Easy compromises and pleasant choices bind the slaves that think they are free. The other road is defined by the rigors your formless spirit truly craves."

He sized me up again, saying, "In time this war will eventually end somehow or another—in consciousness it will not end until you see truly. The magic of their illusion improves while mesmerized minds fall toward the ease of *no-choice*. The free road will close.

"That said, now the natural way is wide open, and leads to immortality, bliss." He challenged me, without a shred of coercion. "It is simple," he said, "Be human. Gayatri is the life raft across the bleak ocean of delusion. Take the mantra, know and love the goddess. Be free and work for the freedom of others. There is nothing else to do."

He held out the photo face down, blue-ink writing on the back. It might have been a birth date. I took it and turned it over, a girl—*the* girl holding iris flowers, smiling! I was confused, a deja vu, a spell. He talked to me.

"I'm going to Nepal in a few days. I am finished here. Twenty-four of us know Gayatri, its depth teaching. You are the twenty-fifth. The five faced goddess will herself instruct and guide you. The photo is of my niece; she lives at the house where I will be staying. It is simple, sparse and sprawling, thirty minutes from Katmandu. There is a lively street culture which still maintains some of the old ways, quieter than the city. I think you would like it. She is also bright, traditional and well-versed in Gayatri shastra.

"It's time for me to recede," he said. My focus was gripped by the image of the girl, though his words burned my ears.

"This will be a good place to contemplate, to be with uncomplicated people, and to die." The tone in his voice had returned to something without an edge.

"I hope you will consider coming," he asked. "There are no rockets so I cannot guarantee you will be completely accepting. I assure you; all will come in time if you choose to make a long visit."

I blurted, "This is exactly the girl in my mind, the one that popped in and then out!"

His expression did not change. "She has a year left in high school. Meanwhile tend to my flat. I won't be returning. Your apartment was a victim of the 'great work.' Your options are easy—now for Dakshina."

What about the girl? Yes, I knew the term *dakshina*, the traditional gift of money or cows, from student to teacher. Vishwamithra had never asked for anything, not even my attention. It was more than I could grasp at once; then there was the girl.

He continued, "When the time is short and choices are important, clarity is critical. You will not see me here after today. As your guru, I offer you a last teaching in the form of this dakshina. The *milk cow* I request is not your attention, ritual service, or your thumb. It is your willingness. Keep this photograph of my niece on your altar, whatever that might be. You will fixate on her and dream of coming to see me. Your mind will do these things because of your feelings for me. Be wary of that tendency, examine it, and criticize it. If you try to drive it away, it will persist, en force. The willingness I ask is to place the picture where it is visible and pay little attention to it.

"*Tapasvadhyaishwara pranidhanani kriya yogaha*, applies here—the friction of awareness is devotion to the Great Self. Discipline yourself and clarity will dawn. Allow the *Tat Savitur* to culture your thought without thinking. That will lead inevitably to your refined intention. Will you give this Dakshina?"

"I want to give what you ask," I said. "My debt to you is far more than that. I can only say with sincerity that I will try." This second blow and bizarre circumstance was as frightening as the bomb. The explosion obliterated my past and my assumptions; the sage had transfigured my future and my expectations. Abruptly he stood as though dismissing me.

"Should I return to the town?" I asked.

"Only when you feel that the time is right. There are some provisions in my modest tree habitat. They are yours. If you temper your appetite the food could last more than a week. I am going."

Knees buckling, I fell at his feet while the ground of his presence slipped away. Holding his ankles, my forehead pressed down as though to hold him in place. He didn't move. I released and sat back on my haunches. He slipped his sandals on, adjusted the straps, and began walking. We moved toward the railroad track that connected the town to the horizon.

"Do your practice," were his last words, right hand raised in *abhyasa* blessing. He smiled long, turned his back to the town, and placed firm steps between two polished steel rails that shined in the waning light.

I watched him follow the track east, pacing himself rhythmically with the wooden ties. He was a dot, then gone from sight. I tried to burst into tears which seemed absurd. Instead I was still, watching the place where I last saw him. Within minutes, the darkening blue sky rested on a crack of dusk riding black silhouettes of trees and fields. The photo was in my hand.

I returned to the oak and felt for the paraffin lantern and matches in my bag. I looked at her picture in the yellow glow of a candle wick, Mata. I did not even have a photograph of her uncle, the birthless sage who talked about dying in Nepal.

Let me receive *by Vitthal Mishra*

Let me receive consciousness, clear and clean,
rushing around and over worldly stones,
wearing down jagged rocks
in a torrent of Awareness.

Let the evils of the world wear smooth
in the flood of my sadhana.
Allow frothing, bubbling schemes to burst
in a bright spate of awakeness.

Teach me the lesson of Ganga
the goddess-presider of rivers
to master the tests and trials of the world
by flowing, flowing, flowing,
bringing life to dry plains,
and constantly returning to the Source.

Part VII: Parampara

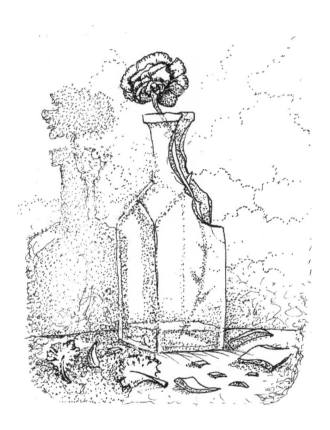

Five vessels *Vitthal Mishra's notes*

An empty vessel receives easily—
The open learner
    has room to accept new knowledge.

A covered container has to be opened—
Close-minded students
    protect what they think they think.

A full flask can't hold anything more—
A bloated brain
    knows everything until it bursts.

Cracks in a jar let the contents dribble-out—
A mind scattered everywhere
    can't hold even one thought.

Poisoned containers taint whatever they hold—
A spoiled thought process
    turns all words and reasons into rot.

ALEK

"OM—OM—OM,"
"Bhur Bhuvah Suvaha
"Tat Savitur Varenyum
"Bhargo Devasya Dhimahi
"Dhiyo Yonah Prachodayat."

There were three sharp raps at the front door. The latch clicked open. Sounds from outside flooded the room and then muffled to quiet again. The metallic contact of the bolt as it set, signaled his arrival. I concluded mantra repetition, touched a small framed photo of Vishwamithra and walked to the vestibule to greet my guest. As expected, it was the policeman, unsnapping and shedding layers of riot gear, piece by piece.

"Come in Alek—I was finishing my prayers." I told him, and turned halfway toward the adjacent room to resume my seat.

Flustered, he cocked one ear over a shoulder while removing his boots, checking that he was clear. Definitely the security agents in the neighborhood should not be consorting with the citizens. Yet here he was again, promptly ten minutes late, as had been our long-time Thursday pattern.

"Sorry, got held up in a zone meeting. I did what you asked and have some questions," he muttered, pulling folded papers from behind a bulletproof vest he had yet to remove.

"They are *our* questions. No apologies are expected. Every effort to live the truth shears clods from the mountain of karma we all share. I have to thank *you*," I said.

My answer put him at ease and he continued the cumbersome task of placing aside the armor that was his uniform. It was a costume in the play called "Security in Dangerous Times." I felt happy to see him loosen straps, leathers, goggles, helmet and gingerly lay his weapon at the foot of the altar. The matt black pipe with an arcing, full clip, shoulder brace, sights, straps, and dormant video screen should have been out of place next to devotional items. It wasn't. The killing device was another kind of candle, wayward statuary, lost and now found. Propellant, explosive lights and the gunsmith's arts would inevitably berth in the radiant source.

I remembered Vishwamithra and thanked him mentally for the armor he gave me, this *Kavacha* called *Gayatri Marga*. It was unclear whether I learned this sadhana from the sage, or if the guru made a transmission directly. It didn't matter. The five lines had become a covering. They say human skin is the largest organ, the third kidney. This mantra functioned in all those ways, protecting, purifying, pleasuring and running in front of me in every interaction. It was a womb-like enclosure that mediated the essence of the world to me.

Mata Gayatri was a wise mother who held me apart from times, events, and attitudes that were patently insane to provide an unobstructed vantage point. While dramas frothed, she brought her children to me. We sat together so she could serve tea and cakes in the form of *Sat-Chit-Ananda*. The apartment where I once listened at the knee of the sage was sanctuary for those that belonged to her. My activities in Vishwamithra's former dwelling drew no attention. Lessons in Gayatri Mantra apparently did not pose a threat to the world-at-large or the daily sessions were invisible to the flattened mindscape around us. This one, Alek, had managed to sustain his depth. He sat near me.

I motioned toward his notebook paper, blue ink spreading into a corner that had absorbed sweat through two layers of black underclothing. He stripped down to a T-shirt and placed the spiral pad aside to dry out. He continued clearing moisture from his forehead and glanced upward for the reassuring presence of the ceiling fan.

He unfolded a stained, dog-eared sheet of lined paper. I recognized my hand-writing.

He said, "Gurudas, it's been six years since you wrote me this and I study it every day before going to work." He read,

"*Steel wires bind a world that's dark*
   You grip them like your very life.

Dawn alights and they're puppet strings
   The wooden doll falls with the stroke of a knife.

With mid-day sun they're chords to strum

You play alone and hum tunes in silence.

By twilight you've become a foolish bard
Who'll sing his songs for anyone.

In starlight you caress the strings
And let them rest.
You're captured by celestial music that's everywhere."

The sweat-saturated notes aired-out on the floor.

Facing me, he said, "I am not a musician of any kind and the ropes seem to get tighter. I don't see the point—there's no end in sight." He was wound up. Every ounce of attention to Gayatri tightened the spring of decision. It had to release.

"Test the practice and see." I said, mentally turning to my teacher, distant in miles, so close in fact. "This is what I live for. Truth grasped firmly by the hand leads the remnant toward conscious fullness. This is not moving sand piles. It's culturing the compost of daily actions so the human tree can grow again. You start."

Settled and cooling, my student adopted a meditative posture. Straight black hair moved slightly in the circulating air. His eyes, closed, sank to a deeper level of awareness. His mouth opened and he spoke the syllables deliberately.

"*Ah, Oh, Um*, beginning, middle and end—the lotus hides the jewel.

"Upset, trapped, on and on and I want out. No patience for lotuses and maybe there are no jewels. Tolerance, I have to tolerate—but how long? The lotus and jewel is the same thing—that's kidding myself. But who gets proof of anything?

"*Bhur bhuvah suvaha...*

"My job—I'm done with it—have to keep it. There has to be something better—every day, anger, push down on it, wait, patience—for what?

"*Tat Savitur Varenyum...*

"Somewhere it's there—blind belief—make the assumption.

"*Bhargo Devasya Dhimahi...*

"Watch, wait. Wait for what? This world's not fit for my kids—not for anybody. Stop judging. Wait."

His ribcage began racking on inhales. Pausing to recover composure, he pulled-in several deep breaths.

"It's stuck, I'm stuck—like blood-sucking, skin frying—like it's crisp, peeling off, raw under it. It hurts—I hate it... I'm sad...my wife, daughter...me. It won't leave me alone, can I leave it? I can't, not now. I'll watch...nothing else to do.

"*Dhiyo yonah prachodayat...*"

He fell away even further, and was someplace else. There was no effort to wipe away tears that streamed from both eyes. His chest convulsed more freely on inhales and exhales. It was like this for ten minutes or so. He breathed, meditated the contradictions he lived, and let the conflict work him, his kriya yoga.

I said, quietly enough to be inside his thought, "Put your head on her lap."

He shook more rhythmically, slumping. His chin rested on his chest.

"It's safe there," I said, "She has you—to protect us all. No death—life is there. Stay, feel her lap, warm, firm, her hand on your face. She has nowhere else to go. Stay longer." We sat this way, opposite one another, seated on the floor, in no rush to move along.

The sound of the fan squeaked a quiet rhythm. There were no noises through windows that opened onto the street. I used to be where he was now—my advanced student, thirty-two year old sergeant of the goons who patrolled the neighborhood—all bedecked in bulletproof vests, black shades, shiny helmet, and boots. Like it or not, they were our cheerleaders and defenders, equally ready with a kind word or baton. He was different from the start.

IT HAD BEEN ONLY DAYS SINCE returning to the sage's flat and taking residence there. I was sweeping up glass shards, assessing the damage to his quarters, anxious, grieving, and expectant at his abrupt exit from my life. While ruminating on the sequence and timing of events that led me to an unlikely and yet inevitable place, I started at the sharp smack of metal against the thin wood door panel.

"Hey!" The voice resonated off bare walls in the vacant apartment. Destruction and resultant population allocations were all fresh and I knew that squatters in sanctioned areas invited official reactions. I expected some kind of notice and tempered my fear reflex. I was in no mood to mix.

I said, "Yes, someone is here. I'm the former tenant's son," the alibi was not an absolute lie, only relative.

"We cleared this area. You need to move on."

I told him I was from another region and came into town to check on the well-being of an aged father. I explained, "He was killed. I'm gathering his effects. Is it possible for a son to arrange personal papers and collect some keepsakes from a dead man?" I said with some force.

He asked my name. I told him *Vitthal Mishra*, which he logged.

He looked at his list, checked off the sage as a casualty of the attack, making a note to the side. I asked him about "a friend" who lived on the other block, me, my address.

"Ashty Hozan, B block...shows as missing, probably killed given that B took a direct hit. You have forty eight hours to identify remains. He scribbled on a separate pad and entered information into the digital notebook. "Take this. Present it to the monitor and they'll give you as much time as you want. See what you can of the victims. They are on ice at the Martial Annex on the southwest corner of the campus. You are lucky to have a couple more days to pay your respects. It'll all be gone after that."

Thanking him, I took the yellow admittance card. He lingered at the door, staring toward the makeshift altar—the one I cobbled together in remembrance of my absent teacher.

"Have a look if you want," I said. He approached more closely, stopped, glanced toward his boots, then up at me.

"It's fine. I'm cleaning so it makes no difference," I said.

He removed his footwear anyway. Shod in socks, he took careful steps toward my dedicated sacred space. It was an oil-rubbed, wooden plank that spanned two roughly-cubed rocks, the whole thing about one arm long and the width of two hands. A folded curtain made a simple runner and held several symbolic objects, precious remnants of what had been: the photo of Vishwamithra's niece named *Dila*, the lamp and prayer book I lifted just two weeks before, and a pair of sandals he left in the apartment. I assumed he had worn them. The flame from the lamp cast a tenuous yellow glow against her framed photo and the *paduka* sandals.

"My grandmother kept an altar," he said, crouching, one knee touching the floor. "May I see these?" He lifted the book, cradled it in his palm and examined it at random. "Sanskrit—can you read this?" He did not look away from these keepsakes. His interest puzzled me.

"No, I'm learning it piecemeal," I said. "At the rate I'm going, it will be a while." I came along side to tell him what I knew about the objects that caught his attention. It was not obvious why weathered slippers, a photo of a girl, and a hand-bound sheaf of yellowed papers would provide any fascination to a police officer.

I offered minimal references to fact, saying, "This is the book my father used to refer to. I only recognize a couple of the *slokas*, a few lines here and there. The girl is a friend's niece. Father had hopes for us, I think. He gave me the picture before he...," I hesitated, "...left...so I have it here as a memento."

"Know her? Or is it just a picture." he asked, at the same time inspecting the cloth cover of the worn prayer manuscript.

"I don't know her. I think the old man was wishing." There was no reason to go into it.

"My *Auntie* may have had this very same book, or one like it. It seems familiar," he said, and made a move to leave, straightening up and backing toward the door. He maintained steady eye contact with the flame that burned to a still, fine point above a bronze oil lamp. He squeezed into mid calf footwear, tucked pant cuffs under leather, and pulled at long laces. He talked between efforts,

"I liked it—her altar. It was more elaborate than yours, covered with little framed pictures and plates of rice, ripe fruit, candy, and flowers. I used to call it religious compost—I wouldn't now. It was like 'home base'—it felt...safe. I don't know why...and I wouldn't dare hazard to touch anything without risking a lightning bolt or a swat on the head."

Coming to his full height, padded by equipment, he asked again, "Which one do you know. Can you say?"

"In the book?" I asked. He nodded, "Yeah, some word or two."

I turned to the Gayatri Mantra, the only lines I felt competent breaking apart.

"What's it mean?" He asked after my word by word reading of the *Devanagiri* script.

I gave him the briefest explanation I could, and added, "It's dense. If you ever feel like getting the long version, come by. I plan on staying here, maybe out back. That is, as long as it's permitted."

The door was open behind him and formed a halo around his padded form. His flesh and bone was a scaffold for the machine. A bare smile formed between the thick vest and his dark shades.

He said, "We need to keep some residents around to discourage looting. I may look in occasionally to see if you are Ok." He left.

That was how we met. The way any paths cross is poignant and completely mysterious. Who can know the miraculous nature of fragmented people, jockeying into position in a race of which they are unaware?

ROOT GURU

OUT OF NINE STUDENTS he was the only cop, the first and the most serious. He used the gun as it was intended, to kill. He was in a force at war with us, all of us and himself. Deepening knowledge amplified his conflicts until they became intolerable. I would lose him if there was no relief. Dramas end when the actors leave, with or without the audience. What was an unaware mind? It was a cocked weapon waiting for someone to own it, to give it a reason. Most men were triggers—inanimate, metallic, spring-loaded reactors. They were "off the shelf mechanisms" ruled by the highest bidder, waiting to be taken in hand and employed, however.

What was murder? Drama excited to its maximum climax, death. What was death with no drama? It was theater played to an empty house, the sound of one hand clapping. An aware mind would only create—it could not destroy. I feared murder, mutilation, blind laws and enslavement as much as anyone. All were the stock in trade of the man sitting here. He was someone caught in a storm between the freedom of doubt and the slavery of certainty. I knew the struggle was tiring. Wisdom only made ignorance more painful—it did not make it go away.

A person awake in his life might create, or kill to protect—they might run to avoid. They might wait and watch. An awakened person could only die *to* something. He could not *just die*. Consciousness is an infinite game. Death is finite. Regardless of beliefs, smashing a light bulb destroys an artifact—the illuminating power remains, unaffected. Consciousness is the source of both.

"...PRACHODAYAT," HE INHALED fully to the collar bones, drinking those syllables for the thousandth time. With eyes shut he looked to the right, as though divining the message.

He said, "I did not put me here for any of this. I did not ask for it, and do not deserve it. Take it away. I don't want it. This uniform-skin sticks to me. It's not mine to shed. Help me peel out of it—there's no other way. If I have to—I'd rather not—it's yours." finishing the prayer, his eyes blinked open.

I said, "*We* are in disguise. *She* has us here at her pleasure. There is movement for you, your wife and children, now. Let's say the mantra."

Om
Bhur Bhuvah Suvaha,
Tat Savitur Varenyum,
Bhargo Devasya Dhimahi,
Dhiyo Yonah Prachodayat.

Gayatri Marga was an infinite work. There could be no "job well done," only "the race well-run." He and I had run it at different paces, on different tracks, with varying goals, and yet, together. Our choices were easy.

"Let me make a proposal." I told him.

Events turned with their own mind. Maybe my teacher, the sage Vishwamithra, found a fulcrum to move the Earth, working our karmas like a cosmic jigsaw puzzle.

"Feel no compulsion to answer right now. Let the fruit fall as it will. Reply at your own speed to what I'm going to present."

He drew his face tight, squinting. My student maintained a suspicious stance, an inbred guard against attack. His trust had to be moment to moment, continuously testing the harmlessness of the other. And he tested me many times.

There are five types of students-as-vessels: empty, covered, full, leaking, or poisoned.

An empty vessel receives easily; that is the advanced pupil.

A covered container first has to be opened; a close-minded student.

A full jar must be emptied to make room; the over-taught learner.

One with holes lets content pour or dribble out; a distracted mind.

A poisoned container taints whatever it holds, affecting the taste or transforming the material into something harmful. That represents a pre-programmed attitude that filters all incoming knowledge and distorts it.

Alek's mistrusting lid was his strength. He had the ability to interact in toxic environments and keep his vessel empty for the truth. That enabled his discriminative intelligence.

The world around us, so-called *modernity*, filled open vessels with tripe or worse. Sloganeering stuffed minds and poisoned them.

Corrosive ideas ulcerated the unsuspecting and made them unable to contain the only source of healing, the food of truth. I was happy enough to pick his locks or bribe the gate keeper for access to his trust. We both knew it was a privilege he afforded me.

I delivered my news. "Time is ripening, currents are mingling. Dila and I are marrying in the spring. We've been engaged for a year. That means a trip to Nepal. My return is uncertain."

Eyes wide, he started to interject.

I said. "Let me finish. Sri Vishwamithra is near the end. I will be there before he...dies...in a word. He has already begun an ideation, a teaching vehicle. I told him I would be there, so it will happen. Here I have eight dedicated students and a dozen more that are so-so. I want you to continue in my place as their guru and thus free me to make the trip. The money from these activities is not too far off of what the government pays you now. This flat costs less than your place. There are two others I might consider as second or third resorts. Without a doubt I prefer your regimented spirit which suits the times. You are tempered by the battle for consciousness. You understand the difficulties in a way that comes naturally to a military mind."

It could have been another blow for him to repulse. Instead, it was the life-giving pain of cold water on frozen flesh. He did not move a muscle and fell again inside himself to take counsel with Gayatri. I did not doubt that he would accept. Joy rose in my chest—a giddy inkling as my guru surged toward another body. Vishwamithra was not a prophet, reading time currents. Neither was he an alchemist, mixing lives and events into the philosopher's stone. He was a carpenter, touching the latent beauty of a wooden plank, running a weathered hand along nuanced grain and honing palaces for souls according to silent dictates. He was that *savitur* which ferried vision out of radiant darkness and tied random stars into constellations. By his example I abided in the mantra, followed stellar movements and resisted final destinations that would stifle the breeze at dawn with its secrets.

Coming events would gestate among evergreen foothills that shouldered Himalayan ranges of rock and snow—flawless white sentinels against cyan skies, rimming patchwork fields. The only road in that region of Nepal was a narrow strip of potholed asphalt—a meandering chord sent from the electrified city, dissipated among isolated farm plots, and finally vanished at the feet of the naked ascetics that cloistered in forests and caves. Our plot was a verdant hectare, away from the metropolis and closer to the mountain.

The sage would use the body's demise to teach. His weathered frame would take-on the mantle of debility as we waited on him. In mind, he would craft a life, his own embryonic vessel, and then die during Dila's second trimester. He would begin a new cycle within her womb—our child. The symmetry thrilled me, sitting there with Alek.

I had given him what was never mine and he only received what was always his, each of us steeped in *Suvaha*—the sweetness that forever pulls the heavy world into *Satyam*, the True, *Shivam*, the Auspicious, and *Sundaram*, the Beautiful.

Om

Bhur bhuvah suvaha
Tat savitur varenyum
Bhargo devasya dhimahi
Dhiyo yonah prachodayat

Om   You are the Author of all.

Bhur   In my hands,
   In my thoughts,
   And in my actions—

Bhuvah   You are the doer of every deed,
   I feel you in every pleasure and every pain,
   You speak in my longing—

Suvaha   In my past, you are my remembering.
   In my present, you are my becoming.
   In my future, you have always been forever.

Tat Savitur Varenyum   You are hidden in the dawn—
   I seek you there to worship.

Bhargo Devasya Dhimahi   You are the life in my mind—
   I contemplate your ways with fascination.

Dhiyo Yonah Prachodayat   You are the fire of sacrifice—
   I pray you accept my daily portion,
      Again,
         And again,
         And again.

i am Your creation, always new.
i am Your love, void of sentiment.
i am only You, the Self— Careening wild in space—Still and constant.

Om.

Notes / Author

THE FAR-AWAY EVENT was impossible until just now. Now it's on the screen, happening everywhere. It showed again and again and again, then slowly, backward, rewinding—then it was an ambient background, slow-moving shapes to complement a news anchor who said *the impossible just now happened*. A nearly perfect *Nikon* was our eye—cameras don't lie, so everyone glued to the screen became faultless witnesses of what was impossible—until today.

At work, grocery, or post-office line no one said anything, knowing that everyone already knew. It was mutual respect for the mourners who were everywhere—eyes that had seen, ears that heard the evening news, the screen in the bar, on the gas pump, over the head of the clerk—it was a global wake with forced attendance, mandatory sorrow. There was more streaming video with many talking heads, the only ones who cut into the silence with authority on the ways and means of nightmares, motives for monstrous acts, profiles of monsters. In fact, the actual nightmare would not happen again. It did not have to. It had become a universal teaching about nightmares, a caution against idyllic islands of happiness that did not include black horizons, flashing ominous lightning bolts of doom. Streaming words and images burrowed deep—a new law of nature that *the impossible can and will happen*. The "proof" was on the screen ten-million times and nobody could get enough.

MEDIA STIRS A POT, tossing trauma into a strange brew of movie-news icons, shock therapy, and coy one-liners. Edited visions brand every mind at once. It's true that bad things have always happened— only now, event-products embed into a million brains at once, like tattoos, so hard to lose once they get needled-in. The full-spectrum attack on perception includes published and broadcast journalism, along with film and commentary. Six media megaliths evangelize the world with a gospel of random violence and futility—confess the nihilistic faith or invite public flogging.

I craved clear guides that could guarantee mental autonomy—a necessity for self-awareness that is more and more on the chopping block of collective thinking. Reality is—and is *Good*, by definition. In spite of corrosive jargon, the mind craves reality. Root scriptures are like Prometheus' gift of fire, which guide, protect, nourish and threaten the gods' authority. *Gayatri Mantra* and *Patanjali's Yoga Sutras* are such teachings, formed when words were divine and effective.

Calling them *Indian* is a convenience—the ideas are universal. Their essence proves itself in experience and practice. A *Rishi, Vishwamithra,* discovered the Gayatri Mantra during meditation a million years ago if one can believe the astronomical timelines. Rishis were great sages, living in an era before our way of measuring time in years. Their contributions included the *Vedas, Puranas, Upanishads* and profound epic stories, notably *Ramayana* and *Mahabaratha.* The traditions were oral, therefore impossible to date.

These beings understood that consciousness *in flesh* was new and delicate—it would require careful tending. They saw urban civilization concentrating power into fewer and fewer hands. Due to the moldable quality of abstract concepts *thought processes* would be easily corrupted, vulnerable to delusion and slavery. Human reason over-writes instinct with invented ideas and mental fabrications. The Rishis gave post-tribal societies a way to see through rationalization-traps, mental colonization, and imperial conceits in order to grasp true reality.

I studied Gayatri and the Yoga Sutras as such remedies using no formal guidance. My method was frequent, long rumination on words and phrases, relying on multiple meanings of Sanskrit vocabulary found in various sources. Working as an illustrator often left my thinking brain free to roam. It allowed long unbroken periods of time gestating what a word implied. Contemplating Sanskrit was one way to overcome rote interpretations offered on-line and in books. That was when I had the following Sai Baba dream.

A DISCHEVELED MAN STOOD on a street corner, preaching with powerful intent and gaining few listeners. I walked closer to find out what it was about, though no one else paid heed. He seemed to have been abandoned; an old fakir, thrown aside as times changed. It was the South Indian spiritual leader *Sathya Sai Baba,* saying the Gayatri Mantra. I repeated the familiar words after him from some distance away. He stopped and smiled, telling me, "I will give you a more powerful Gayatri called *Kaivalya Gayatri.*" I told him, "The Gayatri Mantra you already gave me is enough." A voice said, "You should probably accept what he is offering." I took the advice to be open to his teaching and then awoke.

The dream had a similar theme to an encounter I had with Sai Baba at the ashram in Puttaparthi many years before. The "stars aligned in my favor" and I gained a seat in the first row, coveted among throngs who clamored to get as close as possible to the guru. He entered the hall and strolled through a crowd of fifteen thousand, stopping occasionally to offer a comment or take a letter as had been his pattern every morning for fifty years. On some pauses he made the slow, circular hand motion that signified an impending *vibuthi manifestation.* Bestowing sacred ash from the palm of his hand was the signature miracle, synonymous with his blessing on the recipient. Despite complaints about his miraculous manufacture of small objects, the meaning and impact are more profound than psychology or logic is equipped to explain.

He eventually stood within arms reach. I was rapt, and did not register the telltale movement of his hand as he stood there. Motionless, with palms pressed together, I wanted to avoid the bad form of hurling myself at his feet, as many did. The impending manifestation was not lost on the men around me and they crowded in to receive what I seemed to ignore. He reached toward more willing devotees on either side. The crush from the others jostled my attention to what was happening and I finally stretched out my palms to receive the white clumpy powder. I shared the vibuthi-ash with those around me. It was an ecstatic moment.

SPIRITUAL EVENTS HAVE OCCASIONALLY interrupted my usual ups and downs. Four notable episodes involved: Sathya Sai Baba, the Dalai Lama, *A Course in Miracles,* and a movie by director Peter Brooks on the Indian epic story *Mahabharatha.*

The Holy Man and the Psychiatrist, by Samuel Sandweiss, described eye-opening experiences with Sai Baba in India. The book was loaned to me by a Memphis psychologist who thought I would benefit from the *paranormal research.* Claims by Dr. Sandweiss were unbelievable— the guru resurrected the dead, manifested materials out of the palm of his hand, bi-located, and regularly read peoples minds—which left me two choices: *it was an out right lie,* or *some of it might be true.* If a fraction of it actually happened, it meant that something along the lines of a *second coming of Christ* had occurred in South India. I had to find out more, and immediately called Prakash, the Indian engineer in the upstairs office to hear, first-hand, about this wonder worker.

Over dinner I asked him what he thought of the holy man who, I assumed, had been a household topic during his childhood. Delivering something short of bliss-filled testimony, he said, "Sai Baba is nothing but a magician!" He went on to tell me, "*Swami Vivekananda and Sri Ramakrishna* lived like gods!" The word *god* rolled out as *go-ad*—he urgently advised me to study *the real thing* and not waste time with *the fake,* as he called him.

I studied the books he loaned me about Sri Ramakrishna, a mystic, slightly built and given to ecstatic states—one guru led to another. There were many other saints, lamas and yogis each with stories and core teachings. The Sai Baba spectacle dimmed among the crowded field of miraculous claims that I learned were endemic to India.

A couple of years passed and I went to India. The itinerary included a train trip way south to stay at Sai Baba's ashram, arriving *accidentally* on his 65th birthday. They said two-million people attended. Whatever the actual count, the scale was mind-boggling. Devotees plastered the surrounding hills, jammed dirt lanes, and packed buses that strung bumper to bumper along every approach road. Horns blared, vendors hawked, beggars contorted their bodies for pay, while rank toilet-spots made bio-hazardous waste sites look like picnic areas. Bizarre and pulverizing, India worked its way under my skin. The intense diversity of Indian experiences broke something in me.

Returning North to escape the heat and crowds I unexpectedly received a personal blessing from the Dalai Lama in Macleod Ganj, the Tibetan home in exile. Consistent with the other mind-bending marvels, meeting Tenzin Gyatso was foreshadowed in a pre-dawn dream where the Tibetan leader asked, "What do you want?" Within a couple of days I received a telegram from his office verifying an interview. The higher-altitude hill station was as restorative as the steamy South had been hallucinogenic.

I returned to the United States with a new appreciation for the plastic potential of phenomena. The trip ended my addiction to linear realism. I haphazardly decided to test the useful existence of God by doing *A Course in Miracles* (ACIM) to the letter, as prescribed in the text. Years before I tried reading it, with no success. After India, I succeeded in appreciating the strange logic of ACIM which looped in redundant themes that came across like well-intended brain-washing. Doing the lessons religiously revealed a deeper coherence in everyday events that had been invisible before. It provided a sense of peace and confidence that fate had compassion in it. A couple of years after completing the year-long course, I experienced a dramatic shift in awareness a couple of years after completing ACIM. It lasted about thirty minutes and has not happened since.

The setting was Catholic mass in a beautiful, modernist church in Sarasota, Florida. Returning to my childhood religion was not pleasant. It seemed materialistic and hypocritical after years away from rote religion. Surrounded by retirees, golf clothes, and perfume, resentment worked me over. Sitting in supreme disapproval of the whole thing, I picked up a mantra from an *ACIM* lesson, *Give me your blessing holy son of God,* repeating it continuously and applying it completely to every thing in sight, all of which provoked bitter resentment.

Fifteen or twenty minutes into the mantra, the usual appearance of the room fell away, replaced by something more translucent. With the transformation, a bright, humorous fact shared by all became clear, *every person was an invitation to communion* and there was nothing else. Intensity increased like a fire that had no heat. The beauty became overwhelming. Conventional life seemed like it would burn to ashes. The experience faded and my usual perceptions returned.

In a practical way, I thought Sai Baba and Indian culture might provide a refuge against consumer society for my family. It seemed we could participate socially among diverse people who wanted to follow the guru's moral, ethical, and spiritual precepts. Learning to play *tabla* drums, singing call-and-response *kirtan,* yoga practice and attending events in the Sai organization were part of that process. The effort was short-sighted. Our marriage crumbled under other pressures and the Indian-culture strategy collapsed with it.

After my wife moved away, taking our son with her, I was numb. One night alone, family scattered across the country, I sat surrounded by remnants of what had been a happy home to watch Peter Brook's *Mahabaratha*—a film that condensed the ponderous mythological history of India down to a few hours. The movie presented the vast epic as a series of surreal vignettes. Once the stylized sets and theatrical staging became more familiar, the message staggered me: *There are situations when certain groups are fully committed to destroying every vestige of virtue in the world. It is incumbent upon godly folk to survive by any means at those times.* The god-man in the story, Krishna, instructed the ones he protected to break bonds with conventional, fair-fight agreements. The movie showed rules of war that were entirely stacked against the ones who would be the "virtuous predecessors" of Indian culture and spirituality. The opposing army was vastly superior, led by three immortal heroes. The future of the race depended on the war's outcome—whether it was won in bitter envy or love of truth.

During corrupt times, beauty and goodness endure in traditions that transcend the downward pull of cynicism: great myths, ancient wisdom cultures, the Gayatri Mantra, and the voices for truth beyond appearances.